Urban Disease and Mortality

in

Nineteenth-Century England

Urban Disease and Mortality

in

Nineteenth-Century England

edited by
**Robert Woods &
John Woodward**

**Batsford Academic and Educational, London
St Martin's Press, New York**

First published 1984

Filmset in Monophoto Aldine Bembo by
Latimer Trend & Company Ltd, Plymouth
and printed in Great Britain by
Butler & Tanner Ltd
Frome, Somerset
for the publishers
Batsford Academic and Educational Ltd
4 Fitzhardinge Street
London W1H 0AH

British Library Cataloguing in Publication Data
Urban disease and mortality in nineteenth-century England.
　　1. Public health—England—History
　　I. Woods, Robert　　II. Woodward, John
　　614'.0942　　　RA485

　　ISBN 0 7134 3707 3

First published in the United States of America in 1984 by
St. Martin's Press, Inc., 175 Fifth Avenue, New York, NY 10010
Printed in Great Britain
ISBN 0-312-83434-9

Library of Congress Cataloging in Publication Data
Main entry under title:
Urban Disease and Mortality in Nineteenth Century England.
　　Includes bibliographies and index.
　　1. Urban health—England—History—19th century—Addresses,
essays, lectures.　　2. Social medicine—England—History—19th
century—Addresses, essays, lectures.　　3. Mortality—England—
History—19th century—Addresses, essays, lectures.　　4. Communicable
diseases—England—History—19th century—Addresses, essays, lectures.
5. England—Statistics, vital—Addresses, essays, lectures.
I.　Woods, Robert.　　　II.　Woodward, John (John Hugh)
RA566.5.G7U73　1984　614.4'242　　　84-3474

　　ISBN 0-312-83434-9

Contents

6

List of tables

List of figures

Contributors

Gillian Cronjé—Formerly Research Student, Department of Economic and Social History, London School of Economics and Political Science

Bill Luckin—Lecturer, Department of Liberal and Social Studies, Bolton Institute of Technology

Colin Pooley—Lecturer, Department of Geography, University of Lancaster

Marilyn Pooley—Research Associate, Department of Geography, University of Lancaster

Barbara Thompson—Formerly Research Student, School of History, University of Bradford

Robert Woods—Lecturer, Department of Geography, University of Sheffield

John Woodward—Senior Lecturer, Department of Economic and Social History, University of Sheffield

Preface

Our aim in editing this volume of essays has been to present a variety of perspectives on the decline of mortality in nineteenth-century England and Wales. We have sought to mix the quantitative and the impressionistic, the spatial and the temporal by including the work of historians, geographers and demographers.

Chapter 1 provides a guide to the major factors influencing mortality levels and trends together with an outline of the by now orthodox interpretation by Thomas McKeown which is to be found in his *The Modern Rise of Population* (1976). In its final section it presents a brief summary of the main conclusions of the seven remaining chapters. The second chapter provides a demographic analysis of mortality variations between the English and Welsh registration districts in 1861; it emphasizes the contrasts in conditions experienced, without attempting explanations. Chapter 3 surveys the role of medicine in the nineteenth-century while Chapter 4 examines the changing influence of tuberculosis, the single most important infectious disease of the time. The remaining chapters deal with conditions in specific towns: London, Bradford, Manchester and Birmingham. Chapter 5 focuses on typhoid and typhus as a means of evaluating the impact of the sanitary revolution. Chapter 6 considers infant mortality in particular since in most of urban England deaths to those under one year of age still represented 20 to 25 per cent of all deaths even up until 1900. Chapters 7 and 8 deal with the more general context of the urban environment, with poverty, with the attempts of reformers to improve life chances, and with the evidence for their growing success in the cities of Frederick Engels and Joseph Chamberlain.

Finally, we would like to thank our contributors and Batsford's Tony Seward for their patience, Paul Coles for re-drawing our figures, and Anita Fletcher and Carole Elliss for typing the final manuscript. We also express our thanks to Academic Press for allowing us to reproduce material first published in the *Journal of Historical Geography* Volumes 4 and 8 for 1978 and 1982 in our Chapters 2 and 8. At least in terms of the subject matter of this volume, 1984 may not be as bad as 1884.

Robert Woods and John Woodward
Sheffield, April, 1983

A note on demographic notation

At several places in this volume we have found it useful to employ a form of notation commonly adopted by demographers and statisticians in their work. This brief note is intended to clarify these terms together with a small number of others that frequently appear in the literature on the history of population, public health and medicine.

The demographic reference system known as the *life table* acts as a means of describing population structures. It deals with populations divided up into age groups, commonly five-year age groups, but occasionally single years. To take an example, the probability of dying between age 40 at last birthday and age 45 would be represented by $_5q_{40}$ in demographic notation: 5 refers to the number of years being considered (40–45), q is used for the probability of dying, and 40 is the starting age to be considered. Infant mortality —the probability of dying during the first year of life—would be $_1q_0$ or usually just q_0. More generally, the notation $_nq_x$ is to be found: n is the number of years being considerd (5 or 1 in the above example) and x is the starting age (40 or 0 above). This form $_nq_x$, the probability of dying between ages x and $x + n$, is frequently used in Chapters 1, 2 and 8. Other life table functions which appear in the following pages are l_x, the number of people alive and aged exactly x; $_nL_x$, the average number of people alive in age group x to $x + n$ (n normally equals 5 here); and e_x, the life expectation in years of a person currently aged x (e_0 is the most commonly used as a measure of mortality since it represents the life expectation in years of an infant at birth). For further details on life tables readers are referred to R. Woods, *Population Analysis in Geography* (London, 1979) pages 47–61.

Another important demographic measure which is used in Chapter 2 is the gross reproduction rate (GRR) which indicates the average number of female children a woman is likely to have had on passing through the reproductive years (by convention ages 15–49) (see Figure 2.10). The index I_g which was devised by A. J. Coale in the 1960s deals only with the fertility of married women and ranges from 0 to 1. If I_g is greater than 0.6 it suggests that family limitation is not being practiced by married couples (see Figure 2.11). The American statistician A. J. Lotka was responsible for the definition of the intrinsic rate of natural increase (r) which measures the true rate of natural population growth in the absence of migration (see Figure 2.12).

Mortality, poverty and the environment

Robert Woods and John Woodward

The materialist interpretation of history takes as its fundamental *credo* the notion that social relationships are determined by economic ones; that on the foundation of the dominant mode of production rests the superstructure of a social formation; and that differential access to the means of production leads to the creation of classes which have their own interests and between which there are constant tensions. These tensions are instrumental in the process of transition from stage to stage, that is between modes of production and their associated social formations, they are also linked with the distribution of wealth and general living standards. In pre-industrial societies it is the ownership of and access to land that controls social and economic relations while in industrial societies manufacturing production fulfils this key function. [1]

When applied to nineteenth-century Britain this interpretation emphasizes the role of industrialization and the transition to a mature form of industrial capitalism. It suggests that the development of manufacturing radically altered not only the economy, but also the overall structure of society; that separate social classes were formed which had different degrees of economic and political power and were even distinctive in terms of culture and behaviour. Members of these social classes also experienced different conditions of material life which manifested themselves in terms of regularity of employment, wage levels, housing quality and what would today be called general living standard. The division of labour meant that the simple distinction between employer and employee, whilst persistently sharp, disguised important internal substrata. The capitalist owners; the professionals who met their legal, financial, educational and religious requirements; the petty-bourgeoisie who provided other services often of a consumable variety; the 'labour aristocracy'; the skilled artisans; and the 'labouring classes' each had their own particular life styles and codes of conduct which distinguished them from members of other classes. These distinctive economic functions also provided the basis for the residential separation of social classes in the cities, as work-place and living-place were distanced one from another.[2]

The process of industrialization and the phenomenon of the Industrial Revolution can be viewed in several other ways, however. In Britain the period of industrialization and rapid technological change associated with the development of the factory system had at least two important consequences.

Firstly, it facilitated, led to and even encouraged a period of rapid population growth by loosening the preventive check—the 'prudential restraint on marriage'—and thus allowing nuptiality to rise as non-agricultural employment became more plentiful and independent nuclear families could be formed at an earlier age.[3] The process of industrialization was also linked with that of urbanization and the expansion of the urban system in general via rural–urban migration and ultimately wide-scale rural depopulation.[4] By the mid nineteenth century over half of the population of Great Britain could reasonably be classified as urban and many would in consequence be experiencing the urban way of life for the first time. The growth of the nineteenth-century cities fundamentally affected the everyday environment of the mass of people. There were shops, parks and entertainments, but there was also a new time discipline to adhere to and scarce accommodation to compete for.[5] The urban environment held in store another peril for its residents: it was generally more unhealthy than the countryside. Infectious diseases were more likely to be endemic; epidemics developed more frequently and were easily maintained; poor sanitary conditions meant that food, milk and the water supply were liable to be contaminated; whilst overcrowding provided both a source of psychological tension and an aid to the easy communication of disease.[6]

Our purpose here is to consider mortality itself, to examine its causes and the way it changed during the nineteenth century. The two approaches already outlined suggest that there are also two sets of factors which are important in influencing the level and pattern of mortality, namely the environmental and the socio-economic. Figure 1.1 shows the elements of this argument in a very simple diagrammatic form. It also indicates four of the major ways in which mortality levels could have changed during the nineteenth century. Figure 1.1 therefore provides a model in two parts. The upper half focuses on the factors which are likely to be associated with variations in the level of mortality, and the lower half isolates specific elements which, singly or in combination, could have led to the decline in mortality. The first part of this discussion serves to elaborate the complex mechanism that affects boxes (1) and (2) in Figure 1.1, but above all the manner by which they influence variations in the level and structure of mortality. The second

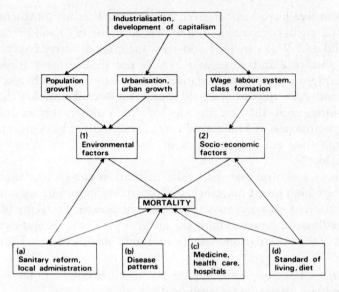

Figure 1.1 A simple model of the factors affecting mortality levels

part will deal with boxes (a), (b), (c) and (d) and will consider, amongst other things, the way in which mortality declined in nineteenth-century Britain.

I

During the nineteenth century the life expectation at birth (e_0)[7] of the average Briton probably increased from about 36 to 50 years. This change was by no means regular or uniform in its occurrence; it varied between age groups, between town and country, within towns and between occupation groups.

However, the precise analysis of these variations is problematic because the civil registration of vital events was not begun in England and Wales until 1837 and in Scotland not until 1855.[8] After these dates age at death and cause of death were recorded in a reasonably systematic fashion although the collection of data on the latter posed many difficulties throughout the nineteenth century. In the period before the first Registrar General's *Annual Reports* were published one has to rely on the work of local actuaries who provided information for the new life assurance companies, some of which was founded on data from parish registers and Bills of Mortality. Table 1.1 shows the l_x columns for four life tables which are appropriate to the nineteenth century. The life table calculated by Joshua Milne for Carlisle, Cumbria, 1780–87, has a life expectation at birth of 38.69 years and infant mortality (q_0) is 154 per thousand live births; that derived by William Farr for Northampton, 1838–44, yields comparable, and similar, levels of 37.62 and 171.2.[9] For England and Wales in 1861 and 1901 these levels were, respectively, 41.74 and 161, and 47.30 and 158. If the figures for Carlisle and Northampton were representative of the late eighteenth and early nineteenth centuries then it would appear that overall mortality changed very little until the last decades of the century. Of course the representativeness of Milne's and Farr's results cannot be demonstrated, although they are compatible with those obtained by Wrigley and Schofield.[10]

Table 1.1 also suggests particular patterns of age-specific mortality with very high infant mortality, high mortality in middle age and, as a comparison of 1861 and 1901 reveals, a reduction finally taking place in the childhood and early adulthood age groups. The static and dynamic aspects of the pattern of age-specific mortality are described in Figure 1.2

Table 1.1.   Four life tables appropriate to nineteenth-century England and Wales (sexes combined)

Age x	Number of persons alive aged x (lx)			
	Carlisle 1780–87*	Northampton 1838–44**	England and Wales, 1861	England and Wales, 1901
0	10,000	10,000	10,000	10,000
1	8,461	8,295	8,393	8,419
5	6,797	6,765	7,309	7,754
10	6,460	6,408	7,069	7,599
15	6,300	6,252	6,918	7,510
20	6,090	6,069	6,688	7,385
25	5,879	5,865	6,421	7,229
30	5,642	5,638	6,144	7,048
35	5,362	5,385	5,846	6,819
40	5,075	5,098	5,522	6,534
45	4,727	4,768	5,191	6,186
50	4,397	4,388	4,823	5,770
55	4,073	3,955	4,410	5,265
60	3,643	3,491	3,866	4,615
65	3,018	2,751	3,295	3,887
70	2,401	1,896	2,516	2,971
75	1,675	1,167	1,753	2,048
80	953	648	972	1,172
85 +	445	323	369	475

Notes: * calculated by Dr Joshua Milne
          ** calculated by Dr William Farr

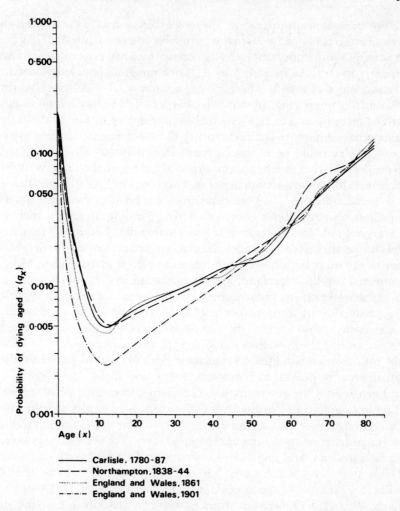

Figure 1.2 The probability of dying at particular ages ($_nq_x$) for selected populations

which shows the probability of dying (q_x, shown on the logarithmically transformed vertical side) for ages 0 to 85. It highlights the particular importance of mortality during infancy and early childhood, and, once again, it seems to suggest the relative lack of change during the first half of the nineteenth century.

This impression needs to be countered for a number of reasons, one of which has already been mentioned above. A second is that the period of industrialization was in all probability linked not only with rapid population growth, but also with growing demographic diversity. Although the towns of pre-industrial England are by tradition thought of as 'demographic sinks' whose populations could not replace themselves without net immigration, the new urban system of the nineteenth century also contained areas that were unable to grow naturally.[11] What is perhaps more important is the increasing disparity between town and country in terms of mortality level. If one imagines population in two distinct units, A and B, where life expectancy in A is declining whilst that in B is improving substantially, but a radical redistribution is also taking place from B to A, then one has an image of Britain in the early nineteenth century.[12] By mid-century these differences between town and country could be measured quite accurately (see Chapter 2) and were the subject of much contemporary comment. In the 1840s William Farr was able to show that many of the rural areas of England and Wales, his 'healthy districts', had life expectancies at birth in the upper 40s as much as 20 years above some of the large industrial towns, such as Liverpool and Manchester, and 10 years higher than London.[13] Further, when one attempts to consider the changing experiences of individual towns the issues become clouded. For example, as we have seen, Milne estimated that life expectancy at birth in Carlisle in the 1780s was 38.69, in the period 1838–44 comparable estimates give a figure of 31.17, that is, a reduction of some 19 per cent in 60 years.[14] By the end of the nineteenth century some of the excesses in this respect had been reduced by increased life expectancies amongst the urban populations. In 1900 the rural districts had life expectancies at birth in the mid-50s whilst the urban areas in general had an average that was in the upper 40s.

Even within the towns there were sharp contrasts to be observed. Taking London and Birmingham in the 1880s as examples, it is the case that amongst the London districts there were clear distinctions in terms of the proportion of the population in poverty. These differences were studied in detail and meticulously set out in Charles Booth's *Life and Labour of the People in London*.[15] Booth's estimates suggest that nearly half (48.9 per cent) of the inhabitants of Holborn (13) and St. George's-in-the-East (18) registration districts could be described as living in poverty, but that only 13.5 per cent of those living in Hampstead (7) would so qualify. When one compares Booth's poverty data with the level of infant mortality by registration districts in the early 1880s one finds a positive, statistically significant relationship (see Figure 1.3).[16]

As one would expect, an increase in the extent of poverty induces an increase in the level of infant mortality, but the relationship is not an exact one. Woolwich (29), for instance, has about a quarter of its population in poverty but only a relatively low level of infant mortality. The relationship described graphically in Figure 1.3 can therefore suggest that poverty and infant mortality are related, but also that other factors are important in controlling the level of infant mortality. It is quite probable that the environmental factor also has a role here for although there are distinctions between the East End and West End in terms of poverty and mortality there are also differences between inner

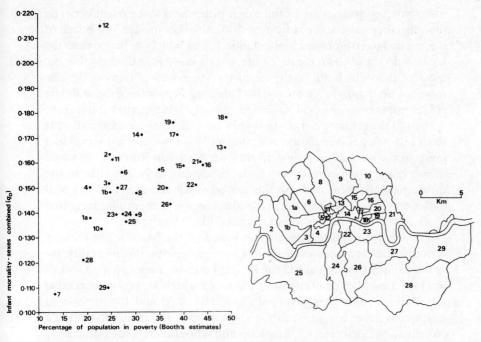

Figure 1.3 The relationship between infant mortality (q_0) and Booth's estimates of the percentage of the population in poverty, London Registration Districts, 1880s and 1890s

and outer or suburban London where mortality may tend to be lower even if conditions of poverty are still common.

Birmingham in the 1880s provides an example of a large rapidly expanding industrial town in which residential segregation was becoming more and more acute. The commercial redevelopment of the central district led to the rehousing of those living in the worst conditions in the poorest courts, but it was preceded by the movement from the remnants of the old Georgian town of the prosperous manufacturers, merchants and professionals to such suburban areas as Edgbaston, Moseley and Handsworth. The net results of these movements was the depopulation of the centre and the rapid expansion of the outer wards of the borough. When one considers the variation in mortality amongst the social areas of Victorian Birmingham it is apparent that deaths from several infectious diseases, like measles and scarlet fever, were virtually nonexistent amongst residents of the more salubrious suburban areas. In the courts of 'back-to-back' houses in the inner wards mortality was higher from all categories of disease.[17] The physical and social environments in which Victorians lived clearly had important influences on morbidity and the likelihood of early death.

Nineteenth-century doctors, demographers and social statisticians were only too well aware of the major differences that existed between the mortality experiences of different occupation groups and hence of the social class component in mortality. It was widely believed that 'the well-to-do classes had a lease of life which was more than double the value of that which fell to the lot of the less favoured citizens.'[18] The *Report on the Sanitary Condition of the Labouring Population of Great Britain* (1842) appears to confirm this view for an earlier period (table 1.2). Although the mean age at death is only equivalent to life expectation at birth (e_0) when a population is stationary[19] it none the less serves as a guide to the level of mortality. In rural areas, such as Rutland, the range of mortality experience between classes appears to be less than in the urban areas, but since during this period rapid urbanization was well under way it is likely that the national average was becoming weighted towards the level of the urban districts, like Manchester.

The work of Henry Ratcliffe on behalf of the Manchester friendly societies also provides examples of occupation-specific mortality estimates.[20] Ratcliffe estimated the life expectation at ages 20 (e_{20}) and 40 (e_{40}) for a number of occupations, some of which are reported in table 1.3. Both the numbers involved (N in table 1.3) and the method of calculation given are grounds for concern over the reliability of these estimates. For example, e_{20} for clerks and schoolmasters suggests that e_0 would be about 33 or 34 years which is particularly low since e_0 for rural labourers might be about 56.[21]

More recent attempts to estimate class-specific mortality have employed the burial records for municipal cemeteries together with techniques of demographic estimation. The results of one such exercise on data for Sheffield, 1860–62, are summarized in table 1.4. Although Sheffield is by no means typical of nineteenth-century England and Wales, the estimates shown in table 1.4 are credible approximations. Life expectation at birth for those in the 'professional classes' may be some 15 years longer than that for the 'skilled workers', although e_0 for the highest social groups was probably not twice that of the lowest.

II

Returning to the model described in Figure 1.1, it is clear that there was only a limited number of ways in which mortality could have declined in the nineteenth century, given that at least some overall decline did occur in the latter part of the century. It is possible that the disease patterns themselves could have changed, case fatality rates could have declined, endemic diseases become less virulent, epidemic diseases less frequent in their incidence. Man's ability to diagnose and effectively cure illness may have improved as may his organization of health care administration in the form of, for example, hospitals and the midwifery

Table 1.2. Mean age at death for selected social classes, Manchester, Rutland and eleven districts, circa 1840

Classes	Manchester	Rutland	Eleven districts*
Gentlemen, professionals and their families	38	52	44
Tradesmen, farmers and their families	20	41	27
Mechanics, servants, labourers and their families	17	38	22

Note: * weighted mean of data from Truro, Derby, Bolton, Leeds, Liverpool, Kendal, Wiltshire, Whitechapel, Stroud, Kensington and Bethnal Green

Source: *Report on the Sanitary Condition of the Labouring Population of Great Britain* (Chadwick Report) (1842, edited by M. W. Flinn, Edinburgh, 1965), pp. 220–27

Table 1.3. Life expectations at age 20 (e_{20}) and age 40 (e_{40}) amongst members of Manchester friendly societies

Occupations	e_{20}	e_{40}	N
Bakers	42	27	44
Blacksmiths	38	24	238
Clerks and schoolmasters	35	21	101
Urban labourers	41	26	428
Rural labourers	45	30	366
Miners	38	24	364
Domestic servants	42	27	138
Spinners	39	24	116
Weavers	42	29	209

Source: H. Ratcliffe, *Observations on the Rate of Mortality and Sickness* (Manchester, 1850) reprinted in R. Wall (ed.) *Mortality in Mid-19th Century Britain* (Farnborough, 1974)

Table 1.4. Generalized estimates of class-specific life expectation at birth (e_0), Sheffield, 1860–62[22]

Classes*		e_0	Level**
1	males	47.1	13
	females	50.0	13
2	males	37.3	9
	females	45.0	11
3	males	32.5	7
	females	35.0	7
4 & 5	males	27.7	5
	females	30.0	5
1–5	males	32.5	7
	females	35.0	7

Notes: * classes are defined as follows: 1, professional–managerial; 2, intermediate non-manual; 3, skilled manual; 4 & 5, semi- and unskilled manual workers
** levels are taken from the West family of model life tables in A. J. Coale and P. Demeny, *Regional Model Life Tables and Stable Populations* (Princeton, 1966)

Sources: estimated from Sheffield Municipal Cemetary Records; see note 22

service. Similarly, developments in local government and public administration in general might have affected the sanitary conditions of the urban environment with the removal and processing of sewage, the provision of an adequate and purified water supply, and the lighting and paving of streets. It is also possible that the general standard of living and particularly the diet of the population improved during the nineteenth century and that it was responsible not only for a reduction in mortality, but in morbidity also. Any one, a number or indeed all of these four broad groups of factors could have had a significant influence in initiating the secular decline of mortality which at least for the urban population began towards the end of the century.

The evaluation of what influence each of these factors had presents a number of methodological and technical problems which have not as yet been successfully solved. One such problem is concerned with the need for direct evidence (which can be associated with temporal and spatial changes in mortality), of changes in these factors. For although such associations do not necessarily provide an indication of causation they are none the less capable of distinguishing plausible relationships from implausible ones. The most obvious and thus most frequently used method of assessing the contributions of the four factors outlined above has been to consider changes in cause-specific mortality and to infer from the aetiology of the diseases concerned what the most probable influences have been on their development. The chief exponent of this method has been Thomas McKeown.[23]

McKeown's argument can be simplified and represented in diagrammatic form. Figure 1.4 shows its main structure. The objective is to explain the overall decline in mortality in England and Wales between 1848–54 and 1901, a period for which there are reasonably reliable vital

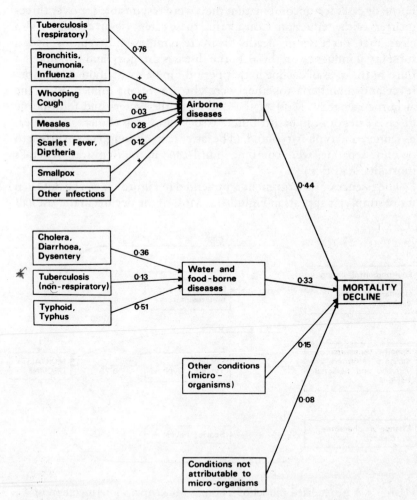

Figure 1.4 Cause-specific influences on mortality decline, England and Wales, 1848–54 to 1901

statistics. During this period overall mortality fell by some 22 per cent
although decline during this period represented only 30 per cent of that
between 1848–54 and 1971. Taking this 22 per cent reduction to equal 1,
Figure 1.4 gives the proportions that are attributable to each of four
major disease combinations. The most influential factor in terms of
disease pattern was the decline in the impact of airborne diseases, which
accounted for some 44 per cent of the late nineteenth-century mortality
decline. A third of the decline can be linked with changes in the influence
of water- and food-borne diseases; 15 per cent with other conditions
attributable to micro-organisms and only 8 per cent with conditions not
attributable to micro-organisms. In accounting for overall mortality
decline one is therefore safe in focusing on airborne, water- and food-
borne diseases for in combination they were responsible for over three-
quarters of the reduction. Considering these categories in detail, it is also
clear that decrease in deaths from respiratory tuberculosis had a
substantial influence on the airborne diseases category and that about a
third of the overall decline in that period can be so attributed.[24] Scarlet
fever and diphtheria together were also important influences on the
airborne category. Most of the decline in the water- and food-borne
diseases category can be attributed to such diseases as cholera, diarrhoea,
dysentery and typhus-typhoid. (The latter pair, although now known to
be quite separate, were combined until 1869 in the Registrar General's
mortality statistics.)[25]

The essence of the argument represented in Figure 1.4 can be put even
more simply; it appears in Figure 1.5. Most of the decline in the last half

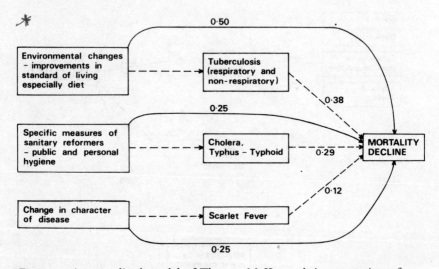

Figure 1.5 A generalized model of Thomas McKeown's interpretation of
the reasons for the decline of mortality in late nineteenth-century England
and Wales

of the nineteenth century is attributable to the reduction in three particular sets of diseases. They are: tuberculosis; cholera, typhus, typhoid; scarlet fever. To account for changes in these particular diseases would be to explain up to 75 per cent of the reasons for the general fall in mortality. The second stage of McKeown's argument is also summarized in Figure 1.5.[26] It is his contention that 'environmental changes' —by which he means improvements in the standard of living, especially diet—were substantial enough to affect mortality from tuberculosis and that in total such environmental changes were responsible for about half of the mortality decline. A further quarter of this decline could be linked with the 'sanitary revolution', that is, the specific measures of the sanitary reformers, which particularly affected public hygiene but are also connected with improvements in personal hygiene. The water- and food-borne diseases are affected here, but especially cholera, typhus, typhoid. McKeown also attributes an additional quarter to changes in the character of diseases themselves, a factor which is thought to be of particular influence in respect of scarlet fever.

A central plank of McKeown's method is the 'argument by exclusion' or the 'Holmesian technique': eliminate the impossible or the improbable and what one is left with must be the answer. In this particular case the positive influence of medicine, health care and hospitals is to be played down if not completely eliminated. Apart from the case of smallpox it is difficult to see how medical science could have had a direct influence on the decline in mortality until the introduction of chemotherapy in the 1930s. Certainly there were changes in the number, distribution, quality and administration of hospitals which, together with the establishment of local dispensaries, must have had a favourable impact if for no other reason than that isolation hospitals were eventually used to segregate the infected from the non-infected.[27]

However, the central problems in any assessment of McKeown's argument remain the need, firstly, to find direct evidence for a rise in the general standard of living during the nineteenth century and to demonstrate the causal link between that rise and the decline in mortality and, secondly, to show the extent of the quantitative contribution of each of the possible factors that might have been involved.

On the first matter, there is still considerable controversy over what has come to be known as the 'standard of living debate' for whilst it is normally agreed that working-class living standards did begin to rise in the late nineteenth century, and possibly from 1840, it is still arguable whether there were significant advances during the first stages of industrial capitalism. If anything the consensus now seems to be that, except for a small section of the labour aristocracy, conditions probably grew worse for the mass of the new urban labour force.[28] However, in the present context this conclusion is often arrived at by a somewhat circuitous route—making inferences concerning living conditions from changes in levels of mortality.[29] We are on firmer ground in the second half of the nineteenth century, for here there is clear evidence of both rising real wages and a falling cost of living.[30] Not only were these absolute improvements, but they seem also to have particularly favoured members of the working classes. At least, that perception was current amongst their betters whose fear of relative deprivation, or, as it has been called more recently, the 'relative income compression phenomenon', was thought by many observers to have been a crucial economic factor in initiating the secular decline of marital fertility.[31]

For the latter part of our period we are able to claim with confidence that general living standards were rising and the overall level of mortality was declining. How may these two variables be causally related? It is apparent from research on contemporary underdeveloped countries that it is possible for life expectancies to increase without the stimulus of economic development and rising per capita incomes—that the substantial changes observed are more likely to be related to improvements in public and private hygiene and to the availability of basic medical care.[32] It is probable that the West European experience, and particularly that of Britain, differs from the norm because of the high incidence of respiratory tuberculosis and the substantial impact that the decline of that one disease had on overall levels of mortality.[33] However, it must also be said that in theory rising living standards should create favourable circumstances for a rise in life expectancy. It is entirely reasonable that such a connection could have operated in the case of England and Wales without that relationship being both a necessary and a universal one.

The second problem to be found in an assessment of McKeown's argument is reflected in Figure 1.5, where the causal links (→) are given numerical weights. These are derived from statements such as that by McKeown and Record: 'the specific changes introduced by the sanitary reformers were responsible for about a quarter of the total decline of mortality in the second half of the nineteenth century' and 'the reduction of mortality attributable to the decline of bowel infection resulted from the specific measures introduced under the sanitary revolution'.[34] This means of directly quantifying the impact of the sanitary revolution, and with such certainty, must render itself open to criticism for, whilst it can be shown quite clearly which diseases were becoming less important as causes of death and indeed what the major influences on those diseases are likely to have been, it is unreasonable to go further and infer that because, for instance, the bowel infections were responsible for a quarter of the mortality decline and that the sanitary revolution was coincident with that decline then the sanitary revolution was therefore specifically and directly the cause of 25 per cent of the mortality decline.

Those now engaged in research on the history of population, mortality, medicine and health care are bound to face these and many other problems. So far, whilst their efforts have been valiant, their analyses and conclusions have often been negative.

III

The essays in this volume have the ambitious task of examining in detail the mortality experience of England and Wales during the nineteenth century, particularly in the period after registration. Some essays follow through the physical deterioration debate into the years before the First World War. The contributions can be divided into three types: those concerning general trends; those dealing with specific diseases; and those analysing the situation in particular towns. Woods (Chapter 2) in his analysis of the data available in the Registrar General's *Annual Reports* for 1861–63, on each of the 631 registration districts, explores the pattern of mortality in England and Wales from a demographic perspective. He makes the initial point that the probability of dying for the five to 14 age group began to decline from mid-century for both males and females as well as in the ten to 24 age group for females. By the last quarter of the nineteenth century this improvement was noticeable for males and indeed the one to four and the ten to 34 age group were showing improvement. Infant mortality, however, did not begin its precipitous fall until after 1900. These variable figures conceal spatial variations, particularly between urban and rural areas. The northern industrial towns, which were made by the Industrial Revolution, had especially high mortality levels. Woods also investigates the possible links between high fertility and high infant mortality, without finding a clear association at mid-century in the period before family limitation became widespread. He concludes his essay with an analysis of the underlying structure of age-specific mortality patterns amongst the registration districts.

Woodward, in following on from the highly statistical analysis in Chapter 2, presents a wide ranging discussion of the factors which were found to be of significance in Woods's essay. Although much of the McKeown analysis is accepted, Woodward does indicate that medicine can be seen as contributing to the fall in mortality. It is clear that the impact of smallpox was diminishing from the mid-eighteenth century, firstly with the more general use of inoculation and, after 1798, with the use of Jenner's cowpox vaccine. This is not to suggest that vaccination was totally accepted or was universally used. Epidemics did occur and local authorities exerted their independence of central control, despite legislation. Public health measures and, ultimately, isolation made their contribution to the reduction in mortality. Although for the major killer diseases effective medical therapies, in terms of antitoxins and artificial drugs derived from the chemotherapeutic revolution, were not available until at least the First World War and often the 1930s, the medical profession did provide assistance in a number of ways. The increasing provision of hospitals, both by voluntary agencies and by the Poor Law, removed from the general population both the acute and chronically sick and by care, rest and good diet returned them to the community to continue to act as breadwinners. Their effectiveness at the local level is more noticeable when viewed as part of a community, rather than at a national level in relation to the total population. Doctors also acted to treat specific sections of the population and, indeed, served the general population through clubs and societies. They also served as members of pressure groups for public health reform and on local authorities, in order to improve their social position. The medical profession also played an important role in the 'physical deterioration' debate at the end of the nineteenth century and helped to extend the area of state activity into the field of personal health.

Cronjé (Chapter 4) examines the particular disease of tuberculosis, the 'white plague', in all its forms. She suggests that the decline in its mortality was not because of effective medical treatment. Between 1851 and 1910 of the four million who died from tuberculosis one third were in the 15–34 age group. Death, though, was far from inevitable for those who contracted the disease and Cronjé attributes the improvement, particularly for women in urban areas, to a combination of factors. Improvements in diet, particularly in the quality of the milk supply, and in housing, coupled with changes in work patterns, increased bodily resistance. She points also to the falling birth rate at the end of the century which, with the above factors, meant fitter women giving birth to healthier babies.

These studies are followed by analyses of individual towns, relating to the general environment and to specific mortality problems. Luckin in his study of London (Chapter 5) concentrates on the decline of mortality associated with typhus and typhoid. He argues that there is a strong case for tracing the medical history of an infection over a short period and in a deliberately delimited area so that relationships can be more accurately examined and regional and national patterns can be juxtaposed. Typhoid showed a substantial and continuous decline between 1871 and 1885, slackening until 1900, whereafter mortality fell rapidly and uninterruptedly. The explanation for this fall cannot be found wholly in improvements in the water supply, as it was only in the 1890s that more than 50 per cent of London's population had access to a constant water supply and then the working-class areas were not always included. The reduction in typhus, again, cannot be wholly accounted for in terms of 'public health' as there was an absence until the 1860s of an extra urban sewage system, and overcrowding was not reduced until at least the 1880s. However, from the early 1870s London, like other English cities, became isolated from fear of infection as migration from urban Ireland declined.

The persistently high rates of infant mortality are studied in an analysis of experience in Bradford by Thompson (Chapter 6). She takes a pessimistic approach, demonstrating the slow improvements in public health, there being no Medical Officer of Health until 1873, after national compulsory legislation, nor any Public Analyst until 1874. Although there is some evidence of improved food supplies— quantitatively and qualitatively—and rising real wages in the 1870s, poverty still remained. Life expectancy did increase with a shift to factory-based worsted production in the 1850s and 1860s, but the lack of domestic sanitary provision, the general disregard for domestic hygiene, and artificial infant feeding maintained high rates of infant mortality among the working-classes in inner city areas, particularly via gastro-intestinal disorders, respiratory infections and premature births. Concern was shown from the 1880s by charitable organizations but to little effect.

The Pooleys in their long-term study of Manchester (Chapter 7) demonstrate the local input of national trends. Downward trends in mortality are interrupted by major peaks during times of trade depression and it is not until the late 1870s that the beginnings of a long-term decline can be discerned. They note that up to 50 per cent of all deaths refer to children under five and that 60 per cent of total lives saved in the second half of the century are in this category. Typhus and typhoid contributed only one-third of the deaths associated with tuberculosis. The new working-class districts did rather better than the old, though with a lessening of differentials over time. However, deaths from respiratory diseases were high in suburban areas where there was an older population. Again they comment, as do the other authors, that public health improvements were unlikely to succeed: traditionally control could only be exerted over levels of exposure to food- and water-borne diseases, and the improvements themselves were patchy.

The final chapter presents a detailed description of the spatial and temporal variations in mortality in Birmingham in the 1880s. It too is sceptical about the precise role of the sanitary revolution and tends, rather, to emphasize the role of poverty and especially housing conditions as a more plausible influence on the overall level of mortality, and its variation over time and through space. Like Luckin's contribution on London it is critical of the McKeown interpretation, at least in its quantitative form (Figure 1.5).

The purpose of this volume has been to bring together geographers, demographers, historians, and social historians of medicine. Although advances in knowledge do not come merely from the combination of disciplines it is hoped that the essays do provide a synthesis, that the importance of information in one essay can be applied to another and that the insights are meaningful. George Rosen, who in a series of essays and books tried to open up the history of public health, mortality and the role of medicine, once stated:

The social history of health and disease is . . . more than a study of medical problems. . . . It requires as well an understanding of the factors—economic conditions, occupation, income, housing, nutrition, family structure and others—which create or influence health problems, and of the ways in which they operate. [35]

The editors trust that the reader will learn a little from these essays and appreciate the many interrelationships with which Rosen was so concerned.

★ 2 ★

Mortality patterns in the nineteenth century

Robert Woods

When attempts were made in the 1840s to calculate the First and Second English Life Tables,[1] life expectancy at birth in years (e_0) was found to be 40 for males and 42 for females.[2] In England and Wales it is now in the upper sixties for men and the mid-seventies for women, but in the Eighth English Life Table (for 1910–12) it had reached, respectively, the low and middle fifties. Between 1840 and 1900 e_0 for males and females probably improved by no more than ten years, whilst between 1900 and 1960 an improvement of at least 20 years was recorded. Although there were substantial changes in mortality in nineteenth-century England and Wales, they were by no means as rapid or as substantial as those that have occurred in the twentieth century.

The aim of this chapter is to explore the pattern of mortality in nineteenth-century England and Wales from a demographic perspective. In this context five general themes will be considered. The first is concerned with overall changes in mortality in the post-vital registration period and deals with England and Wales as a single unit. The second treats the spatial variation in mortality at mid-century and employs the registration districts as its framework. The third deals with the definition of urban places and presents a classification of registration districts which can be used to compare the mortality experiences of urban and rural, small town and large town, and industrial and commercial environments. The fourth seeks to explore some of the relationships which existed between mortality and environment. The final theme is concerned with spatial variations in the structure of age-specific mortality and attempts to identify the essential elements which were creating such widely differing experiences.

I

The changing life expectancy of males and females in England and Wales since 1841 indicates a similar experience to those of the French, Belgian, Dutch and Swedish and indeed to those of North America (Figure 2.1). [3] It is difficult to extend the curve backwards in time before vital registration began, but it is possible to gain some idea of the level of mortality for specific groups or places. Hollingsworth's studies of the demography of the British peerage [4] indicate that e_0 for those born in the late sixteenth century was in the upper 30s, that it declined to about 30

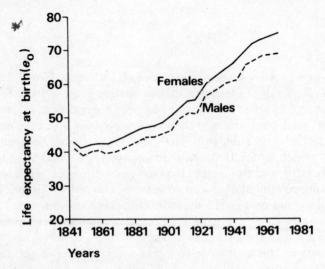

Figure 2.1 Changing level of life expectation at birth (e_0) for males and females, England and Wales, 1841–1970

for those born in the late seventeenth century, and then rose gradually to exceed 50 for the nineteenth-century birth cohorts. Studies by members of the Cambridge Group for the History of Population and Social Structure have revealed not only similar or lower levels of life expectancy, [5] but also have suggested that mortality appears to have fluctuated from time to time, and that there has not been a simple secular decline over the centuries.

It is also clear that the change from life expectancies of 40 to 70 has come about as a result of differential shifts in the balance of age-specific mortality as indicated by an examination of the probability of dying between ages x and $x+n(_nq_x)$ for males and females in England and Wales over the period since 1841 (Figure 2.2). Such changes as did occur in life expectancy during the nineteenth century (left of the vertical line in Figure 2.2) were linked to the decline of mortality in, firstly,

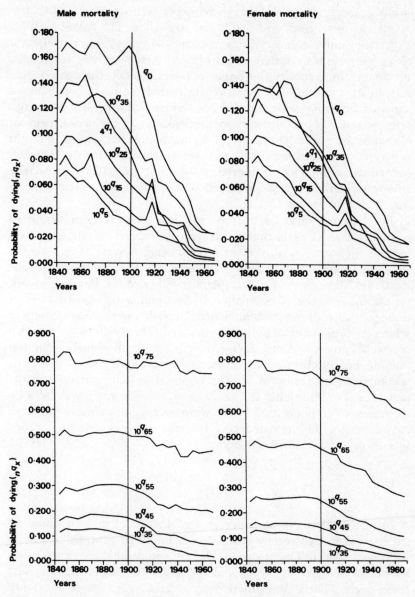

Figure 2.2 Changing age-specific mortality ($_nq_x$), England and Wales, 1841–1970

childhood and, secondly, early adulthood.[6] The probability of dying for both males and females between ages five and ten ($_5q_5$) began to decline from mid-century as did $_{10}q_{25}$ for females. By the third quarter of the nineteenth century $_{10}q_{15}$ and $_{10}q_{25}$ had also begun to decline for males whilst even $_4q_1$ (the probability of dying between ages one and five, that is one and one + four) and $_{10}q_{35}$ were in decline. The 'take-off' in life expectancy only became possible when mortality for the age groups one to 35 had begun to decline and the 'flight path' was only maintained because infant mortality also began a precipitous fall after 1900 (Figure 2.1). Infant mortality (q_0) for males fluctuated about 170 per thousand and that for females around 140 per thousand during the nineteenth century and was one of the major contributors to the maintenance of high mortality during the century. As much as 30 per cent of all deaths occurred to infants who had not yet reached their first birthday. Substantial reductions in mortality amongst the elderly, especially amongst elderly females, produced a new trajectory in recent times (lower part of Figure 2.2).

The patterns outlined provide the basis for an examination of mortality changes in the nineteenth century (Figures 2.1 and 2.2). They indicate the extent of movement and also suggest ways of tackling the vexed question of what caused life expectancy to improve so substantially. McKeown,[7] for example, has followed this line in his work on the modern rise of population by examining the contribution of those particular diseases that influenced mortality in those age groups in which the probability of dying was reduced. The results of this research are well known and are discussed in more detail elsewhere in this volume, but the entire approach has a number of limitations. One of its weaknesses is its failure to identify regional or local variations in the pattern and to distinguish the range of experience which was faced by members of a population who were living in radically different environments. The remainder of this chapter is devoted to a consideration of these particular points.

II

A male baby born in an inner area of Liverpool in 1861 could be expected to live 26 years whilst a female might be expected to live an additional year. In Okehampton, Devon, comparable life expectations would have been 57 years and 55 years for males and females respectively. There was, therefore, as great a range of mortality experience in England and Wales within the 1860s as there was between that of England and Wales as a whole in the 1840s and in the 1960s, namely some 30 years. The magnitude of this discrepancy did not go unremarked by contemporaries,[8] but it has not been possible, until recently, to analyse the underlying regularities in both a rigorous and a comprehensive fashion.

The data provided in the Registrars' General *Annual Reports* together with that in the *Population Censuses of England and Wales* make it possible to construct life tables for relatively small areas of the country—the advent of computers now makes this a feasible undertaking. The system of civil registration, initiated in England and Wales in 1837, was organized so that a superintendent registrar was responsible for the recording of statistics on births, marriages and deaths in each of the 631 registration districts. Although the statistics on births and marriages are rudimentary, every effort was made to record considerable detail on mortality.[9] The *Annual Reports* and *Decennial Supplements* contain information on sex of deceased, age at death and even cause of death. Age at death can be found for 17 age groups, but only 13 are used here.[10] It is unfortunate that such detailed statistics are only available for registration districts for years that can be related to the 1851, 1861, 1871 and 1881 censuses. The *Annual Reports* for 1891 and for subsequent years give age at death by registration counties.[11]

Taking the three years 1861, 1862 and 1863, for example, the mean annual age-specific mortality can be related to the age structure data provided in the 1861 census and thus sex-specific life tables for each of the registration districts can be derived. However, a number of additional problems have to be faced before this can be accomplished. First, an assumption has to be made that as far as mortality and age structure data are concerned under-registration, under-enumeration and misreporting are negligible. This commonly accepted convention has been utilized by Glass and Teitelbaum, for example, to estimate birth under-registration.[12] Second, Anderson raises a potential problem by suggesting that the age-groups used to report mortality are 'too crude for use as the basis of regional life tables'.[13] This seems to be an unreasonable position to take as it is unlikely that life expectancies, for instance, would be significantly different were five-year age groups to be used throughout instead of the ten-year age groups (25–84) that are available. Last, a problem is associated with the nature of the life table itself as an analytical device. The period life table measures life chances at a point in time; it does not give any indication of the true life expectancy of a particular cohort over a number of years. Despite this drawback life tables constitute both a standardized and a most efficient means of measuring mortality. Life expectancy at birth (e_0) provides the most appropriate single number indicator of the whole mortality experience.

A number of techniques have been employed for the construction of period abridged life tables;[14] the one used here is commonly referred to as simple approximation.[15] From the vital statistics on age at death presented in the Registrar General's *Annual Reports* for 1861–63 and the age structures from the 1861 *Population Census of England and Wales*, two life tables can be constructed, using this method, for each of the 631 registration districts which were defined in 1861 (Figure 2.3).[16] The year 1861 is used to represent that period (effectively 1851 to 1881) during which age at death data were published annually by registration districts,

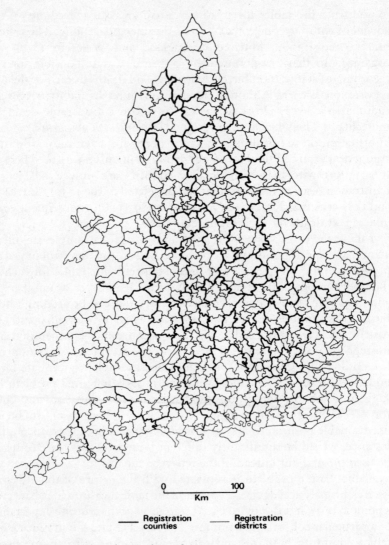

Figure 2.3 Registration district boundaries

and thus the mortality conditions at mid-century. The range of mortality experienced by the population of these 631 districts has been examined by the means and standard deviations of the probability of dying function, $_nq_x$ (table 2.1). It is clear that the normal two to three year discrepancy between the e_0s of males and females is the result of excess male mortality during the first few years of life (0–4, but especially of infant mortality, q_0), and also in late adulthood (over 45) (table 2.1). Female mortality appears to exceed males for the age groups 10–14 to 35–44, possibly attributable to the risks of childbearing and to

Table 2.1. The probability of dying ($_nq_x$) by age groups, England and Wales, 1861 (based on 631 registration districts)

Age groups		Males		Females	
		Mean $_nq_x$	Standard deviation	Mean $_nq_x$	Standard deviation
0	1	0.1466	0.0296	0.1189	0.0264
1–4	2	0.1142	0.0459	0.1107	0.0444
5–9	3	0.0365	0.0134	0.0364	0.0131
10–14	4	0.0221	0.0085	0.0237	0.0083
15–19	5	0.0301	0.0121	0.0356	0.0115
20–24	6	0.0415	0.0157	0.0424	0.0130
25–34	7	0.0854	0.0300	0.0924	0.0208
35–44	8	0.1029	0.0402	0.1047	0.0254
45–54	9	0.1440	0.0504	0.1251	0.0339
55–64	10	0.2428	0.0672	0.2182	0.0487
65–74	11	0.4638	0.0810	0.4266	0.0712
75–84	12	0.8185	0.0797	0.7807	0.0837
85+		1.0000	—	1.0000	—

Sources: calculated from the Registrar General's *Annual Reports* for 1861, 1862 and 1863; *Population Census of England and Wales*, 1861

the ravages of tuberculosis. The standard deviations give an impression of the range of mortality experienced among the 631 observations for each particular sex and age group.

The overall pattern of mortality can be assessed most effectively by using the life expectancy (e_x) function from the life tables. Male life expectancy at birth (e_0) in 1861 for those registration districts outside London (Figure 2.4) can be compared with the London pattern (Figure 2.5). The experiences of Okehampton, Devon, and Liverpool, are also placed in their context. The latter is seen to be but one of a number of districts that had male e_0s less than 35. Bristol, Birmingham, Leicester, Derby, Manchester, Sheffield, Hull and Newcastle registration districts experienced similar conditions, although in none were conditions quite as acute as those in Liverpool. Many of the inner London districts must also be included in this category (Figure 2.5). In contrast, several rural districts in the south, the West Midlands and the south west had male life expectancies at birth of over 50 years. Most of the districts in southern England in addition had e_0s in the upper forties while many of those in north Yorkshire and the northern Pennines had similar expectancies. Only one London registration district falls into this category.

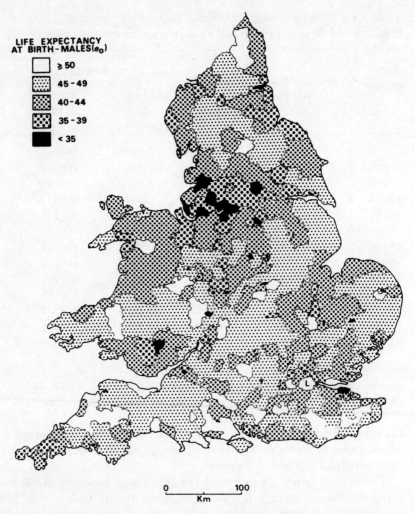

Figure 2.4 Spatial variation in male life expectation at birth (e_0), England and Wales, 1861 (based on registration district units) (L—London has been excluded)

Female life expectancy at birth is closely associated with the male e_0.[17] The overall level of mortality for males and females is similar (Figure 2.6), there being a high positive correlation with the male e_0, on average 2.82 years lower than that for females amongst the set of 631 districts.

Infant mortality (q_0), that element of age-specific mortality, remained high throughout the nineteenth century (Figure 2.2). It is clear that the range of experience between districts was even greater than for life expectancy at birth; that it was greater for males than females; and that q_0 was persistently lower for females than males. An examination of the

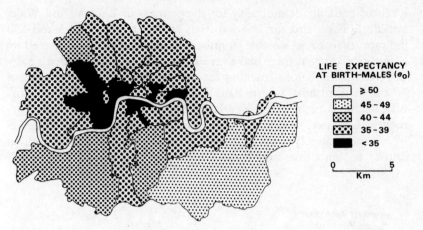

Figure 2.5 Spatial variation in male life expectation at birth (e_0), London, 1861 (based on registration district units)

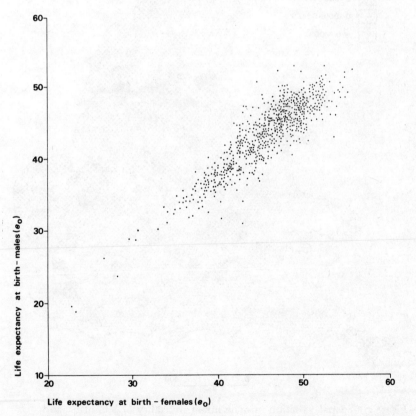

Figure 2.6 Life expectation at birth (e_0), males against females, England and Wales registration districts, 1861

levels of male infant mortality for the districts in England and Wales
outside London and for London itself for 1861 (Figures 2.7 and 2.8)
indicate that in a sizeable number of Lancashire and Yorkshire
registration districts there was a greater than 0.2 probability that a baby
boy would die before reaching his first birthday. Similarly, parts of
North Staffordshire, North-East Warwickshire, South Wales, Cornwall, Cambridgeshire and Kent together with Norwich, Great Yar-
mouth, Leicester, Nottingham and Newcastle-upon-Tyne had levels
which were equally as high although, surprisingly, only one London
district fell into this category. Districts with the lowest male infant

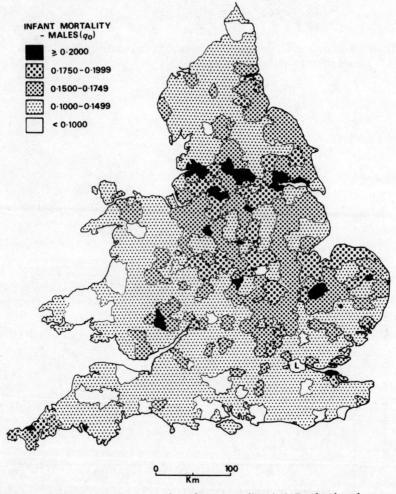

Figure 2.7 Spatial variation in male infant mortality (q_0) England and
Wales, 1861 (based on registration district units) (L—London has been
excluded)

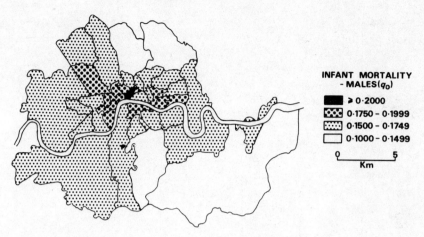

Figure 2.8 Spatial variation in male infant mortality (q_0), London, 1861 (based on registration district units)

mortality were to be found in the south, the south west, Wales and the north Pennines. Unlike the case of life expectancy at birth, the relationship between male and female infant mortality, whilst positive and strong, is less significant.[18] It is possible, therefore, that q_0 for males could have been relatively high in particular districts, whilst that for females was relatively low (Figure 2.9).

The patterns and relationships are complex (Figures 2.3 to 2.9) and remain extremely difficult to explain. These complexities will be approached here in a highly simplified, exploratory and partial manner. The first approach considers the often hypothesized association between firtility and infant mortality; while the second deals with the role of urbanization.

In societies where infant mortality is high, fertility is also likely to be high to compensate for the loss and to provide replacements where otherwise a population might not be able to maintain its numbers naturally. In addition, if fertility is high and women are having high parity births during their forties, the chances of stillbirths, together with high infant mortality, will also be substantially increased. Therefore, there could be a significant relationship between infant mortality and fertility.[19]

Although there are problems associated with the measurement of mortality in nineteenth-century Englans and Wales they are only slight when compared with those involved in the measurement of fertility. Indices such as the total fertility rate or the gross reproduction rate cannot be measured directly until well into the twentieth century, because information on age of mother at the birth of each child was not collected during the nineteenth century. An indirect standardization

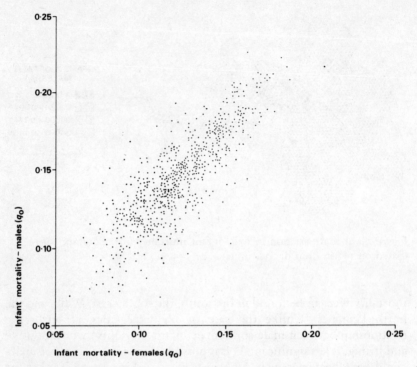

Figure 2.9 Infant mortality (q_0), males against females, England and Wales registration districts, 1861

technique will be used here as a means of estimating the gross reproduction rate (GRR), ie the number of female children an average mother might be expected to have on passing through the reproductive ages 15 to 49.[20]

The statistical association between female infant mortality (q_0) and the gross reproduction rate (GRR) shown for the 631 registration districts is relatively weak (Figure 2.10) and even though the correlation coefficient between them is positive and significant at the 95 per cent level, the coefficient of determination is only 0.75. Moreover, the gross reproduction rate is probably a poor measure of that particular aspect of fertility which is likely to be influenced by mortality in infancy or early childhood. A. J. Coale's index of marital fertility may be superior in the circumstances.[21] The relationship between $_4q_1$ (the probability of dying between ages one and five) for females and Coale's index of marital fertility (I_g) has been calculated (Figure 2.11). The coefficient of determination now increases to 5.62($r = -0.237$ and $_4q_1$ (females) $= -0.203 I_g + 0.249$).

The combined effects of fertility (GRR) and mortality (e_0 sexes combined) levels on population growth rates, as measured by the intrinsic rate of natural growth (r), have been determined (Figure 2.12).[22] The isolines ($r = 0.00$, $r = 0.01$ and $r = 0.02$) link points with

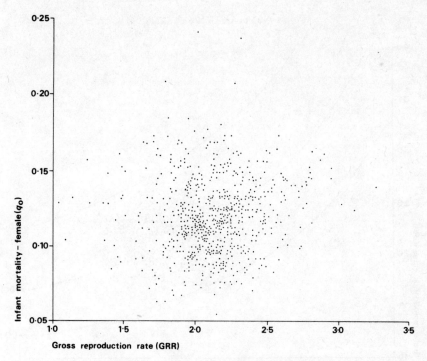

Figure 2.10 Female infant mortality (q_0) against gross reproduction rate (GRR), England and Wales registration districts, 1861

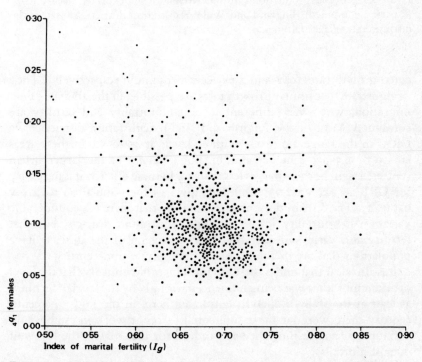

Figure 2.11 Mortality of female children aged 1–4 ($_4q_1$) against index of marital fertility (I_g), England and Wales registration districts, 1861

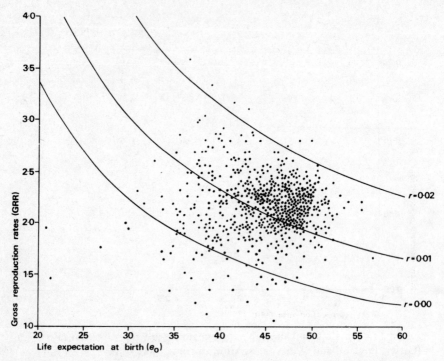

Figure 2.12 Gross reproduction rate (GRR) against life expectation at birth (e_0, sexes combined), England and Wales registration districts, 1861 (*r* is the intrinsic rate of natural increase)

equal growth rates (0, 1 and 2 per cent per annum respectively). They demonstrate that similar growth rates are possible, in the absence of net migration, when very different levels of mortality and fertility are combined. Most of the English and Welsh registration districts have GRRs in the range 2.0 to 2.5 with e_0 levels at 45 to 50. In these areas $r = 1.0$ to 1.5 per cent per annum, but in many of the larger urban centres, as will be shown, e_0 is less than 40. In these districts it is necessary for GRR to exceed 1.75, 2.00 and upwards for population to grow naturally. The distribution suggests not only that there is a considerable variation in mortality levels amongst registration districts, but that fertility also varies considerably. Indeed, several of the districts have populations that are unable to grow naturally at mid-century.

It is also clear that under these circumstances it is unlikely that the level of infant mortality was being influenced strongly by the level of fertility, at least at the scale of analysis employed here. In the mid nineteenth century there were far more influential forces at work in establishing variations in infant mortality and indeed for that matter the levels of overall mortality.

III

The urban districts are likely to have the highest mortality (and therefore lowest e_0) and the rural districts the lowest, and those districts which mainly consist of small towns or suburban environments are likely to occupy an intermediate position (Figures 2.4 and 2.7). This broad generalization was certainly clear to most contemporaries; it is obvious in the writings of Edwin Chadwick and William Farr, for example, just as it is implicit in the work of the sanitary reformers.[23] However, to define 'urban' and 'rural' in practical terms and to specify what exactly it was about the urban environment in the nineteenth century that made it less healthy, raises far more complicated issues.

The definition of 'urban' has always been problematical. Is it to mean non-agricultural, non-rural, or should it be used to characterize a place's built environment, and hence, refer to an area that is continuously built-up, or a distinctive legal entity? Should the term 'urban' be approached via 'urbanism', i.e. a particular and distinctive 'urban way of life'?[24] These questions raise difficulties which can only be side-stepped, or tackled indirectly, if a practical definition of 'urban' is to be devised which will enable registration districts to be grouped into categories. In the late nineteenth and early twentieth centuries these difficulties were faced by social statisticians such as T. A. Welton and A. L. Bowley.[25] Bowley took a very pragmatic approach by using a critical population density of over 30 per 100 acres (74.13 persons per sq. km.). A registration district was rural if less than 50 per cent of its population lived at such densities; urban or suburban if the entire district was above that critical density; and was placed in an intermediate category if over 50 per cent of its inhabitants were living in places above that level.

An even simpler version of this approach will be employed here (Figure 2.13). Those districts with population densities in excess of 1,000 persons per sq. km. stand out very clearly and may confidently be regarded as urban places. By using such a critical density most of the large towns in England and many of the small ones, such as Exeter, Salisbury and Canterbury can be distinguished. However, this ability is largely a function of the configuration of registration district boundaries, which in many cases combine a small town with a surrounding rural area (see Figure 2.3). It is possible to identify the town of Bury St. Edmunds, but not that of Lincoln, merely because the former is defined by a single registration district whilst the latter is contained within a predominantly rural district. Despite this drawback the greater than 1,000 persons per sq. km. category provides a simple yet effective way of distinguishing the continuously built-up areas of Liverpool, south-east Lancashire, the West Riding of Yorkshire, the Black Country and of London. At the other extreme of the range those registration districts with population densities of less than 100 per sq. km. can be regarded as

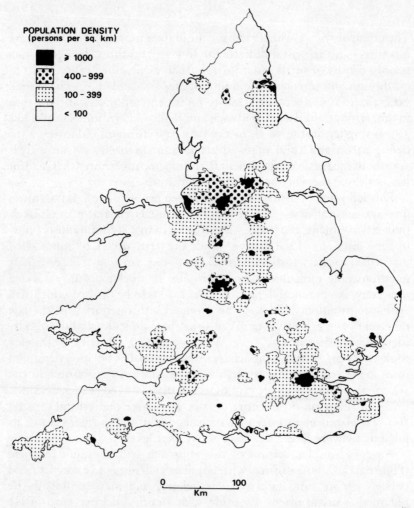

Figure 2.13 Classification of urban areas by population density, England and Wales, 1861

predominantly rural. Thus, most of England and Wales can be considered rural in the mid nineteenth century, although a majority of the population was concentrated in non-rural districts.[26]

This simple classification raises many difficulties, but one of the most troublesome involves the identification of suburban areas or areas in which there are large numbers of industrial villages. Much of County Durham, South Wales, Derbyshire, Nottinghamshire, Leicestershire and the Home Counties might be regarded as containing mainly urban populations, that is, those who do not gain their livelihood from agriculture or economic activities related to agriculture. In the first two areas coal mining predominated, in the third mining and the textile industry were important and in the fourth the influence of the metropolis was all-pervading. The division of the population density classes into those over 400 but less than 1,000 persons per sq. km. and those over 100 but less than 400 persons per sq. km. makes it possible to distinguish several highly urbanized registration districts round Newcastle-upon-Tyne, Leeds, Bradford, Manchester, Sheffield, Birmingham and Bristol, and to identify also several more small towns like Chatham–Rochester, Eastbourne, Colchester, King's Lynn, Bath and Cheltenham (Figure 2.13). The lower density of the two intermediate classes picks out the coalfield areas of South Wales, South Lancashire and the coal-based industrial belt which is associated with the York–Derby–Notts coalfield, but which extends southwards to incorporate Leicester and the industrial districts north of Coventry. The outer-metropolitan area of suburbs and small towns also falls into this class.

The classification of registration districts in terms of population density, as outlined above, can only provide a crude and arbitrary means of tackling the problem of defining 'urban' and 'rural' areas, and the above analysis represents just one simple solution.

IV

The annual league tables of death rates that were published by local Medical Officers of Health and the Registrar General, and which appeared regularly in the press, tended to confirm the contemporary view that towns were unhealthy places when compared with rural areas and that the largest urban areas were the most unhealthy of all. To what extent was this actually the case in the mid nineteenth century?

As an illustration, taking the life expectancy at birth of males it can be shown that there is a fairly strong inverse relationship between male e_0 and population density, once the latter has been transformed logarithmically.[27] It is obvious that although the association is a significant one statistically, it is quite possible for the same e_0 to be found in places with a range of different population densities (Figure 2.14). As population density increases so life expectancy declines, but only down to an e_0 level of about 35 after which point there was little variation in life expectancy. If the classification employed previously (Figure 2.13) is used here then it appears that it is amongst 'rural' registration districts that the most clearly distinguishable inverse association occurs and that in districts with population densities in excess of 400 per sq. km.—the 'urban' areas—life expectancy was universally low. Life expectancy for males in the rural districts was usually in the 40s and varied with population density; for the urban districts it was in the 30s, but did not change consistently with population density.

A considerably less ordered pattern is found when dealing with infant

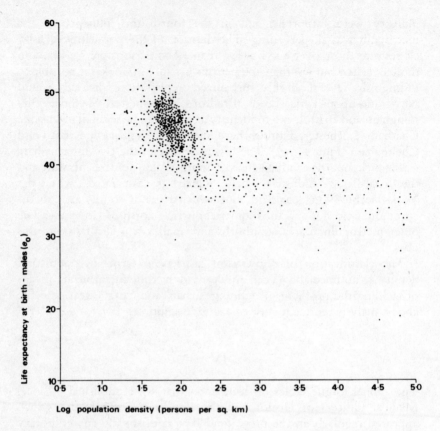

Figure 2.14 Life expectation at birth (e_0) against log population density, England and Wales registration districts, 1861

mortality. The scatterdiagram (Figure 2.15) of male infant mortality (q_0) and log population density displays a fan-shaped distribution which suggests that districts with high population densities are also likely to have higher infant mortality, and that those in the 'rural' category could experience a considerable range of q_0 values, some of which were just as high as those to be found in the 'urban' districts.[28] Those districts with q_0 values less than 0.1 are all 'rural' in character, although those with male infant mortality in excess of 0.2 are likely to be 'rural', 'intermediate' or 'urban'.

The significant points to emerge from this analysis are that Victorian social statisticians were quite right to distinguish between urban and rural places in terms of their mortality. Generally there was a clear association, but nevertheless the link via population density was by no means as clear-cut as might first be imagined.

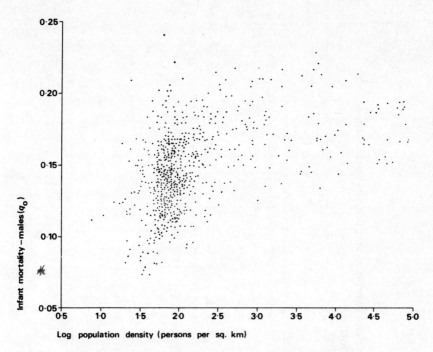

Figure 2.15 Male infant mortality (q_0) against log population density, England and Wales registration districts, 1861

V

It is apparent, therefore, that there were considerable spatial variations in the mortality experience of England and Wales's mid nineteenth-century population and that although there are regularities to be identified, they do not lend themselves to any simple explanation or interpretation. An additional means of searching for order might be provided by an analysis of how age-specific mortality varied spatially, but since 12 age-groups are being dealt with some means of summarizing their interconnections must be found before the analysis can be made. Both principal components analysis and factor analysis provide means of isolating the fundamental structures in a set of inter-correlated variables, that is, they symbolize the statistical associations by substituting a small number of summary components or factors for a large number of variables.[29] In this particular case it is necessary to define 12 age-specific mortality variables and to calculate matrices of correlation coefficients (12×12) using the set of 631 registration districts with one matrix for male $_nq_x$ and another for female (table 2.2). Over the set of 631 registration districts the correlation between q_0 (variable 1) and $_4q_1$

Table 2.2. Correlation coefficients between $_nq_x$s for males (above the diagonal) and females (below the diagonal), England and Wales, 1861 (based on 631 registration districts)

Age group	variables	1	2	3	4	5	6	7	8	9	10	11	12
0	q_0 1	—	0.599	0.409	0.239	0.203	0.047	0.094	0.266	0.373	0.467	0.526	0.381
1–4	$_4q_1$ 2	0.580	—	0.636	0.328	0.228	0.125	0.258	0.522	0.601	0.666	0.662	0.459
5–9	$_5q_5$ 3	0.441	0.582	—	0.434	0.344	0.253	0.330	0.413	0.419	0.431	0.399	0.250
10–14	$_5q_{10}$ 4	0.078	0.142	0.358	—	0.452	0.394	0.379	0.355	0.370	0.323	0.347	0.139
15–19	$_5q_{15}$ 5	0.058	−0.043	0.162	0.312	—	0.603	0.510	0.389	0.347	0.292	0.269	0.119
20–24	$_5q_{20}$ 6	0.027	−0.098	0.128	0.278	0.458	—	0.603	0.411	0.306	0.203	0.150	−0.027
25–34	$_{10}q_{25}$ 7	0.185	0.109	0.206	0.307	0.430	0.409	—	0.667	0.579	0.468	0.333	0.067
35–44	$_{10}q_{35}$ 8	0.325	0.386	0.302	0.179	0.247	0.246	0.414	—	0.778	0.693	0.535	0.284
45–54	$_{10}q_{45}$ 9	0.429	0.537	0.325	0.133	0.121	0.114	0.323	0.490	—	0.775	0.679	0.386
55–64	$_{10}q_{55}$ 10	0.451	0.591	0.285	0.096	0.027	−0.003	0.209	0.517	0.613	—	0.754	0.463
65–74	$_{10}q_{65}$ 11	0.388	0.540	0.248	0.038	0.037	−0.017	0.183	0.383	0.542	0.574	—	0.494
75–84	$_{10}q_{75}$ 12	0.288	0.324	0.125	0.025	0.048	0.033	0.083	0.241	0.352	0.380	0.427	—

(variable 2), for example, is 0.599 for males and 0.580 for females, whilst that between $_5q_{20}$ (variable 6) and $_{10}q_{55}$ (variable 10) is 0.203 for males and −0.003 for females.

The use of factor analysis on the correlation matrices for male and female age-specific mortality yields three important factors in each case, although those factors in combination account for 71.1 per cent of the variance between $_nq_x$s for males and 62.0 per cent for females (table 2.3). Examination of factor loading matrices for males and for females provides the most straightforward means of interpreting each of the factors (tables 2.4 and 2.5).

The principal factor to be isolated in the case of male $_nq_x$ distinguishes adult mortality from that in other age groups, but particularly the mortality of those aged 35–64. The second factor is strongly associated with infant mortality and that in early childhood while the third loads heavily on mortality in the 10–24 age group. As far as male $_nq_x$s are concerned, therefore, the mortality experience can be summarized by three distinctive and unrelated elements, namely, and in order of importance: adult mortality; infant and child mortality; and teenage and early adulthood mortality. As for female mortality, once again three distinctive factors are isolated; the first is associated with mortality in the 45–74 age group, the second with that in the 15–34 age group and the third with the one–14 age group. These factors can be labelled as follows: late adulthood, adulthood, and childhood mortality. The second factor corresponds well with the effective female reproductive period and suggests that it might more appropriately be labelled as 'mortality associated with the risks of childbearing'. When the patterns of factor loadings for males and females are compared it seems that in both cases, adult mortality is the most influential in creating distinctions between levels of age-specific mortality. In terms of the second factor, infant and child mortality is more significant for males than for females, whilst for the latter it is the risk of mortality in childbearing that takes second place. The third factors, which are even less important, also have some overlap in their loading pattern, though here the emphasis is on childhood mortality amongst females and early adulthood mortality amongst males.

The full value of this method of analysing the structure of mortality can be shown by turning to spatial variations and by considering the role of environmental factors in influencing the level and pattern of mortality. Factor analysis is capable of yielding factor scores which measure the importance of each factor in each of the spatial units that have been employed to construct the original correlation matrix. In this instance the 631 registration districts in England and Wales for 1861 provide the spatial framework and once again the sexes can be treated separately (Figures 2.16 and 2.17).

Factor scores equal to or above +1.0 indicate that the age-specific

Table 2.3. Results of factor analysis on $_nq_x$ for males and females, England and Wales, 1861 [31]

Factors	Males			Females		
	Eigen-value	Percentage of variance	Cumulative percentage	Eigen-value	Percentage of variance	Cumulative percentage
1	5.557	46.3	46.3	4.226	35.2	35.2
2	1.933	16.1	62.4	2.080	17.3	52.6
3	1.044	8.7	71.1	1.138	9.5	62.0
4	0.709	5.9	77.0	0.781	6.5	68.5
5	0.595	5.0	82.0	0.701	5.8	74.4
6	0.547	4.6	86.5	0.556	4.6	79.0
7	0.380	3.2	89.7	0.528	4.4	83.4
8	0.344	2.9	92.6	0.507	4.2	87.7
9	0.284	2.4	94.9	0.463	3.9	91.5
10	0.219	1.8	96.8	0.419	3.5	95.0
11	0.201	1.7	98.4	0.343	2.9	97.9
12	0.188	1.6	100.0	0.257	2.1	100.0

Table 2.4. Factor loadings from analysis of age-specific male mortality

Age group variables		Factor loadings—males		
		Factor 1	Factor 2	Factor 3
0	1	0.0708	0.7963	0.0950
1–4	2	0.3597	0.7905	0.1432
5–9	3	0.0808	0.6355	0.4757
10–14	4	0.0559	0.3524	0.6816
15–19	5	0.1768	0.1196	0.7854
20–24	6	0.2696	−0.1398	0.7986
25–34	7	0.6579	−0.0909	0.5954
35–44	8	0.8116	0.2043	0.3321
45–54	9	0.8072	0.3708	0.2186
55–64	10	0.7395	0.5209	0.1053
65–74	11	0.5730	0.6338	0.0729
75–84	12	0.3204	0.5956	−0.1584

Table 2.5. Factor loadings from analysis of age-specific female mortality

Age group variables		Factor loadings—females		
		Factor 1	Factor 2	Factor 3
0	1	0.5167	−0.0316	0.5191
1–4	2	0.6150	−0.1595	0.6324
5–9	3	0.1759	0.1255	0.8585
10–14	4	−0.1272	0.4846	0.5604
15–19	5	0.0040	0.7723	0.0594
20–24	6	−0.0154	0.7801	−0.0114
25–34	7	0.2498	0.7282	0.0907
35–44	8	0.5971	0.4181	0.1552
45–54	9	0.7504	0.1813	0.2165
55–64	10	0.7990	0.0243	0.2140
65–74	11	0.7856	−0.0097	0.1179
75–84	12	0.6504	0.0173	−0.0842

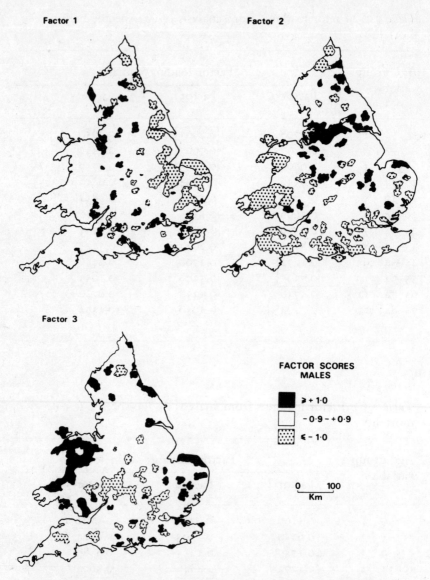

Figure 2.16 Factor scores, male mortality (L—London has been excluded)

mortality of a registration district is closely and positively represented by
that particular factor whilst scores of less than or equal to —1.0 suggest a
strong, but inverse relationship. For example, factor 1 most closely
represents the mortality of adult males so it should be possible to reveal
in which registration districts it is relatively more important and in
which it is relatively less important than other forms of male age-specific
mortality (table 2.4). Low negative scores (≤ —1.0) on factor 1 for

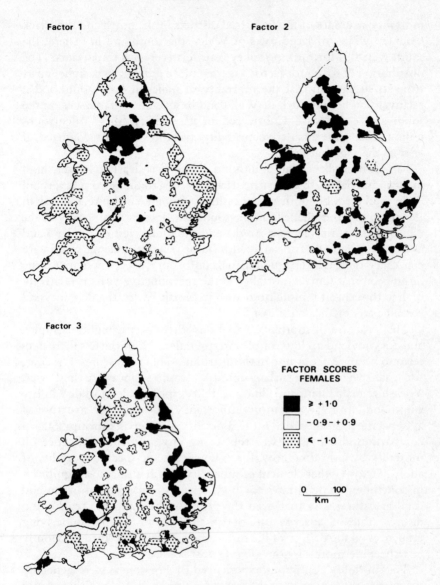

Factor 1

Factor 2

Factor 3

FACTOR SCORES
FEMALES

■ ≥ +1·0

□ -0·9 - +0·9

▨ ≤ -1·0

0   100
Km

Figure 2.17 Factor scores, female mortality (L—London has been excluded)

males are to be found mainly in the eastern counties of England, whilst high positive scores (≥ +1.0) occur in many of the large urban centres, such as Birmingham, Liverpool, Manchester and Newcastle-upon-Tyne as well as several of the smaller southern towns like Exeter, Chichester, Reading and Cambridge (Figure 2.16). Bath, Southampton, Brighton and Eastbourne also fall into this category. In terms of factor 2, male infant and child mortality is a particularly significant element of the mortality structure of the industrial districts in the north and the Black Country while for large parts of Wales, the south and in general the south west this form of mortality is of relatively less importance. The distribution of scores for factor 3 is even more difficult to decipher apart from its suggestion that the mortality of males in early adulthood is relatively higher in much of Wales and in several coastal towns on the south and east coasts. Considered in its entirety, these calculations indicate that some distinctive mortality structures can be recognized, at least at the regional scale.

Female mortality in late adulthood (factor 1) is clearly relatively high in the industrial north and particularly that area running from Liverpool in the west through southern Lancashire into west Yorkshire, to Leeds in the north east and Sheffield in the south east (Figure 2.17). Many of the registration districts in East Anglia and the south west of England and Wales are negatively associated with factor 1. As far as factors 2 and 3 are concerned there is little sign of spatial conformity, except perhaps for the impression that female mortality in the reproductive years is relatively high in those most remote rural areas in North Wales, the Pennines and certain parts of the south east.

The structure of mortality variations, therefore, is highly complex and does not lend itself to simple interpretation. None the less there does seem to be some patterning in the distribution of factor scores. It is clear, for example, that in urban-industrial south Lancashire and west Yorkshire male infant and child mortality, and female mortality in late adulthood, are relatively more important elements in the structure of age-specific mortality than is the mortality of other age-groups. Such a comparison also makes clear the strong environmental influence on mortality by indicating how, for instance, the age-specific mortality of adults (factor 1), that element of mortality which is the most significant in controlling general rates for both sexes, varies between urban and rural areas in a way that even the problems of using the registration district scale of analysis cannot obscure. Some of the underlying influences on the pattern of life expectancy at birth described previously now become more obvious (Figure 2.4).

The mortality conditions experienced by Londoners were generally worse than those in most of the rest of England and Wales, although not necessarily worse than those to be found in the large provincial towns (Figures 2.18 and 2.19). Therefore, it might be expected that many of the London registration districts would show high and positive factor scores on those factors which played the most important part in creating high levels of total mortality. Most of the London districts, for example, have factor scores ⩾ + 1.0 on factor 1 and the high mortality of adult males is a relatively important element in the overall structure of mortality. In the case of factor 2 it is clear that for the inner area of London high male infant and child mortality is significant and at this level of analysis there is little to distinguish the east end from the west end. Furthermore, for

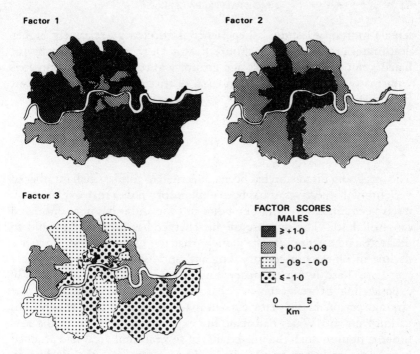

Factor 1

Factor 2

Factor 3

FACTOR SCORES
MALES

■ ≥ +1·0

▨ + 0·0 - +0·9

▦ - 0·9 - -0·0

▩ ≤ -1·0

0   5
  Km

Figure 2.18 Factor scores, male mortality, London, 1861

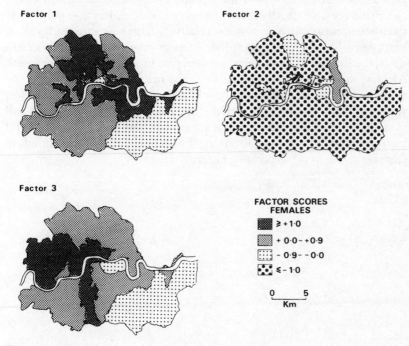

Factor 1

Factor 2

Factor 3

FACTOR SCORES
FEMALES

■ ≥ +1·0

▨ + 0·0 - +0·9

▦ - 0·9 - -0·0

▩ ≤ -1·0

0   5
  Km

Figure 2.19 Factor scores, female mortality, London, 1861

female mortality London's experience is affected by relatively higher death rates in the adult age groups (factor 1), though the mortality of females in their reproductive age groups was relatively low compared with many of the more isolated rural districts, even in the south east (factor 2) (Figure 2.19).

VI

The foregoing discussion has been concerned to fulfil a small number of very limited objectives; it has been exploratory rather than explanatory; it has been limited to only one point in time and it has not considered cause of death. The purpose of this chapter has been to raise and to illustrate one essential point, namely that the experience of mortality decline in nineteenth-century England and Wales was highly place-specific. Those living in many rural districts in 1861 were already experiencing life expectancies that would only be reached by the 'average person' in the 1920s; even in 1931, 20 of the 84 county boroughs in England and Wales had male life expectancies at birth in the low fifties, a figure which the inhabitants of several rural areas had attained some seventy years previously.[32] The reasons for the decline in mortality in the post-vital statistics period can only be understood by an appreciation of conditions which are highly heterogeneous and of the fact that over time the diversity of experience diminishes, so that in late twentieth-century Britain there is relatively little variation in levels of mortality, although there are still differences between social classes.[33] In short, the strong environmental influence on mortality in the nineteenth century, which is closely linked with the urban-rural dichotomy, has faded away to near insignificance whilst the socio-economic influence, although it has become weaker than it was in the last century, is still evident today. There seems to be strong support here for the general interpretation of the variations in mortality patterns presented in Chapter 1 (see p. 21 especially Figure 1.1).

★ 3 ★

Medicine and the city: the nineteenth-century experience

John Woodward

The growth of civilization means the growth of towns and the growth of towns means, at present, a terrible sacrifice of human life . . . . The fact is that in creating towns, men create the materials for an immense hotbed of disease, and this effect can only be neutralized by extraordinary artificial precautions.[1]

The historian who approaches the problems presented by the demographic history of Britain during the nineteenth century is faced with an almost intolerable number of factors to consider. Social status, work experiences, quality of housing, extent of amenity, size of family, access to and quality of food supply and medical treatment: these are but a few of the factors influencing the life chances of an increasingly urbanized and industrialized population. The intention of this chapter is to examine the role of medicine in contributing, or not doing so, to alterations in those life chances (particularly in urban areas) during the nineteenth century. It is necessary to state at the outset that medicine does not merely encompass the relationship between a patient and a doctor, where scientific knowledge is used in an attempt to cure a disease. On the one hand this definition excludes the preventive contribution that medicine and its practitioners can make at a public and personal level. On the other, not all disease is treated by a registered medical practitioner; the unregistered can make contributions, as can self-treatment by the patient. Indeed, this final aspect still remains of key importance in understanding the practice of health today. Therefore, the official statistics of disease mortality on which so much reliance has been based for historical analysis, from the implementation of the Registrar General's office in 1837, do not inform the historian who needs to take cognisance of the non-fatal attacks of illness, both infectious and non-infectious, from which the sufferer recovers. The recovery may or may not have been due to active medical intervention. In short, 'an iceberg of disease of unknown, though probably vast dimensions existed in the nineteenth-century urban context'. Equally, 'medicine is not only what the physician does. The majority of all cases of illness—the minor ailments—are never seen by a physician. They are treated by the patient himself or by his relatives.'[2] It is worth emphasizing that 'not only is disease related causally to the social and economic situation of the given population, but the health care received also reflects the structure of a society, particularly its stratification and class division. Rank has its privileges in illness as in health. From antiquity to the present, the social class of patient has in various ways affected the medical transactions related to his illness.'[3]

I

The role of medicine, with these qualifications and observations, can be analysed using a number of bench marks against which to judge its contribution. Throughout the nineteenth century the population of England and Wales grew at over one per cent per annum, rising from 9.2 in 1801 to 17.9 in 1851, 32.5 in 1901 and 36.1 millions in 1911. As the population increased the balance altered from rural to urban. After 1851, when the changeover point occurred, the most rapid growth was to be found in those regions based on textiles, ship building, coal mining and iron and steel. From the 1840s to the 1870s crude birth rates fluctuated between 34.8 and 35.8 per thousand while the secular decline in fertility is apparent from the 1870s and the 1880s.[4] Crude death rates changed little between 1841 and 1871, whereafter decline set in.[5] Life expectation at birth (e_0) began to rise significantly from the 1860s: for example, the 1838–54 birth cohort had an e_0 of 39.9 years for males and 41.9 years for females; while the 1901–12 cohort had e_0s of 51.5 and 55.4, respectively.[6] The decline in infant mortality was particularly noticeable from 1900 onwards, but not before.

The causes of the reductions in mortality which appear as the cause of death in the official statistics have been analysed in the well-known series of articles and books by Thomas McKeown and his associates.[7] Comparing the decades 1851–60 and 1891–1900, of the lives saved the proportions attributable to each of the major disease categories were: all forms of tuberculosis, 47.2 per cent; typhus, enteric fever and simple continued fever, 22.9 per cent; scarlet fever, 20.3 per cent; diarrhoea, dysentery and cholera, 8.9 per cent; smallpox, 6.1 per cent; and whooping cough, 2.3 per cent. Diphtheria actually increased by five per cent. A parallel movement was seen in Scotland though there a significantly greater contribution was made by typhus and typhoid (33.0 per cent) and diphtheria did decline (15.0 per cent).[8] On an age basis the most notable features were, first, a substantial reduction in all age groups from tuberculosis and from the typhus and enteric group; second, a substantial reduction in childhood mortality from scarlet fever; third, a reduction in mortality from the diarrhoeal diseases in all age groups apart from childhood up to the age of four years; fourth, a decline in mortality from smallpox in children up to the age of nine years.

Thus, according to McKeown, non-infective conditions appear to have contributed only about eight per cent to the decline in mortality, though the reduction may be illusory because of errors in certification. It is therefore the reduction in air-borne and food- and water-borne infective conditions which is significant. In the case of tuberculosis and smallpox McKeown suggests that mortality was declining before civil registration.

As McKeown takes a very narrow definition of the role of medicine in contributing to the perceived decline in mortality it is possible to argue that no effective therapies were available for most of the diseases until well into the twentieth century. The 'white plague' of tuberculosis registered a decline before the identification of the tubercle bacillus by Koch in 1882. An initial anti-toxin was ineffective and it was not until the introduction of streptomycin in 1947 and the BCG immunization programme from 1954 that active medical therapies were available. The mortality attributable to bronchitis, pneumonia and influenza increased in the second half of the nineteenth century, followed by a major decline after 1901. Yet, chemotherapy in the form of sulphonamides was not introduced until 1938 and was only really effective in the case of lobar pneumonia. Although a decline in mortality from whooping cough was evident from the 1870s effective treatment awaited the introduction of sulphonamides in the late 1930s and preventive immunization in 1952. No reduction in measles was forthcoming until after 1915 and no treatment for it by chemotherapy until 1935. A decline in mortality from scarlet fever was noticeable after 1863 and although the causative streptococcus was identified in the 1880s effective treatment was awaiting, yet again, the introduction of sulphonamides in the 1930s. Deaths from diphtheria peaked just before the end of the nineteenth century. The causative organism was isolated in 1889 and anti-toxins became available from 1894, though it has been argued that immunization may not have been the only contributor to the subsequent decline in mortality. Mortality from smallpox exhibited great variations, though on a declining trend. Inoculation had come into use during the eighteenth century and after the introduction of the techniques pioneered by the Sutton brothers became more widespread, thereby contributing to a decline before the beginning of the nineteenth century. [9] Cowpox vaccine, discovered by Jenner, came into widespread use in the early nineteenth century and free vaccination became available in 1840 through the Poor Law authorities and was made compulsory in

1854, with further legislation in 1871 and 1898. Cholera, as an epidemic disease, struck for the last time in 1865, even though there were no effective treatments available.[10]

On these grounds, therefore, McKeown fails to find any benefit from medical intervention, apart from smallpox. In the case of scarlet fever there was a change in the nature of the causative organism. As an explanation of the decline in mortality he turns to improved nutrition as the causal factor. It is possible to argue that the Industrial Revolution brought improvements in real wages to many sections of the population and that, in particular, the last twenty years of the nineteenth century were years of gains as food prices fell. However, a cautionary note should be brought in at this point. As Oddy has demonstrated recently it is difficult to find major shifts in food consumption patterns at the end of the nineteenth century. Firstly, there is no positive evidence to show that there was any secular increase in heights or weights of school children. Secondly, working-class diets were still composed principally of carbohydrates and any movement towards proteins was limited to small increases in the consumption of dairy products rather than meat.[11] Yet, of course, any better nutrition, however small, would give greater resistance to viral and bacterial infection. Though here again, the qualification must be entered that in a number of instances the nutritional state of the body can be diminished by disease and that muscles will be metabolized. Infections of the stomach and gut and of muscles selectively affect the already undernourished and the disease may act cumulatively on the body. Again, although food adulteration may have come under scrutiny after 1872 many food processes, for example condensed milk and roller milled flour, may well have been less nutritious and in some instances harmful to the consumer. Interestingly, bovine tuberculosis appeared to respond to the pasteurization of milk from the late 1880s, but the extent of the consumption of cow's milk by children and of general access to pure and unadulterated milk supplies for the population as a whole is difficult to establish.[12] Yet the question remains, whether small improvements in nutrition coupled with smaller completed families did allow some gains in health. Thus far, a somewhat depressing picture has been painted of the role of medicine and of the qualification related to nutrition. Yet, perhaps it is mistaken to see medicine in such restricted terms as only based on active and effective drug therapy. Medicine and its practitioners have a much wider role in the life of the people. Indeed, was all therapy ineffective? — particularly in cases of non-fatal disease, where treatment could enable an individual to resume his role at work and in the family. The restoration of health would also mean that the body was depleted no longer and would resist attacks from the other, perhaps fatal, diseases. Is it possible that medicine contributed at the very least to the stabilization of the mortality rate and then ultimately succeeded in reducing that rate?

It is customary to argue that the medical profession was small and elitist during the nineteenth century and that few people had access to treatment as fees could only be afforded by the wealthy. In the eighteenth century it is clear that the patient was in control of the medical transaction and that patient domination implied that physicians had no choice but to tailor their theories and remedies to meet the expectations and requirements of their genteel clients.[13] The patient himself determined even the nature of illness. In particular the patient's understandable desire to be cured of his symptoms, rather than be diagnosed of his disease, had an indelible impact on contemporary theories of virology and pathology. Medical knowledge revolved around the problems of the prognosis and therapy of symptoms, rather than the diagnosis and analysis of diseases. Symptoms were not regarded as the secondary signs of internal pathological events, but rather as the disease itself.[14] However, from the early nineteenth century, developments in medical knowledge helped to produce a shift in the balance between doctor and patient. Increasingly, scientific knowledge based on relating symptoms to changes in the vital organs became available. This development and knowledge was taken up from France and particularly from the Paris hospitals where extensive post mortems and clinical examinations were taking place. The shift from observation to examination meant that the doctor defined the problem and the solution.[15]

Such advances could have had even greater significance if the medical profession as a whole had been larger, better trained, more equitably distributed and better organized. Before the passage of the Medical Act of 1858 the organizational structure of the profession was in a state of near chaos. There were 19 different licensing bodies, three of which were particularly important. In 1800 there were 179 fellows, licentiates and extra-licentiates of the Royal College of Physicians in England, by 1847 there were 683, of whom just over three-quarters practised in London. Some 80 per cent of all London physicians held College licences, but only 23 per cent of provincial doctors were so qualified. Of the 14,700 medical men recorded in the 1851 census there were 1,700 who claimed to be physicians. In the mid nineteenth century some 8,000 practitioners held a surgical licence, but only 200 were fellows of the Royal College of Surgeons. However, there were few who practised purely as surgeons, most were surgeon-apothecaries. The Apothecaries Act of 1815 empowered the Society of Apothecaries to grant licences for medical practice, over 6,000 of which were granted by 1834. In the years after the passage of the 1858 Act it is possible to be more precise about the numbers of medical practitioners, their relative preponderance and distribution. The doctor:population ratio in 1861 was 1:1,392; 1:1,547 in 1871; 1:1,721 in 1881; and 1:1,500 in 1891.[16] The number of medical men graduating per annum reached about 1,200 by the 1880s. These national ratios do conceal considerable regional and local variations,

however. In London in 1861 the ratio was 1:514; in Wales it was
1:1,769; and by 1886 it was 1:726 in Brighton; 1:939 in London;
1:1,232 in Bristol; 1:1,564 in Liverpool; 1:2,209 in Glasgow; 1:2,593
in Sheffield; and 1:3,908 in Salford. Within these urban areas there are
also likely to have been considerable variations. For example, in 1914 in
London, Shoreditch had a ratio of 1:5,000 while in Kensington it was
1:500.

It is important to appreciate, however, that these figures should not be
confused with doctor:patient ratios. It is possible to argue that
during the second half of the nineteenth century more and more people
came under the attention of a general practitioner. The commonplace
observation that the poor could not afford the fees of doctors and
therefore had little or no contact with the medical profession has been
challenged by Peterson, in her recent study of the mid-Victorian
medical profession.[17] Doctors in urban areas often had to compete
strongly for practice and income. Although the general practitioner
would be looking for middle-class clients he often had to depend on
others for his income. The average fee for an ordinary visit as late as 1910
was just under 3s.[18] Fee schedules for the 1870s and 1880s show them to
be as low as 1s. for an ordinary visit, while practitioners appearing before
a House of Lords committee in 1890 indicated that fees of 1s. to 2s. 6d.
were common and that general practitioners did not expect to get as
much as 3s. 6d. a visit. Treatment might even be free, in fiction at
least. For example, Sir Arthur Conan Doyle, who was himself a general
practitioner in Portsmouth in the early 1880s, had his character Stark
Munro charging poorer patients 1s. 6d. a visit and on one occasion a
gypsy family was treated free of charge.[19]

In addition to such practice there were other opportunities to reach
the working classes. Firstly, there was contract or 'club' practice which
grew up from the 1830s. Medical clubs, a sort of self help for the poor,
were encouraged by local Boards of Guardians; fraternal societies and
working men's clubs sometimes established sick clubs for their members. Some of these medical clubs were founded entirely from weekly or
quarterly subscriptions; others were subscribed through private philanthropy. Some clubs had a single doctor who served all members,
while others had a panel of doctors. The fees varied. In the 1830s they
ranged from 2s. to as much as 7s. 6d. per person per year; in the 1880s
minimum fees were nearer 3s. Additional fees were charged for 'extras'
such as maternity care, insurance certificates, and the care of broken
bones. Provident dispensaries were a similar form of working-class
medical self help combined with philanthropy—out-patient clinics
where subscriptions and contributions paid for drugs and the balance of
the income was divided among participating medical men.

Secondly, government employment led medical men into many areas
of practice: as medical officers of health from 1848, into public

vaccination from 1840, as prison and gaol medical officers, police and militia surgeons. There was a plethora of such appointments, including certifying factory surgeon under the legislation of 1853; port sanitary officer; post office doctor. Perhaps the greatest number were involved in Poor Law work. Appointment as a Poor Law medical officer was common for a general practitioner, often on a part-time basis. Although the Poor Law Amendment Act did not specifically cover the sick, local authorities did appoint medical officers, as they had done before 1834, but although there were general medical orders in 1842 and 1847 there was no mandatory provision until 1868. This sector of employment totalled about 2,300 in 1840, 4,000 by 1870 and 5,000 by the mid-1880s.

At the time of the establishment of the Ministry of Health in 1919 the posts available to medical practitioners at a full-time and part-time level had expanded to encompass school medical and dental officers; pensions medical officers; and tuberculosis officers. Many practitioners held more than one post. As many as 1,700 were certifying factory surgeons; 2,000 were post office medical officers; while 16,000 out 21,000 general practitioners worked within the national health insurance scheme of 1911.[20]

II

Although members of the medical profession acted as individual general practitioners, which may also have involved them in part-time work as medical officers to a variety of agencies, many were also involved in the medical care provided by hospitals. Here, once again, we are on uncertain ground. We can follow two lines in assessing the role of hospitals in the nineteenth century. The first is concerned with the provision of hospital beds and the extent to which hospital care could cover the needs of the people. The second line involves an evaluation of the positive contribution of hospitals to the decline in the death rate; a contribution which McKeown, amongst others, thought was negligible if not harmful.[21]

The first of these lines is relatively more straightforward. In 1861 there were about 14,800 beds available in voluntary hospitals; 29,500 in 1891; and 43,221 in 1911. In the sector administered through the Poor Law there were 50,000 beds in 1861; 83,280 in 1891; and some 154,000 in 1911. By 1861 there were about 900 hospitals of which some 650 would be better described as ordinary workhouses. By 1891 the total had risen to 1,666 of which 713 were Poor Law institutions, and by 1911 the total was 2,187 with 625 Poor Law. In terms of bed provision per thousand of the total population, in 1861 total accommodation in voluntary hospitals amounted to 0.73 beds per thousand, with 0.33 in general, 0.26 in teaching and 0.10 in special hospitals. The remaining 0.04 constituted provision for infectious diseases, tuberculosis, maternity cases and cases of chronic sickness or infirmity. Workhouses provided 2.49 beds per thousand population. By 1891 general hospital provision had trebled to 0.94 beds; special accommodation for infectious diseases increased to 0.38 beds; and by 1911 the most marked expansion had occurred in general hospitals and hospitals for infectious diseases.[22] On the whole these figures would support the view that voluntary hospitals did well in keeping up with urban population growth during the nineteenth century. This observation also appears to be valid locally. In his recent summary Cherry has indicated that the ratio of in-patients per thousand local population was consistently over five in Manchester, for instance, and could reach as high as 16 in Leicester by 1800.[23] From 1800 to 1820 these ratios were maintained, though from then to 1870 the position did deteriorate, but not catastrophically. At no time did the ratios fall below 12 per thousand in Worcester and Cambridge; below seven in Bristol and Leicester or, at the extreme, 3.2 in Manchester.

Cherry has also proceeded to develop the second line of enquiry outlined above by examining the beneficial, or otherwise, influence of hospital care. The pessimistic views of McKeown and others for the eighteenth and early nineteenth century had already been challenged by Sigsworth[24] and Woodward,[25] who argued that 'it is impossible to measure positively their [the voluntary hospitals] contribution as the necessary data are not available; and yet a negative effect on mortality would seem to be unlikely'.[26] In general 'the conclusions to be reached about the experience of the voluntary hospitals during the eighteenth and nineteenth centuries . . . are favourable towards their contribution to the health of the community. The hospitals did achieve what appears to be a remarkable degree of success in treating their patients and the mortality remained at a low level throughout the period, generally being under ten per cent of the patients admitted.'[27] Cherry's own study covers seven provincial hospitals[28] which despite surgical and medical limitations, together with those of space, equipment and trained staff, attempted to treat a wide range of diseases and injuries throughout the nineteenth century, most of which were beyond cure at that time. Cherry's conclusions tend to support those of Sigsworth and Woodward for although in-patient mortality rates had increased by the 1870s this was probably related to increased patient pressure, and thus the treatment of only the most serious cases in hospital, together with a widening of the range of cases for which treatment was attempted. Given these considerations it is surprising that average rates did not greatly exceed the 7.64 per cent level estimated for the four major hospitals in 1880. Hospitals did become increasingly more successful in treating industrial and other accidents, and in helping the sick poor who were particularly prone to respiratory and debilitating diseases. 'Additionally, the hospitals played a vital role in curing those with less critical injuries for, with large sections of the poor living at or near subsistence levels, the prolonged illness or absence from work of family breadwinners could have had disastrous results for whole families.'[29]

A perspective that develops a traditional preoccupation has been suggested even more recently by Hamilton, based on his analysis of the records of the Glasgow Royal Infirmary.[30] From the 1870s the increased success of many long-established operations, together with an increase in the range of new surgical methods, can be associated with the introduction of antiseptic precautions and the improvement in hospital cleanliness, but also, and here Hamilton places great emphasis, with improved host defence caused by improved nutrition in the community. All three of these influences were working to the same end and appeared at the same time. However, as would be expected the evidence presented is not conclusive. The rise in United Kingdom real wages from 1850; the generalized annual death rate from compound fracture of the upper limb in Glasgow Royal Infirmary, 1842–1900; and the annual number of deaths from typhus in Glasgow from 1855 are related one to another. The first-mentioned shows a continuous rise, but is hardly particular to Glasgow; the second displays increase to a peak in the late 1860s (26 per cent) and decline thereafter, but the means of estimating the 'average trend', against which comparisons are made, are not specified; and the third shows decline interrupted between 1860 and 1873 by substantial peaks and is used as an index of 'social conditions'. The emphasis in Hamilton's interpretation may be misplaced—like many before him he has failed to prove the unproveable—but it nonetheless serves to illustrate the factors involved and to demonstrate both the absolute increase in the number of surgical operations undertaken and their relatively greater chance of success by the end of the nineteenth century compared with mid-century.[31] Evidence from Glasgow has also been used to demonstrate how hospitals came to accept fewer cases of certain diseases by the 1900s. The voluntary infirmaries actually treated fewer and fewer cases of pulmonary tuberculosis, although other respiratory diseases did increase.[32] In the poorhouses the sick were often admitted only at an advanced stage of illness, 'beyond the expectation of a cure', and only a relatively small proportion of the total cases were so dealt with. Such institutions had little effect, therefore, apart from isolation. However, in the latter years of the nineteenth century admission of acute cases became more common.[33]

Much of the early work on the voluntary hospital movement also considered the contribution of the dispensaries.[34] These institutions 'provided care on an outpatient basis, including home visiting and, in their general economy, they resembled in many ways the health centres of today'.[35] The dispensary movement effectively began in the eighteenth century and declined sharply, particularly after 1911 with the introduction of National Health Insurance, as their functions were taken over increasingly by the outpatient departments of the voluntary hospitals.[36] The dispensaries were probably of most significance between 1770 and 1850 during which time they competed with the hospitals in most large English towns, but they provided a service which was new and important, especially for the urban poor. After 1850 the voluntary hospitals began to take over their role, often by merger or, in certain cases, the dispensaries provided the nucleus for the foundation of a new hospital.

III

Nineteenth century medicine, ... was regulated more in accordance with normality than with health; it formed its concepts and prescribed its interventions in relation to a standard of functioning and organic structure, and physiological knowledge—once marginal and purely theoretical for the doctor—was to become established ... at the very centre of all medical reflexion. Furthermore, the prestige of the sciences of life in the nineteenth century, their role as model, especially in the human sciences, is linked originally not with the comprehensive, transferable character of biological concepts, but, rather, with the fact that these concepts were arranged in a space whose profound structure responded to the healthy/morbid opposition.[37]

The end of the nineteenth century saw the coalescence of a number of events in both the medical and social fields. Medicine itself was becoming more scientific and was requiring greater expertise. The advance of scientific knowledge was to initiate a change in the aims of medical treatment from the alleviation of suffering towards cure (though a cure had virtually always been claimed), but there was also occurring a fundamental change in the attitude of British society, as represented by both local and central government, with regard to its responsibility to the health of the community at large and ultimately to the individuals within it. *Ad hoc*, permissive legislation over a disparate range of sanitary and health problems was, in the early twentieth century, replaced by a co-ordinated, though not wholly complete, system of control and intervention. As a corresponding feature of this growth in state activity members of the medical fraternity had gained control over their own sphere of influence (by registration since 1858), but they also became influential as public servants in the public health movement and as a lobby for reforming legislation at both the national and local levels. During the hundred years that followed the reform of the Old Poor Law in 1834 state intervention in health care first expanded dramatically with the public health movement—the sanitary revolution so called—and then shifted its emphasis to become preoccupied with personal health and the well-being of individuals and families.[38]

Although the final stages in this long process only came in the 1940s, and thus lie beyond the range of the present volume, some important advances were made before the First World War, and the origins of the shift of emphasis are to be seen even in the Victorian era. The 'profound structure', as Michel Foucault terms it, altered slowly in response to a variety of forces, but its ultimate impact on mortality through medical science, the organization of personal health care and the creation of a state social security system was probably substantial. [39]

It has been argued that by the turn of the century there were developing pressures for greater collective activity by the State and that this was reflected in the provision of health services. 'The changing patterns of state medicine evolving in the personal health services during the first decade of the twentieth century were closely linked to the new concepts of a national society.' [40] There appear to have been three sources for these 'new concepts'. First, political pressure emanated from a more effectively organized working-class movement. [41] Second, a new attitude of 'social imperialism' became common amongst members of the political élite; an attitude related to the needs of empire and the view that the welfare of the working class depended on imperial strength. [42] Third, and closely linked to the second, was the growing debate over national deterioration which developed from the 1880s and became acute from the early 1900s as a result of evidence from the screening of Boer War recruits and the publication of Rowntree's and Booth's surveys. [43] The new concepts themselves are probably best represented in the 1904 report of the Inter-Departmental Committee on Physical Deterioration. The committee's recommendations pointed to the need for active intervention by the State and highlighted the major contribution that medical science had to make. There were particular recommendations for the introduction of a programme of health education, especially in schools and for mothers, for the wider development of a system of health visiting and for the provision of meals for school children, as well as medical inspection. [44] Further evidence of the need to extend health care was available: for example, the reports of the certifying factory surgeons emphasized the poor physical development of many adolescents and not just those from the poorest homes. The way forward had thus been opened for a shift in emphasis away from public health towards the provision of personal health care. 'The personal health services evolved from the broadening concept of communal needs and functions in twentieth-century society. Pressures which had pushed the problems of life of the working-class man to the fore had gradually created a public recognition that sanitation alone was not the answer to communal health. Medical treatment services were necessary for special classes of the community who required care which they were unable to supply for themselves.' [45]

IV

The practical form which this change in attitudes took may best be explored by examining one particular aspect of mortality and the way it was tackled by the State and other responsible agencies. As has already been remarked,[46] infant mortality remained high throughout the nineteenth century and only began to decline in the twentieth, but mortality in early childhood began to fall in the 1860s and 1870s. While the working child had been protected by factory legislation, infants remained unprotected. The Infant Life Protection Act of 1872 had been passed to protect infants in the care of persons other than parents, particularly on 'baby farms'. However, many abuses continued until the Act's extension in 1897. As regards the care of infants, information was being built up relating to feeding.[47] Breast-feeding was encouraged by a number of organizations. The first 'goutte de lait' for the distribution of free milk was opened in St Helens in 1899 and was soon followed by Liverpool (1901), Battersea (1902) and Finsbury (1904). The Medical Officer for St Pancras, London, established a school for nursing mothers in 1907, and an infant clinic was opened in Liverpool in the same year. Infant clinics, schools for nursing mothers and milk depots were to be the basis of a child welfare service. It was local authorities rather than central government which initiated these schemes and employed a number of trained nurses and others as health visitors to oversee the early days after birth. Huddersfield, for example, created a child welfare service in 1905 by appointing two lady health visitors, initiated payment for the notification of births within 48 hours, and established a pure milk depot and an experimental day nursery. National action on these issues was somewhat more tardy, however, but the Local Government Board did publish a report in 1910 which recommended the need for study of all infant deaths, the value of health visiting, education in infant health, and the training of midwives.[48]

The 1902 Midwives Act created the Central Midwives Board, which was required to keep and publish a role of midwives, make rules for their training and examination, and regulate their practice. The Act determined that no woman might 'habitually and for gain attend a woman in childbirth otherwise than under the direction of a qualified medical practitioner unless she be certified under the Midwives Act'. Maternal mortality appears to have declined once the Act was enforced although, as usual, there is no good reason to impute a single causal link.[49]

The growing responsibility of the State for the infant at and after birth marked a turning point in the evolution of personal health services. Now attention needed to be focused on the years between infancy and employment, namely on the schoolchild. At the local level the London School Board appointed their own medical officer in 1890, and in 1893 Bradford appointed a medical superintendent of schools, an example soon to be followed by Salford and Halifax. In the early 1900s the physical degeneration debate and the reports of the Inter-Departmental Committee, based as they were on firm information about the poor health of elementary school children, helped to establish the school meals programme (given legislative support from 1906) and eventually, after 1907, the medical inspection of children immediately before, at the time of, or as soon as possible after their admission to a public elementary school. Medical inspection only served to confirm how widespread was schoolchildren's poor health, but ultimately it also led to the free treatment of minor complaints amongst such children.[50]

V

The tenor of this evaluation of the role of medicine has been, like the volume itself, tentative rather than conclusive; it is difficult to see how medicine could have made an immediate and direct contribution to the decline in mortality in the nineteenth century—or in the period before the First World War, for that matter. However, medicine did contribute in other ways: by providing a network of medical practice; by example; by encouraging public health measures; and by facilitating a move towards personal health. Even if the spectacular advances in applied medical science or the organization of health care were not to be found in the nineteenth century, their origins are certainly there with Jenner, Lister, Koch and Pasteur; the voluntary hospital movement; the registration of medical practitioners; Chadwick, Farr, Simon and Newsholme; and ultimately with the cumulation of individuals' efforts towards the same goal. By the end of the nineteenth century there existed a recognizable positive concept of health, rather than a simple negative concept of the absence of ill-health. Indeed, as Newman commented, it was possible to assert that 'the sound mind in the sound body, the full capacity and opportunity of labour, the true *joie de vivre* which springs from all-round health, may in some larger and more liberal measure become established in the homes of the English people'.[51, 52]

Appendix to Chapter 3

Select list of health-related legislation, reports and advances

1798	Smallpox vaccination
1831–32	Central Board of Health
1833	Factory Act
1834	Poor Law (Amendment) Act

1837	Registration of births, marriages and deaths (start of civil registration in England and Wales)
1840	Vaccination Act
1842	Report on the sanitary condition of the Labouring Population of Great Britain (Chadwick Report, Flinn (1965))
1848	Public Health Act
1858	Medical Registration Act
1868–71	Royal Sanitary Commission
1872	Public Health Act
1882	Robert Koch discovers tubercle bacillus
1885	Medical Relief (Disqualification Removal Act)
1886	Medical (Amendment) Act
1888	Diploma in Public Health compulsory for medical officers of health
1890	Diphtheria anti-toxin discovered
1898	Alwirth Wright develops typhoid vaccine
1899	Compulsory notification of infectious diseases
1902	Midwives Act
1904	Report of the Inter-Departmental Committee on Physical Deterioration
1904	First use of diphtheria toxoid
1906	Education (Provision of Meals) Act
1907	Education (Administrative Provisions) Act
1909	Ehrlich isolates salvassan for use against syphilis (start of chemotherapy)
1911	National Health Insurance
1912	Neosalvassan
1915	Notification of Births Act
1918	Maternity and Child Welfare Act
1919	Ministry of Health

⋆ 4 ⋆

Tuberculosis and mortality decline in England and Wales, 1851–1910

Gillian Cronjé

I

Tuberculosis has been called 'the white plague', and this description, with its deliberate reference to the Black Death of earlier centuries, indicates the disease's dominating position in English mortality in the Victorian era. Consumption—phthisis, or pulmonary tuberculosis, as it was alternatively known—killed more people, especially in young adulthood, than any other disease in the nineteenth century. Yet by the first decade of the twentieth century the giant, if not vanquished—it was not until the 1950s that tuberculosis ceased to be a serious problem—was at least somewhat dwarfed.

By 1910 it became possible for social and medical administrators realistically to discuss mechanisms for the compulsory registration of tuberculosis victims, living as well as dead. Half a century earlier, when every family might expect to have some first or second-hand experience of tuberculosis, the enormity of this task would have defeated a social system which regarded the disease as part of the fate of the poor, the ill-housed, the under-nourished and the sickly. The steady fall in tuberculosis death rates, well established by 1870, was achieved almost entirely in the absence of effective medical treatment: it was only after the Second World War that mass prevention and cure campaigns became significant. Although there was great uncertainty about the nature and cause of tuberculosis, it is clear that women, in particular, benefited from improvements in tuberculosis mortality and that by the end of the nineteenth century urban areas were beginning to fare better than their country counterparts, reversing an earlier disadvantage (see Chapter 2).

After the identification of the tubercle bacillus by Robert Koch in

1882, health authorities gradually ceased to believe that the disease was a matter of inherited, constitutional susceptibility—of a 'tubercular diathesis'. They came to accept that specific public health measures—a clean milk supply, the isolation of infectious cases, the enforcement of particular public hygiene requirements, and health education—could help to lessen the impact of tuberculosis. Yet many of the underlying social and economic causes, which made tuberculosis the most serious of all endemic diseases in the second half of the nineteenth century, were still identified in the inter-war period as preventing its elimination Elimination only came with the changes which occurred in the wake of the Second World War.

Tuberculosis, because it was infectious, claimed victims from all classes, although a disproportionate number of them were poor. A wide range of economic, social and demographic variables which influenced tuberculosis mortality must be considered, and such complexity does not allow for simple explanations. The following discussion, rather than trying to provide answers, outlines the areas of major interest and some of the questions that they raise. This chapter first describes the medical aspects of tuberculosis, then examines the statistics, nationally and regionally, and considers the contrasts in mortality between town and country; in conclusion, it discusses the relative importance of the major factors affecting tuberculosis mortality.

II

Tuberculosis affects not only the lungs, as phthisis; but also every part of the body, particularly the intestinal tract, bones and joints, and lymph nodes—the form known in the nineteenth century and before as scrofula. Phthisis is largely an adult disease, whereas, in the nineteenth century, the bulk of the victims of extra-pulmonary tuberculosis were infants and young children. Tuberculosis is found in a number of mammals besides humans—most notably, in the present context, in cows. Bovine tuberculosis bacilli, although often associated with extra-pulmonary tuberculosis, can cause the disease in all the forms which 'human' bacilli are capable of producing. [1]

The bacilli are most commonly disseminated through the sputum expelled by sufferers in coughing or spitting—the droplet method of infection—or through food or objects contaminated in this way. The seriousness of this mode of infection depends on the degree of close physical contact between the sick and the healthy; for this reason, the adequacy of housing and the extent of overcrowding is a particularly important consideration in programmes designed to prevent the spread of the disease. Other relevant factors are the standards of cleanliness and degree of crowding in workplaces, and the extent to which measures of public hygiene are enforced.

Another common route of infection is through the consumption of contaminated food, particularly of milk originating from tuberculous herds. This source is likely to have its greatest impact on children, the population group consuming the largest quantity of liquid milk, and the one among whom infection from bovine bacilli is the highest.[2] The incidence in Britain of tuberculosis of bovine origin has been found in the past to vary considerably from area to area. Tuberculized milk can be very widespread. A survey carried out in Manchester in the late 1890s[3] found that 17.6 per cent of samples from the city's milk supply of country origin were infected, but only 5.5 per cent of samples from milk produced in Manchester itself—no doubt because urban cowsheds were subject to stricter regulation and inspection than those in the country. An inter-war study[4] showed that, in parts of Scotland, cases of infection from bovine bacilli occurred far more commonly than in England and Wales. The mortality from bovine tuberculosis in Glasgow, where milk was heat-treated, was a quarter of that in the rural areas which supplied the milk.

The problem of infected herds relied for its solution largely on the willingness of government to take measures to eliminate or control this source of bacilli. It was also a function of the readiness of individual consumers to take the precaution of boiling milk; and this depended on the extent of their education and awareness of the dangers of infected milk. Income was another important consideration: milk could easily become infected as a result of storage in dirty or contaminated conditions, particularly in the small general corner shops from which many working-class households bought their supplies.[5]

Once the bacilli enter the body, they multiply and set up foci of infection, causing necrosis of the surrounding tissue and forming lesions and cavities. Depending on the extent of the individual's natural or acquired resistance, the infection can at this stage be contained by calcification of the affected areas and the eventual destruction of bacilli; or it can become progressive, with further dissemination of bacilli and necrosis of vital tissue resulting, eventually, in death.

Death from tuberculosis is far from inevitable. However, the balance between the seriousness of the initial infection, the degree of resistance possessed by the sufferer, and his general state of health and standard of living, determines the outcome of the infection. Tuberculin tests, which were developed as a diagnostic tool in the early twentieth century, indicate whether an individual has ever suffered from tuberculosis, even if the infection has subsequently been contained or overcome. Surveys carried out in the early twentieth century revealed extremely widespread exposure to infection. One, conducted in London in 1930–31,[6] showed that 58.3 per cent of the children in the sample aged between 10 and 15 reacted positively to the test, while among the 14- and 15-year olds, the proportion was as high as 82.2 per cent. Other surveys indicated almost universal exposure in European cities[7] where, on average, 20 per cent of children had been infected by the time they were two; 50 per cent by the time they were five; 90 per cent of children under 15; while 97 per cent of adults reacted positively to a tuberculin test. The frequency of infection varied according to time, place and sample. Yet, it is clear that most people were able to overcome an initial infection, and did not develop progressive and ultimately fatal tuberculosis, because they possessed innate resistance, or a degree of resistance acquired as a result of previous infection which conferred some protection against subsequent illness. [8]

Innate or acquired resistance both reduces the risk of contracting tuberculosis and allows the sufferer successfully to contain an established infection and to prevent the rapid formation of large numbers of eventually fatal secondary lesions. 'Childhood' forms of tuberculosis, in which initial infection leads to a rapid and severe spread of bacilli, were given infrequently as causes of death among adults in nineteenth-century England and Wales. A slowly progressive pulmonary form, lasting for months or years, was more common. Nineteenth-century estimates of the duration of tuberculosis tended to lengthen as the century drew on, from a suggested 12 months in the mid-decades[9] to three, four, or even five years at the end of the period. [10] This improved prognosis was, probably, largely due to earlier recognition of phthisis. Rises in general standards of living probably also played a part, enhancing the individual's resistance, while better medical care came a long way behind. [11]

Tuberculosis could be controlled effectively only when the sources of infection could be neutralized or removed. This realization was the driving force behind the anti-tuberculosis movement, formed in the last decade of the nineteenth century, which launched the clean milk campaign and the sanatorium movement. Treatment in specialized hospitals first became available, for those able to pay, in the mid nineteenth century. [12] The attempt to make some form of sanatorium treatment more widely available gained momentum only after the 1882 demonstration that tuberculosis was infectious; but the response in terms of hospital beds was very inadequate as late as 1910. [13] The majority of tuberculosis sufferers received hospital treatment in the Poor Law infirmaries which, by the end of the nineteenth century, often afforded treatment that was good by prevailing standards. A few sufferers gained admittance to the handful of specialist hospitals, such as the Brompton Hospital for Consumption and Diseases of the Chest in London; most other voluntary hospitals were unwilling to accept patients suffering from what was widely regarded as an incurable disease. There were, indeed, few specific measures that could be taken, apart from efforts to alleviate some of the more distressing symptoms of tuberculosis.

Despite the new campaigns to tackle the tuberculosis problem, there was little change in the approach to treatment that had become established in the mid nineteenth century.[14] The medical profession, although recognizing the 'pre-disposing causes' of tuberculosis, felt that there was not much they could do about these evils, which arose out of poverty or ignorance or were the result of an inherited or acquired susceptibility to the disease. Bad housing, inadequate nutrition, poor ventilation, insufficient clothing, insanitary conditions, the inappropriate feeding of infants and young children, and general disability due to bad health, were all identified as closely associated with tuberculosis.

Some forms of tuberculosis, especially those affecting bones and joints, were increasingly treated by surgical intervention, particularly with the improvement in surgical techniques in the latter part of the nineteenth century. In general, however, treatment was aimed at strengthening the whole constitution against an inherited or acquired susceptibility to the disease. This overall approach consisted primarily in the provision of a suitable, nourishing and substantial diet, often supplemented, particularly for hospital patients, by cod-liver oil, whose curative properties were highly esteemed.[15] Other important aspects of treatment were considered to be fresh air and sufficient exercise, together with good ventilation, suitable climate and adequate clothing. At the end of the century, with the sanatorium movement, there came a greater emphasis on the open-air method of treatment, linked to an attempt to educate sufferers to observe essential rules of hygiene, and to care adequately for themselves.

III

During the sixty years 1851–1910, nearly four million people in England and Wales were recorded as having died of tuberculosis,[16] accounting for nearly 13 per cent of total mortality. More than one-third of these deaths occurred in the 15–34 age group, and over 40 per cent of all the deaths among young adults were attributed, in the official records, to tuberculosis. Those aged 20–24 suffered most of all: in this age-group, almost half of all deaths were classified as being from tuberculosis.

The aggregate figures not only conceal great changes in the incidence of tuberculosis over time but also obscure important differences in mortality among males and females. These two variables are closely related since, as tuberculosis deaths declined continuously, an increasing proportion occurred among men rather than women—a reversal of the 1851 position, when slightly more women than men died of the disease (see table 4.1). The proportion of deaths from tuberculosis was falling for both sexes in every decade; but it was falling faster for women than for men.

Within the young adult age group (15–34), the pattern is broadly similar: a faster decline in tuberculosis deaths for women than for men.

Table 4.1.   Tuberculosis deaths as a percentage of total deaths for males and females at all ages and at young adult ages (15–34), England and Wales, 1851–1910

	1851–60	1861–70	1871–80	1881–90	1891–1900	1901–10
Males, all ages	15.2	14.2	13.6	13.0	11.7	11.6
Females, all ages	16.3	14.9	13.5	12.4	10.3	9.9
Males, 15–34	44.2	43.3	40.6	40.2	37.5	38.2
Females, 15–34	49.3	48.5	44.9	42.5	37.3	37.9

Source: calculated from Registrar General's *Decennial Supplements*, 1851–1910

Consequently, by 1901–10, a greater proportion of male than female deaths resulted from tuberculosis. There are also some variations in the pattern. Firstly, the female advantage in the young adult age group became evident at a later date than among the population as a whole, that not only were young women affected most severely by tuberculosis, but that they suffered from adverse circumstances which were especially persistent. Secondly, for both sexes, the proportion of deaths from tuberculosis rose slightly in 1901–10; indicating that, for young adults, the causes underlying the more general improvement in the figures no longer operated with the same force as previously.

While the age and sex-specific patterns of tuberculosis are complex, one feature dominated their configuration in the second half of the nineteenth century: this was the considerable decline in tuberculosis over the period (table 4.1). Population increased greatly in the second half of the nineteenth century, while the total number of tuberculosis deaths actually fell. The decennial death rates —the number of deaths measured as a proportion of the living population (table 4.2) —show the extent of this fall. [17]

The male death rate nearly halved over the six decades, falling at a continuously accelerating pace. The female improvement was even greater, with a 60 per cent reduction in the death rate by 1901–10. Female rates persistently declined faster than male rates, but there were particularly great improvements in the last two decades, when almost half the reduction during the entire sixty years occurred (table 4.3). The general improvement in the standard of living that is known to have taken place after 1870 seems to have had a great influence on the number of tuberculosis deaths. There was no change in the medical approach to

Table 4.2. Annual mortality from all forms of tuberculosis per thousand living at all ages among males and females, England and Wales, 1851–1910[17]

	1851–60	1861–70	1871–80	1881–90	1891–1900	1901–10
Males	3.5	3.4	3.1	2.7	2.3	1.9
Females	3.5	3.2	2.7	2.3	1.8	1.4

Source: Registrar General's *Decennial Supplement*, 1901–10, Part III, p. ccviii

Table 4.3. Percentage decline in annual mortality from all forms of tuberculosis per thousand living among males and females (a) over 1851–60; (b) over previous decade, England and Wales, 1861–1910

	1861–70		1871–80		1881–90		1891–1900		1901–10	
	(a)	(b)	(a)	(b)	(a)	(b)	(a)	(b)	(a)	(b)
Males	2.9	2.9	11.4	8.8	22.9	12.9	34.3	14.8	45.7	17.4
Females	8.6	8.6	22.9	15.6	34.2	14.8	48.6	21.7	60.0	22.2

Source: based on Table 4.2.

the disease, nor any extension of treatment sufficiently dramatic to account for a decline in the mortality statistics on this scale. It was, however, either an improvement that benefited women more than men; or, perhaps, other male-related conditions simultaneously worsened to prevent a faster reduction of male tuberculosis death rates.

The pattern of phthisis deaths, which accounted for 60 to 80 per cent of total tuberculosis deaths, was much the same as for the disease as a whole (table 4.4). Again, male death rates almost halved, while female rates fell by two-thirds. The acceleration in the rate of decline is very clear in the male phthisis statistics up to 1900 (table 4.5); while although the falls demonstrated in the female data were considerable, and more rapid than for men, the tendency to acceleration was not so clear. Very great improvements in the rates occurred in 1891–1900, particularly for women; but, during the following decade, the rate of decline for both sexes was lower than it had been for some time, as the vigour of the force that had markedly reduced the impact of phthisis on both sexes was apparently slackening.

Table 4.4. Annual death rates from phthisis per thousand living among males and females, England and Wales, 1851–1910

	1851–60	1861–70	1871–80	1881–90	1891–1900	1901–10
Males	2.7	2.6	2.4	2.0	1.6	1.4
Females	2.9	2.6	2.1	1.7	1.2	1.0

Source: Registrar General's *Decennial Supplement*, 1901–10. Part III, p. ccvii

Table 4.5. Percentage decline in annual mortality from phthisis per thousand living among males and females (a) over 1851–60; (b) over previous decade, England and Wales, 1861–1910

	1861–70		1871–80		1881–90		1891–1900		1901–10	
	(a)	(b)	(a)	(b)	(a)	(b)	(a)	(b)	(a)	(b)
Males	3.7	3.7	11.1	7.7	25.9	16.7	40.7	20.0	48.1	12.5
Females	10.3	10.3	27.6	19.2	41.4	19.0	58.6	29.4	65.5	16.6

Source: based on Table 4.4.

Forms of the disease, other than phthisis, showed much slower rates of decline (table 4.6). Male death rates fell by about a third over the 60 years, female rates by somewhat less. Furthermore, decline was very slow, with the mid-decades of the period particularly lacking in improvement among females (table 4.7). Indeed, there was an actual increase in female mortality from these forms of tuberculosis in 1871–80, followed by a very small decrease in the following decade. These anomalies may be explained, in part, by the fact that most extra-pulmonary tuberculosis deaths occurred in the first five years of life, while phthisis was predominantly a disease of young adults: the interaction between sufferer and environment is likely to have been different according to age. However, the accuracy of the statistics for extra-pulmonary tuberculosis deaths is also to some extent in doubt. It was sometimes difficult to diagnose cause of death, especially in very young children; this was particularly so at a time when there was widespread prejudice against post-mortem examinations. Increasing accuracy of diagnosis over time may have made the decline in these deaths appear smaller than it actually was.

Table 4.6. Annual death rates from extra-pulmonary tuberculosis per thousand living among males and females, England and Wales, 1851–1910

	1851–60	1861–70	1871–80	1881–90	1891–1900	1901–10
Males	0.8	0.7	0.7	0.7	0.6	0.5
Females	0.6	0.5	0.5	0.5	0.5	0.4

Source: calculated from Registrar General's *Decennial Supplement*, 1901–10, Part III, pp. ccvii–ccviii

Table 4.7. Percentage decline in annual mortality from extra-pulmonary tuberculosis per thousand living among males and females (a) over 1851–60; (b) over previous decade, England and Wales, 1861–1910

	1861–70		1871–80		1881–90		1891–1900		1901–10	
	(a)	(b)	(a)	(b)	(a)	(b)	(a)	(b)	(a)	(b)
Males	4.8	4.8	7.9	3.2	11.9	4.0	16.7	5.5	31.9	18.2
Females	14.3	14.3	7.4	−7.9	7.9	0.5	11.9	4.3	24.8	14.6

Source: based on Table 4.6.

The age-specific pattern of all types of tuberculosis mortality was very different from trends in general death rates. The normal pattern in the nineteenth century was for high death rates in infancy and early childhood, a steady fall through later childhood and adolescence, remaining low, although gradually rising, through young adulthood, followed by a significant rise in the 35–44 age group, reaching a peak at the higher ages. By contrast, tuberculosis rates, after conforming to the general trend until adolescence, began to rise in the 10–14 age group, reaching a sharp peak in young adulthood. They then declined, although towards the end of the 60-year period another, very muted, peak tended to occur in later life.

Within this pattern, the male and female rates differed, as can be seen from evidence on the 1881–90 decade (table 4.8). The increased incidence of tuberculosis mortality began at an earlier age for females

Table 4.8. Percentage of total tuberculosis deaths occurring in each age group among males and females, England and Wales, 1881–90

	0–4	5–9	10–14	15–19	20–24	25–34	35–44	45–54	55–64	65–74	75+	All ages
Males	25.2	3.8	2.7	5.9	8.5	17.6	15.9	11.4	6.4	2.3	0.3	100
Females	22.5	4.5	4.9	9.0	10.3	19.7	14.6	8.3	4.3	1.7	0.3	100

Source: calculated from Registrar General's *Decennial Supplement*, 1881–90, p. 415

than males, and after continuously higher rates, reached a more marked peak. One reason for this distinct trend among girls may have been the onset of puberty.[18] It is also possible that standards of living among girls were worse than for boys, whose earning power and economic potential needed to be safeguarded. However, as boys took up employment, this female disadvantage would tend to be counteracted, in part, by the greater exposure of men to infection and by the increased physical strain imposed on them. A second difference between men and women is evident in the age at which peak mortality occurred. There was, by 1891–1900, a tendency in both sexes for the highest death rates to occur later in life (table 4.9) — the trend was rather stronger for men than for women, and it is noticeable that, as the age of peak female mortality changed in 1891–1900, it was accompanied by a far lower death rate than for men.

The shift in the age of peak mortality may suggest that the conditions of early childhood were crucial to an individual's later ability to resist tuberculosis: a well-established but contained infection resulting from a poor standard of living could become reactivated in adulthood. Similarly, an inadequate diet in childhood could seriously impair the adult's resistance. As diet and other conditions improved, these circumstances probably acted with less force on each subsequent generation. This led, at any one time, to the presence of fewer unhealthy young adults, though to relatively more older individuals having greater susceptibility to tuberculosis, because their childhood circumstances had been worse than those of succeeding generations. A second contributory factor may have been an amelioration of adverse conditions at work and at home in each successive decade, so that vulnerable young adults were less likely to develop the disease. The fact that male peak rates changed more than female may indicate that working conditions improved rather more rapidly than those in the home.

IV

The previous section has indicated the extent of tuberculosis in England and Wales as a whole in the second half of the nineteenth century, has described its rate of decline, and has shown that its age- and sex-specific impact was far from uniform. The national trends were generally evident in the separate counties for, in every registration county, the tuberculosis death rates fell consistently, usually at a faster rate for women than for men, with a distinct slowing down in the rate of decline in the last years of the period. However, the national figures also obscure very great differences in the severity of the death rates in each county, and geographical variations are also evident in the sex incidence of tuberculosis deaths.

Table 4.9. Age of peak phthisis mortality among males and females, and annual death rates per thousand living experienced at that age, England and Wales, 1851–1910

	1851–60		1861–70		1871–80		1881–90		1891–1900		1901–10	
	Peak age	Death rate	Peak age	Death rate	Peak age	Death rate	Peak age	Death rate	Peak age	Death rate	Peak age	Death rate
Males	20–24	4.1	35–44	4.2	35–44	4.1	35–44	3.6	45–54	3.1	45–54	2.8
Females	25–34	4.6	25–34	4.4	25–34	3.6	25–34	2.8	35–44	2.1	35–44	1.6

Source: calculated from Registrar General's *Decennial Supplement*, 1901–10, p. ccviii

The Registrar General's records divide England into 45, and Wales into two, registration counties (see Figure 2.3). The age-standardized tuberculosis death rates for these registration counties reveal several 'black-spots'. In Lancashire, the West Riding of Yorkshire, Northumberland, South Wales and North Wales, both males and females experienced particularly high tuberculosis death rates; while in Worcestershire and Rutland, the lowest rates in the country for both sexes were being recorded. Just how great was the difference between a 'good' and a 'bad' county can be seen from a comparison between the age-standardized death rates for Lancashire and Worcestershire (table 4.10) — the Lancashire figures are about 50 per cent higher than those for Worcestershire.

The counties which experienced the highest male tuberculosis mortality were not identical with the counties with high female mortality. Cornwall, for example, with its notoriously unhealthy tin mining industry, Sussex, and, particularly, London, had in all six decades among the highest male, but not female, death rates. In contrast, Suffolk and Cumberland exhibited high mortality rates for women, but not for men. There were also great dissimilarities in male and female experience in counties with relatively low mortality rates: in Middlesex, Somerset and Hertfordshire, the female rate alone was distinctly less than average, while in Lincolnshire, Dorset and Monmouth the male rate was similarly distinguished. Clearly, the geographical pattern of high tuberculosis rates was not simply a reflection of the distribution of urban and rural areas.[19]

The tendency for female tuberculosis death rates to fall faster than male, leading to an excess of male deaths by the end of the century, was present in varying degrees in the registration counties. In contrast to phthisis, extra-pulmonary tuberculosis led to roughly similar numbers of male and female deaths. The phthisis statistics show that in 1851–60, in 39 of the 45 registration counties female deaths were higher than male — the six exceptions were London, Hampshire, Middlesex, Hertfordshire, Cornwall and Warwickshire. Cornwall was probably a special case because of the tin mining industry.[20] The London statistics must be treated with caution, for here, as to a lesser extent in all large urban areas, the concentration of voluntary hospitals and Poor Law institutions may have distorted the figures and rendered them unreliable. By 1861–70, the number of counties with higher female rates had fallen to 32, and in the next two decades there was a further fall in those with higher female death rates, with industrial-urban counties showing a particular tendency for male to overtake female rates. The decisive shift occurred in 1891–1900, when only four registration counties had higher female than male phthisis death rates: Dorset, Lincolnshire, Monmouth and South Wales.

The shift to older age groups of peak mortality, already described on

Table 4.10. Annual tuberculosis death rates per thousand among males and females in Lancashire and Worcestershire Registration Counties, 1851–1910

	1851–60		1861–70		1871–80		1881–90		1891–1900		1901–10	
	M	F	M	F	M	F	M	F	M	F	M	F
Lancashire	4.2	4.0	4.0	3.6	3.6	3.0	3.0	2.4	2.6	2.0	2.2	1.6
Worcestershire	2.6	2.8	2.3	2.2	2.2	1.9	2.0	1.6	1.9	1.3	1.5	1.1

Source: calculated from Registrar General's Decennial Supplements, 1851–1910

the national level, was reflected in the county rates, but to widely varying extents. This was true, in particular, of the male statistics: in some cases there was a difference of 20 years between county and national peak ages, with South Wales, Monmouth and Cornwall notably conspicuous. In predominantly urban counties, peak ages were generally similar to, or higher than, the national average; in rural counties, however, male, and to a lesser degree female, tuberculosis mortality tended to peak at a further lower age than the national average.

While the conditions that encouraged the faster fall in tuberculosis rates appear to have been present throughout England and Wales, they operated with considerable variations in the different registration counties. Those who lived in industrial-urban counties gained a disproportionate share of the improvement for, as the century progressed, rural areas were apparently falling further behind urban registration counties in their rate of improvement. The theory that urban areas in particular fostered tuberculosis, and that rural life afforded some protection against the disease, was an important part of nineteenth-century explanations of regional variations in the rates. The standardized death rates for the registration counties certainly seem to support this view, for counties with a clearly urban character—above all, London, Lancashire and the West Riding of Yorkshire—show, throughout the period 1851–1910, persistently high phthisis death rates for males and, to a lesser extent, females. Predominantly rural areas, in contrast, such as Rutland and Hereford, consistently reported relatively low rates, again particularly for males.

The Registrar General's *Decennial Supplement* for 1891–1900 identified an 'urban' and a 'rural' group of registration counties.[21] Two groups have been selected from this classification, to allow comparisons to be made between the tuberculosis death rates in town and country.[22] The urban group comprises Lancashire, London, Middlesex, Monmouthshire, Northumberland, Nottinghamshire, Staffordshire, the East Riding and the West Riding of Yorkshire; the rural group, Buckinghamshire, Cambridgeshire, Cornwall, Herefordshire, Huntingdonshire, Lincolnshire, North Wales, Norfolk, Oxfordshire, Rutland, Shropshire, Somerset, Suffolk, Westmorland and Wiltshire.

The phthisis death rates for these two groups of counties differ in certain respects (table 4.11), and divergences in male and female death rates already evident in other contexts are again clear. Male rates in the rural counties were, in every decade, 20 per cent or more below rates in urban counties. After a slow start in the 1850s and 1860s, male mortality rates declined at the same rapid pace in both town and country, so that by 1901–10 they were about half the 1851–60 level. However, the rural advantage was very much smaller among females, for whom the difference in death rates between the two sets of counties was never more

Table 4.11.   Crude phthisis annual death rates per thousand living among males and females, urban and rural registration counties, 1851–1910

Decades	Urban		Rural	
	Males	Females	Males	Females
1851–60	2.8	2.8	2.3	2.7
1861–70	2.8	2.6	2.2	2.4
1871–80	2.7	2.1	1.9	2.0
1881–90	2.1	1.7	1.5	1.6
1891–1900	1.9	1.3	1.3	1.4
1901–10	1.5	1.0	1.1	0.9

Note: annual death rates are not age-standardized

Source: calculated from Registrar General's *Decennial Supplements*, 1851–1910

than eight per cent. In 1891–1900, female rates in rural areas actually exceeded those in urban counties; the great decline in the rates among women in this decade apparently affected urban far more than rural counties. However, in 1901–10, the rural county rates fell faster than the rates for urban counties. By this decade long-term improvement had reduced female phthisis death rates to about one-third the 1851–60 levels.

Phthisis mortality for both sexes declined at an accelerating rate in the urban registration counties. In the rural counties, the female rate of decline showed a greater tendency to fluctuate, but, as for the urban counties, it exceeded the male. For death rates, as distinct from their rate of decline, the pattern differed: female phthisis death rates in the urban areas were below male rates after 1860. The rural picture is quite different: here female rates were persistently above male rates until 1901–10.

The statistical data thus bear out the contemporary belief that rural areas escaped more lightly from tuberculosis than urban counties. However, the female advantage over males, while evident in the towns, was not present in the country. There was a far greater similarity between urban and rural female death rates than between male rates in the two areas. The crucial factor for women may have been conditions in the home—about two-thirds of women spent their days at home rather than at an external workplace—and their health must have been greatly affected by housing conditions. Sanitary improvements may have had a particularly significant impact on them. Men, on the other hand, were far more vulnerable to sources of infection outside the home. They travelled more, visited public houses and other places of entertainment far more frequently than women and, above all, worked outside the home. Rural conditions may in all these respects have been better than urban.

The tendency of tuberculosis sufferers to return home to die, typically from urban to rural areas, was sometimes mentioned in the nineteenth century as being a possible distorting influence on the statistics, a phenomenon which was thought to apply with particular force to female domestic servants, many of whom were of country origin.[23] Migration of this kind would have artificially worsened the rural rates by inflating them with a number of deaths caused by urban, not rural, conditions. Thus, it is possible that the general rural death rate was increased by between five and six per cent, and that female tuberculosis mortality in the 15–34 age group was increased also by 11 to 15 per cent. The rural areas, in fact, may well have enjoyed a greater advantage over the urban areas than the official records suggest. A further difference between urban and rural rates is in the age of peak mortality: in the country, the men and women who died of tuberculosis generally did so at an earlier age than in towns (table 4.12). Moreover, in the urban areas, male rates showed a more pronounced tendency to peak at a later age than female rates.

Other forms of tuberculosis, mainly affecting children, also indicate a rural advantage, albeit decreasing over time (table 4.13). These death rates declined at a far slower pace than in the case of phthisis, male rates exceeding female rates to a greater extent in the town than in the country. However, the problem of accurate diagnosis for these forms of

Table 4.12. Age of peak phthisis mortality among males and females in urban and rural registration counties, and annual death rates per thousand living experienced at that age, 1881–1910

| Decades | Urban | | | | Rural | | | |
| | Males | | Females | | Males | | Females | |
	Peak age	Death rate	Peak age	Death rate	Peak age	Death rate	Peak age	Death rate
1881–90	35–40	4.2	35–44	2.9	25–34	2.9	25–34	2.9
1891–1900	45–54	3.4	35–44	1.7	25–34	2.0	25–34	1.6
1901–10	45–54	3.9	35–44	2.3	35–44	2.2	25–34	2.0

Note: age-specific death rates are available for the registration counties only from the 1881–90 decade

Source: calculated from Registrar General's *Decennial Supplements*, 1881–1910

Table 4.13. Crude extra-pulmonary tuberculosis death rates per thousand living among males and females, urban and rural registration counties, 1851–1910

Decades	Urban		Rural	
	Males	Females	Males	Females
1851–60	11.1	8.2	6.7	5.3
1861–70	10.5	7.7	6.6	5.3
1871–80	9.6	7.6	6.2	5.1
1881–90	8.9	6.9	5.7	4.8
1891–1900	7.7	6.1	4.9	4.4
1901–10	5.9	4.9	4.0	3.7

Note: death rates are not age-standardized

Source: calculated from Registrar General's *Decennial Supplements*, 1851–1910

tuberculosis should be noted; a problem which may well have been particularly acute in rural areas where medical facilities were more rudimentary.

The connection between all forms of extra-pulmonary tuberculosis in children and the consumption of tuberculized milk has been referred to earlier. The available nineteenth-century data appear to indicate that the consumption of milk depended to a large extent on wage levels.[24] In addition, there is a significant positive correlation between wage levels and abdominal tuberculosis rates—a type of extra-pulmonary tuberculosis closely connected with infected milk: counties with the highest rates of abdominal tuberculosis were also generally high wage counties.[25] The correlation between wage levels and abdominal tuberculosis rates in the registration counties in 1851–60 is 0.4 for males and 0.5 for females—both statistically significant results—and in 1901–10, the correlations are 0.5 and 0.6 respectively.[26] The two counties which most clearly failed to conform to this pattern were Cumberland and Westmorland, both high wage counties with low abdominal tuberculosis rates. Exclusion of these counties gives a correlation of 0.6 for both sexes in 1851–60 and 0.7 in 1901–10. One reason for the divergence of Cumberland and Westmorland may be that their milk supply was less tuberculized than elsewhere; for, in adjacent Northumberland and Durham, the abdominal tuberculosis rates were the highest in the country. However, factors other than the availability of tuberculized milk may also have had an important influence on abdominal tuberculosis in the most severely affected 0–4 age group: the practice of breast feeding, and the length of time this was continued may, for example, have been subject to wide regional variations.

Thus, the overall course of tuberculosis death rates throughout England and Wales was consistently downwards. Despite the many variations, there was a sustained fall in the mortality of both sexes and all age groups, a decline often attributed to rises in living standards. If this is so, what weight should be assigned to its various components—better diet and housing, improved hygiene and conditions at work? Moreover, what importance should be given to factors such as migration and changes in fertility?

Within the general pattern, some important and persistent variations are evident. Most notable is the differing degree of severity of tuberculosis mortality in the registration counties, and divergences in the extent to which males and females were affected. The more rapid decrease in tuberculosis rates among females than among males is also a prominent feature in the national and regional trends. Consideration is now given to some of the possible influences on the death rates.

V

Five major areas of economic growth can be distinguished in the second half of the nineteenth century: the Northern textile counties, the North-East coalfield, Birmingham and the Black Country, Glamorgan and the South Wales coalfield, and London and the Metropolitan counties, all suffering from high tuberculosis mortality. It would be reasonable to assume that there was a causal connection; counties showing the lowest tuberculosis rates in each decade were almost wholly rural, though the factors that might contribute to such an explanation could not at the same time have accounted for the high rates for both sexes in North Wales, for males in Sussex, or for females in Suffolk and Cumberland. The set of causes which gave rise to the prevailing tuberculosis rates must have been as diversified as the economic and social circumstances of the populations in each county.

Two inter-related approaches to understanding the pattern of tuberculosis mortality between 1851 and 1910 suggest themselves. Firstly, it may be argued that the disease was primarily connected with social factors such as diet, housing and occupation. Secondly, structural factors, such as migration and levels of fertility, might contribute to an explanation of the regional variations in tuberculosis rates.

Dietary standards improved in the second half of the nineteenth century, with real wages rising particularly after 1870, just at the time when the major falls in tuberculosis mortality became evident. Towards the end of the century, imported food supplemented and improved the diets of many sections of the population—the import of tinned, and later frozen, meat represented a particularly valuable addition in the important field of first-class proteins. Imports of meat tripled between 1870 and 1890, and increased by another 50 per cent between 1890 and 1910, while imports of butter and margarine more than doubled between 1880 and 1910.[27] Food was the largest single item in working-class budgets, and as such was closely related to levels of poverty. Moreover, considerable differences in standards of nutrition were shown by an 1863 Privy Council survey[28]—diet varied according to wage levels, especially with regard to first-class proteins, and this may be related to regional variations in tuberculosis mortality.

Diet is a factor likely to have been particularly important during short-term crises such as the Lancashire 'cotton famine' of 1861–64. While for 1861–70 as a whole, phthisis death rates in Lancashire fell, in 1864–7 the yearly rates rose for both men and women. Moreover, in Salford, male phthisis rates were higher in 1861–70 than in 1851–60, while female rates declined only very slightly, and the evidence indicates that these adverse effects continued into the following decades. By contrast, in the rural Lancashire district of Garstang, the tuberculosis death rates fell continuously and steeply over the whole period. This experience suggests the extent to which an acute economic crisis could affect the tuberculosis death rate. Diet may also in part explain differences between male and female mortality: from nineteenth-century evidence, it appears that in families, men, whose ability to work it was imperative to maintain, were given the most and best of the available food, leaving women and children more likely to be inadequately nourished and vulnerable to illness.[29]

Housing may have had a significant influence on geographical variations in tuberculosis mortality, particularly among females, the group likely to have been most severely affected by adverse conditions of this nature. The importance of housing is suggested by inter-war studies. The Tyneside medical authorities, whose area suffered the highest tuberculosis death rates in the early twentieth century, remarked that 'such a degree of overcrowding as is found in many parts of Tyneside ... is conducive to a high incidence of tuberculosis'.[30] A 1930–31 investigation in Jarrow and Blaydon, moreover, indicated a definite relationship between tuberculosis and overcrowding.[31]

Clearly, an important cause of bad housing, and of other conditions giving rise to tuberculosis, was poverty, though the connection between poverty and poor living conditions was not straightforward. Over-crowding could be caused by a variety of factors arising from the economic structure of a region, such as, for example, transport facilities and the pattern of land ownership. The presence in an area of a large proportion of low-quality housing is likely to have had a particularly long-term influence on the level of tuberculosis mortality: housing was not nearly as responsive to changes in prosperity as was diet, nor could even sweeping government action lead to rapid improvement.

Nevertheless, housing improved considerably in the second half of the nineteenth century, with a rise in the quality of new building, a reduction in excessive overcrowding and increased government regulation bringing better sanitation and water supply. Throughout the period, increases in the number of houses seem to have more than kept pace with population growth. It is, however, unlikely that the improvement was sufficient nationally to explain the fall in tuberculosis mortality. The spread of tuberculosis could only be checked by the isolation of sufferers to a considerable extent, and by the implementation of hygienic measures. Working-class housing, in which shared bedrooms were the rule,[32] could not easily provide these facilities. Moreover, there were considerable variations in housing standards. The 1884-5 Royal Commission on Housing revealed great overcrowding among the poor and casually employed and, contrary to the national trend, in parts of central London the housing situation grew acutely worse in the second half of the century.[33]

The high female tuberculosis rates in Lancashire and the West Riding of Yorkshire, where there were large numbers of working women, suggest that differences in the levels of female employment may have played a part in determining regional variations in female mortality. The strain of both running a home and doing a job may have heightened susceptibility to the disease. It cannot, however, explain high female rates in counties such as Suffolk and Cumberland, where the employment of women was no higher than the national average. Studies carried out in Britain and the United States in the inter-war decades have also tended, on balance, to discount the suggestion that working women, simply because they worked, suffered more from tuberculosis than full-time housewives.[34]

However, conditions of work, as distinct from the mere fact of employment, undoubtedly influenced tuberculosis mortality, for example in the textile industry. These circumstances must have affected men in particular—unhygienic working conditions and specific factors such as silica dust are known to encourage tuberculosis infection. Nineteenth-century occupational mortality statistics indicate that workers in some occupations suffered from exceptionally high rates of tuberculosis mortality; these included tin miners, inn and hotel keepers, potters, earthenware workers and workers in metal trades. Casual and poorly-paid occupations—for example, costermongering and portering—may have attracted those already suffering from ill health. In contrast, the highly-paid occupation of printing was also particularly subject to tuberculosis. Modern studies of occupational mortality stress the role played by poor working conditions, especially excessive crowding in the workplace, in encouraging the spread of tuberculosis.

Regional differences in levels of fertility may have produced variations in tuberculosis rates among women. Childbearing, particularly if frequent, aggravates the development of tuberculosis, creating exceptional physical strain and impairing general health. The restriction of families would reduce the danger to women of death from tuberculosis, as would the practice of allowing a longer interval between each child. The general birth rate began falling in the 1870s, and the trend towards later marriages among some sections of the population, and smaller families, may have led to the deferment of the birth of the first child. This reduced, for some, the risk of tuberculosis by avoiding the danger of physical strain in the vulnerable 15–24 age group. When the age-specific death rates for registration counties become available, in 1881–90, the counties with the highest female tuberculosis mortality certainly show also a tendency to reach peak rates at earlier than average ages. Urban counties such as South Wales and the West and East Ridings of Yorkshire, in particular, exhibited this trend. Most mining communities experienced high fertility rates, and the three registration counties with major mining activity—County Durham, Northumberland and South Wales—also had exceptionally bad records of female tuberculosis deaths; in Durham and South Wales, moreover, peak rates occurred at ages lower than the national average, suggesting the interrelation of high fertility, early childbearing and high tuberculosis death rates. Regional variations in fertility, however, are likely to account only partially for differences in the tuberculosis death rates. Birth control, although practised throughout the period, became more widely practical only after about 1870, and was in any case confined to a minority of the population until the 1890s. However, it may have helped to accelerate the reduction in tuberculosis mortality, particularly in the urban areas, not only by reducing the direct risk to women, but also by allowing improved standards of diet, housing and education.

Migration has sometimes been put forward as a possible cause of regional variations in tuberculosis rates. It has been suggested, with reference to the twentieth century, that migrants were a physically select group, whose departure therefore lowered health standards in rural areas.[35] Possibly, this process may be reflected in the mortality rates for some areas such as Wales, which suffered high tuberculosis rates in the nineteenth century. Yet the greater healthiness of the rural counties for much of the period, combined with the poor record of the areas receiving migrants, suggests that this was not a general influence. It may, however, have become more important in the 1870s and 1880s, when the volume of movement from the countryside reached its peak in absolute terms, with a continued heavy outflow to the end of the century. This coincided with the slight worsening in the relative position of the rural counties. The great improvements in rural tuberculosis in 1901–10 may also be partly connected with a slackening in the rural exodus.[36]

In conclusion, this survey has shown that no single cause influenced the rapid changes in tuberculosis mortality between 1851 and 1910, or explains the various patterns that have been described. Housing, diet and occupation must have been factors of profound significance. There is some evidence that housing in particular affected underlying mortality, influenced geographical variations and gave rise to differences between male and female mortality.[37] Long-term changes such as the trend to smaller families indirectly improved living standards and so lessened susceptibility to tuberculosis. Simultaneously, diet and working conditions grew very much better, further strengthening resistance to the disease and reducing the risk of contact with sufferers. Housing, however, was less open to regulation than occupation and less responsive to increased prosperity. A rise in housing standards far greater than would have seemed realistic to nineteenth-century reformers was needed before overcrowding ceased to affect the death rates. The phthisis death rates in 1901–10 were certainly a very great advance on the figures of 60 years earlier. However, they still represented a very heavy loss: through death and disablement of the sick, tuberculosis deprived the economy of a section of the labour force at its most productive age. As the general tide of social evils ebbed, housing became relatively more important in its significance, and was increasingly the problem which defeated efforts to eliminate tuberculosis—a problem which was not to prove simple or easily to be resolved.[38]

Evaluating the sanitary revolution: typhus and typhoid in London, 1851–1900

Bill Luckin

From the early sixteenth century typhus and typhoid caused calamitous suffering among European communities.[1] Epidemic typhus swept through towns and villages during periods of warfare and famine: typhoid struck more insidiously whenever and wherever infected water or rotten food were consumed. The two diseases, invariably and erroneously conflated by medical men, were, together with smallpox and the infections of childhood, pre-eminent among those post-plague causes of death which kept mortality at such continuingly high levels between the later seventeenth and the early nineteenth centuries.[2]

Very little is known in precise terms about aggregate mortality from the two diseases in eighteenth-century England but, in the case of typhus, it seems likely that the benefits gained from the alleviation of famine conditions were counterbalanced by the onset of urbanization and by the concentration of unprecedentedly large numbers of the very poor into overcrowded homes and public institutions. Popular terminology—'jail fever', for example—indicates a correspondence between the emergence of the disease as a 'social problem' and the growth, from the mid eighteenth century onwards, of agencies—hospitals, workhouses, houses of correction, prisons, asylums—committed, as recent scholarship has begun to demonstrate, to the management and 'treatment' not only of the sick but also of the deviant and the straightforwardly poverty-stricken.[3]

The history of typhoid during the eighteenth century is even more obscure than that of typhus, but it is probable that the growth of population in towns and the increased scale of facilities for the supply of water and food led to high levels of mortality from the disease. The village, or closed community, which drew its water from the same polluted stream or well year after year could expect to lose a fixed proportion of its population every summer and autumn; and, in towns, where techniques of water purification were either unknown or only crudely applied, epidemics were likely to be more widely disseminated.[4]

Both diseases continued to thrive in the nineteenth century. Country and capital were severely afflicted by typhus in 1801, 1816–19, 1837–8 and 1846–7, when the pressure of war and demobilization, extreme poverty and uncontrolled Irish immigration provided an ideal environment for the spread of the infection.[5] Death from typhoid at this time was more likely to occur as a result of a regular annual endemic cycle than during an epidemic onslaught, but mortality in urban regions, like that from other water-associated infections such as dysentery, diarrhoea and cholera, nevertheless reached very high levels. After mid-century, however, mortality from typhus and typhoid began its final decline, leading to a very great alleviation in human suffering—mainly though not exclusively concentrated among the poor—and also contributing to continued demographic growth.[6]

Although it is undesirable to isolate the quantitative from the experiential in the social history of disease, this essay will address itself primarily to the question of why it was that typhus and typhoid, which destroyed so many lives between the sixteenth and the mid nineteenth centuries in England, should, by the early twentieth, have been claiming so few. If demographic questions of this kind are to be satisfactorily settled, it might be argued that the historian should examine a disease, and particularly as ecologically complex an infection as typhus, for a period of a century or more, in order to reveal the changing relationship between vector, host and environment, and also to chart the complex rhythms of dormancy and recrudescence. However, there is also a strong case for tracing the natural history of an infection over a much shorter period, and in a deliberately delimited geographical area. This latter approach makes it possible to juxtapose the regional against the national pattern; to undertake a detailed analysis of the final phase of an epidemiological downswing; and to analyse concepts which have traditionally dominated discussion of 'fever' and its demographic significance. Each of these aspects is explored in this essay, beginning with a brief account of the principal characteristics of typhus and typhoid, and an explanation of the inability of so few medical practitioners to make a firm distinction between the two conditions until the later nineteenth century.

I.

Typhus is a rickettsial infection which thrives in conditions of acute social dislocation, poverty and overcrowding and is principally, though not exclusively, encountered during the cold months of the year.[7]

Rickettsia prowazeki, the infectious organism, which was first isolated in 1909, is transmitted from person to person by the body louse. The *rickettsiae* are ingested when the louse draws in blood from an individual already suffering from typhus; then, when this blood meal has been digested, the micro organisms are ejected with the faeces. In crowded and dirty living conditions, where lice and fleas proliferate, surface lesions, caused either by the bite of an insect or by the scratching of a persistent irritation, are inevitably common; and typhus is most usually spread when the *rickettsiae* contained in the faeces of lice are rubbed into broken skin. Once the disease has been contracted, the sufferer is afflicted by a severe headache and a very high temperature; and the entire body, except for the face, the palms of the hands and the soles of the feet, becomes rapidly disfigured by angry red spots. During an intense epidemic the case fatality rate may rise to more than 50 per cent; but during the nineteenth century it probably ranged between about 20 and 45 per cent.[8]

Unlike typhus, typhoid is a disease of the faecal–oral route, and is usually spread via infected water, milk and food.[9] There is no vector and transmission is always due either to passage from an already infected individual or from a carrier of the disease. Typhoid flourishes in all those circumstances in which the faeces of sufferers or immune carriers come into contact with extensively distributed supplies of food and drink. In contrast to typhus, typhoid has traditionally affected a wide range of both poor and relatively affluent, particularly in societies in which water and foodstuffs have been exempt from effective public health regulations. Once the infection has been contracted, the patient becomes listless, loses appetite and then develops a high and sustained fever, which is often accompanied by profuse diarrhoea. This diarrhoea, leading to abdominal haemorrhage, is the most frequent terminal event in the illness. Typhoid, during the nineteenth century, was most common during the summer and autumn and case fatality was lower than that for typhus, fluctuating between about 15 and 20 per cent.[10]

The typhoid sufferer, like the individual who has contracted typhus, is liable to display a red rash, although its nature and distribution are, in fact, quite distinct. It was this symptom which persuaded most doctors before the later nineteenth century that the two conditions were identical. However, from the 1830s, a number of pioneers, notably W. W. Gerhard in America, P. C. A. Louis in Paris and Sir William Jenner in London, had drawn attention to prominent clinical differences between the two diseases, and especially to the fact that diarrhoea was never encountered in typhus.[11] Yet it was only in 1869 that William Farr at the Registrar General's Office felt that it had become possible to collect separate national statistics for the *Annual Reports*. This failure to differentiate between the diseases makes it necessary to examine mortality attributable to them in two periods, before and after 1870.

Mortality from typhus and typhoid, during the first period, was recorded as typhus; during the second, it was registered under typhus, typhoid and, a third category—simple continued fever. By the end of the first period typhus had gone into a steep decline as a cause of death and, during the second, it was replaced by typhoid as the most prevalent of the adult 'fevers' in nineteenth-century Britain. Simple continued fever was of only limited statistical importance for a single transitional decade, the 1870s. In addition, there is strong evidence in favour of redistributing the mortality attributable to it to typhoid—a convention which has been followed in this essay. [12]

Combined mortality from typhus and typhoid in London between 1851 and 1870 is plotted with mortality for the rest of England and Wales in Figure 5.1. Although it is not possible to make a definitive separation between the two infections during this first period, data from

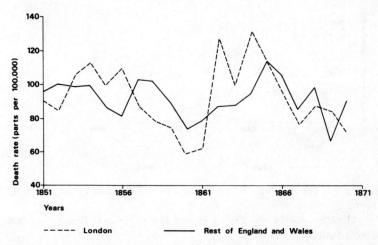

Figure 5.1 Mortality rate (parts per 100,000) from typhus and typhoid, London and the rest of England and Wales, 1851–70

the London Fever Hospital, the only institution which accepted large numbers of working class fever patients before the 1870s, together with the observations of several medical officers of health, suggest that typhus probably accounted for a substantially higher proportion of mortality from the two diseases during the 1860s than the 1850s. [13] This pattern is clearly revealed in Figure 5.2 which analyses the type of fever recorded for about 18,000 patients admitted to the London Fever Hospital between 1851 and 1870. Only once in the 1850s, during the recession associated with the end of the Crimean War in 1855–6, did contemporaries record that London had been afflicted by epidemic typhus. [14] However, from 1862 until 1870, the disease returned with

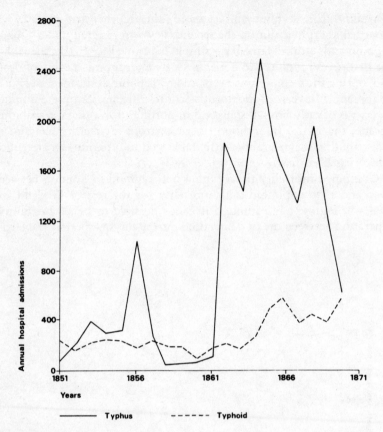

Figure 5.2 Typhus and typhoid admissions to the London Fever Hospital,
1851–70.
Source: Charles Murchison, *The Continued Fevers of Great Britain* (London,
1884, third edition), pp. 52–3

unexpected ferocity and in 1869 and 1870 it was accompanied by an
epidemic of the less fatal, jaundice-like infection, relapsing fever —
popularly and aptly known as 'famine fever'.[15]

Throughout this period typhoid was an endemic or sub-epidemic
rather than a consistently epidemic infection. Intermittently, though,
during the 1850s, it may have accounted for as high an annual death toll
as typhus. These peaks are probably inadequately documented in the
London Fever Hospital records, since typhoid was a less visibly
traumatic disease than typhus and a smaller proportion of total sufferers
were admitted to hospital.[16] In particular, middle-class victims were
unlikely to be accurately represented in public hospital records since
they were reluctant to enter any institution such as the London Fever
Hospital, which was partially reliant upon charitable funds. Neverthe-

less, the testimony of several medical officers of health, from a wide geographical area within the capital, implies that intermittently during the 1850s, annual aggregate mortality from typhoid may have been greater than that from typhus.[17] District and hospital statistics, during the 1860s, give the impression that mortality from the disease rose above its typically endemic norm to reach sub-epidemic proportions. The data from the London Fever Hospital indicate that between 1863 and 1870 deaths from typhoid followed the upward movement of typhus, although at lower absolute levels.

The reduction in mortality from typhoid during the second period requires only brief description, following the decline of epidemic typhus from about 1870. Figure 5.3 shows the pattern for the capital, set against that for the rest of England and Wales. The decline between 1871 and

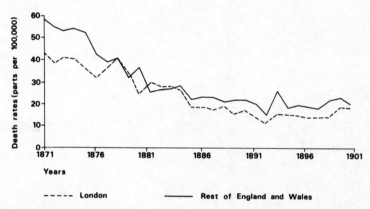

Figure 5.3 Mortality rate (parts per 100,000) from typhoid in London and the rest of England and Wales, 1871–1900

1885, despite fluctuations, was both substantial and continuous. However, from 1885 until the end of the century the rate of improvement slackened and little further progress was made either in the capital or in the rest of the country during the 1890s.[18] It was after 1900 that mortality was rapidly and uninterruptedly reduced to levels which, by 1910, were beginning to approximate to the more sanguine expectations of the mid twentieth century.

A more detailed representation of mortality from the two diseases in London between 1851 and 1870 is set out in table 5.1 and Figure 5.4. since typhoid accounted for a higher proportion of aggregate mortality from the two infections between 1851 and 1860 than between 1861 and 1870, Figure 5.4 almost certainly underestimates deaths from typhus during the 1860s. Thus, during the 1850s, only Shoreditch and

Table 5.1. Mortality from typhoid and typhus in London registration districts, 1851–1900 (death rates in parts per 100,000)

Districts	Typhus and typhoid 1851–60	1861–70	Typhoid 1871–80	Typhus 1871–80	Typhoid 1881–90	Typhoid 1891–1900
Kensington	61	54	21	5	22	10
Chelsea	77	70	29	6	16	13
Westminster*	87	81	32	6	23	27
Marylebone	68	61	27	4	18	13
Hampstead	65	31	20	—	19	11
Pancras	72	67	29	4	23	16
Islington	77	76	32	6	24	13
Hackney	83	71	33	7	27	13
St Giles	93	100	23	3	19	13
Holborn	78	100	30	6	19	16
City	104	136	48	7	29	18
Shoreditch	132	120	34	7	20	16
Bethnal Green	102	119	36	8	21	19
Whitechapel	116	135	42	6	39	13

St George in the East	100	152	35	10	17	17
Stepney and Mile End	101	123	32	8+	25	18
Poplar	70	113	32	5	24	19
St Saviour**	92	98	32	6	15	17
St Olave×	103	101	34	7	20	17
Lambeth	76	85	35	7	25	12
Wandsworth	66	60	27	5	16	12
Camberwell	56	64	32	3	15	10
Greenwich	91	104	41	5	30	20
Lewisham	57	56	25	3	12	8
Woolwich	—	—	34	7+	12	4
London	87	89	30	5	18	12

Notes: * includes St George Hanover Square, Westminster; St Martin's, Westminster; St James and Strand districts
** includes St Saviour, St George and Newington
× includes St Olave, Bermondsey and Rotherhithe
+ doubtful value

Sources: Registrars General *Annual Reports* and *Supplements to Annual Reports*

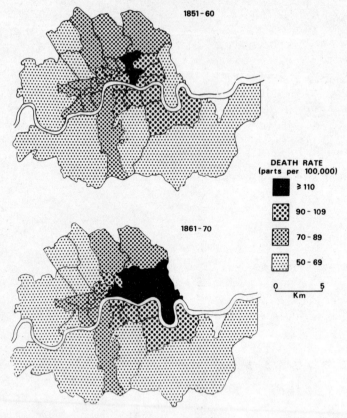

Figure 5.4 Mortality rate (parts per 100,000) from typhus and typhoid, London registration districts, 1851–60 and 1861–70

Whitechapel experienced a combined death rate from typhus and typhoid of more than 110 per 100,000 population. Yet, between 1861 and 1870 no East End district was exempt from very serious epidemic mortality from the two diseases, with typhus quite definitely claiming the bulk of the deaths.[19] The most telling illustration of this deterioration is provided by Poplar. In the earlier period its combined death rate from the two diseases was relatively low, comparable to that of such relatively affluent western and south western districts as Kensington, Marylebone and Wandsworth. However, as during the 1860s, the western, north western and south western suburbs marginally improved their position; while Poplar, like the rest of the East End, was severely afflicted by epidemic typhus.

The decline in mortality from typhoid between 1870 and 1900 is shown in table 5.1. The differentials in mortality between the poorest and the more affluent districts were now far less pronounced, especially after 1880, than had been the case for typhus during the preceding 20 years. In fact, by the beginning of the twentieth century, typhoid had ceased to be a major epidemic infection in the capital. A poor district in the East End, like Shoreditch, which had been particularly ravaged by both diseases during the 1850s and 1860s, had, by the 1890s, become very nearly totally immune from typhus and now only occasionally experienced annual death rates from typhoid of more than 15 per 100,000 population.

II

The decline of typhus has usually been explained in terms of an interraction between rising standards of living and the impact of the sanitary revolution—a long-established and inexplicit term covering large-scale improvements in drainage, water supply and housing, and associated levels of personal hygiene. When seeking to account for the decline of the disease after 1870, different historians have emphasized different variables subsumed under this generalized concept. Thus, Creighton argued that an improved housing stock and greater communal attention to cleanliness had probably been less important than an increasingly healthy diet.[20] George Rosen gave primacy to increased supplies of water which, so he contended, allowed more regular washing of both bodies and under-garments.[21] In the most rigorous analysis so far undertaken, Thomas McKeown and his colleagues have drawn attention to three related components: the direct effects of the systematic cleansing of the urban environment, improvements in diet, and the possibility of a favourable change in the relationship between host and parasite.[22] The emergence of a convincing and comprehensive account of the decline of typhus has clearly been inhibited by a number of conceptual and empirical difficulties. Therefore, in this section, existing, and often overlapping, explanations of the national reduction in mortality from the disease will be surveyed in the light of developments in the capital between about 1870 and 1900.

Whether as a means of cleansing the individual home, removing filth from enclosed streets and alleys, or raising levels of personal hygiene, an improved water supply has invariably occupied an important role within the traditional schema. In London, demographic pressure ensured that daily *per capita* supply declined marginally between the 1820s and 1850.[23] Consumption rose from 21 to 23 gallons per head per day during the 1850s, but the next 20 years witnessed little improvement and the water companies were under strong and persistent pressure to extend constant supply and to increase the meagre amounts delivered to the poorer areas for domestic purposes. By 1880 there had been an improvement, with *per capita* consumption within the capital as a whole rising to about 26 gallons per day.[24] If increases on this scale could be identified in those working class districts which had been most heavily affected by typhus during the 1860s, it might be possible to argue that this amelioration had played an important part in reducing the incidence of the disease in the 1870s. Yet detailed analysis of the evidence cannot support such a conclusion. The great bulk of the water consumed in the eastern and northern districts was supplied by the New River and East London companies and, since these two concerns 'shared' many areas, statistics for aggregate supply from each company to individual registration districts are not available. However, a moderately reliable estimate of water consumption in the typhus-prone region as a whole — the eastern, inner city, inner northern and north eastern suburban districts shown in Figure 5.4 — can be calculated. *Per capita* consumption in these districts rose from approximately 20 gallons per day in 1850 to 24 gallons by the mid-1870s.[25] This finding must, however, be set against the fact that it was only in the 1890s that more than 50 per cent of the total population in this region gained permanent access to the company-supplied water and that even at this late juncture, 31 per cent of all Londoners, and as many as 55 per cent of all customers of the New River Company, were still without constant supply.[26] It would clearly be rash, in the light of such statistics, to postulate a widespread change in working class washing habits, whether of bodies or of clothes, until a decade or so after typhus had entered its final decline.

Emphasis has also traditionally been placed on improved drainage. The period of intensive construction of sewers in the capital, both by district and municipal authorities, beginning with the Chadwickian initiative in the late 1840s, and culminating in the completion of the main drainage project in the mid-1860s, undoubtedly witnessed the transportation of very large quantities of refuse from closed inner city areas to the larger external environment.[27] Yet in the absence, until the mid-1860s, of an efficient means of extra-urban sewage disposal, or even moderately reliable methods of water treatment, any reduction in mortality from typhus which may have flowed from less insalubrious living conditions in the inner city, was almost certainly cancelled out by an increase in mortality attributable to water-transmitted infections. This hypothesis is supported not only by the rising share of deaths from typhoid within combined mortality from typhus and typhoid but also by the timing and intensity of the water-transmitted cholera epidemics which afflicted the capital in 1849, 1853–4 and 1866.[28] According to this interpretation, the systematic drainage of the inner city districts which was undertaken during the sanitary revolution may indeed have reduced mortality from typhus but only at the short-term cost of a deterioration in water supplies drawn from river sources which were still too close to major sewer outlets.[29] Once the main drainage system had been completed in the mid-1860s, London certainly became a cleaner and a healthier place in which to live and, in this sense, there can be little doubt that improved sewerage was a necessary, though not a sufficient, condition for the eradication of epidemic typhus.

The next strand in the traditional argument concerns the provision of housing and on this issue the Metropolitan evidence may be briefly and categorically summarized. Neither contemporary medical specialists, nor urban historians, have been able to point to any significant reduction in overcrowding until about 20 years after typhus had ceased to be an epidemic threat.[30]

The possible impact of an improved diet is a complicated issue. The East End suffered extreme poverty, involving malnutrition and even occasional cases of starvation, during the extended typhus epidemic of the 1860s.[31] In the light of trends now generally accepted for the country as a whole, it seems unlikely that standards of living failed to rise marginally when typhus waned for the last time in these same areas during the 1870s.[32] Twentieth-century epidemiologists and medical historians are undecided, however, as to the relationship between fluctuations in nutrition and changes in communal resistance to typhus, especially when nutrition is isolated from the generalized nexus of poverty—the overcrowding and vagrancy in which the disease was observed to flourish in the nineteenth century.[33] It is certainly unwise to seek links, however tentative, between, for example, the price of bread and the incidence of typhus in the capital during the 1850s and 1860s.[34]

The evident shortcomings of the argument that either the impact of the sanitary revolution, or rising standards of living, can adequately account for the sudden and dramatic decline in mortality from typhus after about 1870 are thrown into even sharper relief when the Metropolitan statistics between 1851 and 1880 are set against those for other large centres of population in England and Ireland.[35] Table 5.2 seeks to compare mortality rates from typhus, as well as changes in those rates, in 22 conurbations of more than 100,000 population at the census of 1881. Since the figures for 1851–60 and 1861–70 refer to typhus and typhoid combined, and those for 1871–80 to typhus alone, there is clearly a lack of comparability between the second and fourth columns. Yet, even if the conservative estimate is made that as few as 50 per cent of all deaths from typhus and typhoid in the 1860s were in fact attributable to typhus, only two communities—Belfast and Dublin—reveal an annual average reduction of less than the remarkably high figure of 60 per cent during the 1870s. This is a decline sufficiently large, sudden and generalized throughout the majority of urban areas, to hypothesize that it may have been an 'autonomous' change in the nature of the disease itself, rather than numerous uncoordinated programmes of reform, directed at differing environments, which precipitated the once-and-for-all extinction of epidemic typhus in nineteenth-century England.[36] When, however, the case fatality rate for the disease during the early

Table 5.2. Mortality from typhus and typhoid in selected towns, 1851–80 (death rates in parts per 100,000)

Major towns	1851–60	1861–70	Percentage change	1871–80	Approximate percentage change
Belfast	—	123*	—	91	—26
Birmingham	107	79	—26	2	—97
Blackburn	157	110	—30	1	—98
Bolton	107	95	—7	2	—98
Bradford	98	106	+8	5	—95
Brighton	91	53	—42	—	—96
Bristol	99	93	—6	3	—98
Dublin	—	130*	—	96	—26
Hull	124	144	+16	1	—99
Leeds	109	141	+29	11	—92
Leicester	137	80	—42	1	—99
Liverpool	154	222	+44	58	—73
London	87	89	+2	5	—94
Manchester	124	170	+37	18	—78
Newcastle	99	128	+29	14	—78
Nottingham	105	85	—19	2	—98
Norwich	104	90	—13	—	—98
Oldham	90	85	—5	—	—98
Preston	109	84	—23	—	—98
Salford	83	135	+63	1	—97
Sheffield	132	139	+5	8	—88
Stoke	92	97	+5	—	—96
Sunderland	80	92	+15	33	—64

Note: * 1864–75
Sources: Registrar General's Annual Reports and Supplements to Annual Reports;

nineteenth century, when aggregate mortality was high, is compared
with case fatality during the later decades of the century, when mortality
had been so greatly diminished, the result—a rate consistently fluctuating between about 20 and 45 per cent—does not indicate that the
infective *rickettsiae* were becoming less virulent.[37] There is, in other
words, no evidence to support the view that *rickettsia prowazeki* was
undergoing a modification during the later nineteenth century similar to
that proposed by McKeown and Record for the haemolytic streptoc-
cocus responsible for the propagation of scarlet fever.[38] Epidemic
typhus was certainly becoming rarer after 1870, but the chances of
survival for the individual who contracted it, during the 1890s for
example, were no higher than they had been for his or her predecessors
at mid-century.[39]

Nevertheless, what of the vector? Is it conceivable that there may have
been a sudden diminution in the body louse population, or a favourable
shift in the relationship between body louse and *rickettsia*, which resulted
either in fewer lice coming into contact with susceptible humans, or the
same number of lice transmitting *rickettsiae*, though to less destructive
effect?[40] Unfortunately, it is not possible to locate evidence which
would either support definitively or contradict the hypothesis that the
relationship between the body louse and *rickettsia prowazeki* did undergo
a modification of this kind; but the stability of the case fatality rate
among human sufferers from typhus makes it improbable that such an
ecological event did occur. Yet there is a case for proposing that, from
the early 1870s, the great English conurbations were becoming
increasingly insulated from foci of infection and, hence, also from
regions in which there were high concentrations of body lice—notably
in urban Ireland (table 5.2). The final column of table 5.2 demonstrates
that typhus continued to thrive in Dublin and Belfast, and that among
English urban areas the disease was declining less rapidly in those trading
and seaborne centres in the north east and the north west which had
natural and continuing links with Ireland.[41] The wider context within
which this 'lagged' effect should be located is one in which, taking
England and Wales as a whole, the number of Irish-born residents had
risen very rapidly from just 300,000 in 1841 to just over 600,000 in 1861,
but had then remained static for the next four decades at around half a
million.[42] In London, the Irish-born accounted for nearly five per cent
of the total population in 1851, just under four per cent in 1861, 2.1 per
cent in 1881 and 1.6 per cent in 1891.[43] It would clearly be a caricature of
social and epidemiological history to use these figures to argue that
successive waves of epidemic typhus in nineteenth-century Britain were
determined by the 'flow of infection' from Ireland, or that the decline of
the disease coincided symmetrically and causally with diminishing
immigration after 1860. Nevertheless, once it had run its full epidemic
course, the extended and final outbreak of typhus could be reactivated

only by a large-scale movement of infected lice-carrying individuals from centres of population where there continued to be a high incidence of the disease. Such centres were to be found in Dublin and Belfast at precisely that time when, had it conformed to the general periodicity observable during the first 80 years of the century, the disease would have been expected to recur in the great English cities. However, this time, typhus did not return. This remission is more likely to be understood by an analysis of short-term fluctuations in rates of migration from Ireland to urban England than through a generalized appeal to a supposedly monolithic and nationally uniform sanitary revolution.

The decline of typhoid during the final 30 years of the nineteenth century may be more briefly considered. Despite incompatibilities between the measures undertaken to reduce mortality and the theories which supported them, the conscious efforts of doctors and professional epidemiologists played a more significant role in this process than had been the case with typhus. Throughout this period epidemiology continued to be shaped by a broadly miasmatic theory of disease, according to which small-scale outbreaks of typhoid were believed to be transmitted via the vapours which emanated from badly constructed privies and water closets.[44] The programmes which were undertaken as the practical expression of these beliefs undoubtedly reduced much mortality which would now be attributed to person-to-person infection. There was, therefore, no functional contradiction between a predominantly miasmatic conception and the emergent and more 'scientific' approach which emphasized the specificity of disease.

From about 1870, improvements in company filtration techniques ensured that unsafe water ceased to be widely suspected by public health workers and, subsequently, attention was directed towards other ways in which the disease was believed to be spread. Unsafe milk and foodstuffs were energetically tracked down in the 1870s and 1880s;[45] contaminated shellfish and water-cress were frequently implicated in the 1890s;[46] and, by the end of the century, investigators were beginning to understand the role of the immune carrier.[47] Attention was briefly redirected in the 1890s to puzzling differentials in district mortality rates from typhoid. The possibility that the disease had once again been transmitted via public water supplies was widely canvassed. Shirley Forster Murphy, the first medical officer of health to the London County Council, pointed to the probability that districts which were supplied from the Lea were likely to suffer higher mortality than those supplied from the Thames and, more specifically, that the reservoirs and filters of the East London and New River Companies were inadequate to the task of providing safe water when the Lea was in flood.[48] Murphy's methodology was sophisticated and revealing. He demonstrated, by applying Booth's data on poverty to the incidence of infectious disease for each of the metropolitan districts, that in the case of typhoid, and typhoid only, complex environmental shortcomings were more significant than differentials in real income.[49] This was a telling formulation of several of the aetiological differences which had long been thought to exist between typhoid and typhus, as well as an explanation of the frequently observed phenomenon whereby typhoid had invaded even the most respectable and hygienically scrupulous of middle-class homes.[50]

In addition, by the 1890s compulsory notification and hospitalization in public institutions administered by the Metropolitan Asylums Board had been added to routine inspection and epidemiological analysis at district level. Thirty per cent of all metropolitan typhoid sufferers, by the end of the decade, were receiving treatment as in-patients.[51] The geographical spread, and mortality from outbreaks, of the disease were reduced by this extension of hospital provision to that section of the working class just above that officially stigmatized as 'pauperized'.[52] Thus, the London experience suggests that McKeown and Record's generally pessimistic conclusions *vis-à-vis* the impact of hospitalization on infectious disease during the nineteenth century as a whole may be in need of modification.[53] It is worth noting that, by the end of the century, the public fever hospitals had been augmented by local bacteriological laboratories which facilitated a more rapid identification of localized outbreaks.[54] The steady elimination of typhoid during the final 30 years of the century proceeded despite, rather than because of, the initiative of any unifying municipal body with responsibility for the whole of London. The powers of the Metropolitan Board of Works had been deliberately restricted in this sphere by the Act of 1855 and, after 1889, the medical officer of health to the London County Council occupied no more than an advisory position in relation to the still intensely independent and localist vestries. A closer and more effective control over the environment may be traced to the enthusiastic involvement of a network of specialists who came into contact with one another through a variety of professional and scientific bodies which had their headquarters in the capital. The water supply improved consistently, with only intermittent set-backs, between 1870 and the formation of the Metropolitan Water Board in 1902. This improvement occurred not through Government surveillance exercised by the Board of Trade, but as a result of the collaboration between William Farr at the Registrar General's Office and the eminent theoretical chemist and water analyst, Edward Frankland—a relationship which began during the cholera crisis of 1866 and which survived, in the face of acrimonious opposition from the water companies, for the next 15 years.[55] Frankland may well have exaggerated the dangers of the Thames and the Lea as long-term sources of supply,[56] but without his regular reports on chemical and bacteriological quality, stringent and quasi-compulsory

Metropolitan water standards would not have been adopted. Once the safety of the water supply had been finally and compulsorily ensured, mortality from typhoid could be eroded by other means. The Metropolitan Association of Medical Officers of Health, reporting on specific epidemics, pressing for more rigorous protection of food and milk, and rebuking recalcitrant vestries, complemented and extended the efforts of Frankland and Farr.[57] The influence of these individuals, operating within a still largely informal administrative network, and undertaking regular measures to control not only typhoid, but the whole spectrum of infectious diseases, should not be underestimated.[58]

Typhoid, therefore, seems to have been brought at least partially under control by the campaign launched against it by doctors, epidemiologists and public health workers, while typhus, a more complex, socially traumatic and threatening disease, was less tractable. The two infections, frequently and understandably confused by contemporaries, and later unhelpfully bracketed together as 'dirt diseases' by historians of public health, reacted quite differently to attempts at coordinated containment. At the explicit level this essay has attempted to confront some of the ambiguities and contradictions of the orthodox, 'classic' sanitary revolution; implicitly, it has touched upon a deeper and more enduring problematic—the troubled issue of agency in history.[59]

A note on sources

In all but the last of the *Supplements* to the *Annual Reports* which apply to the period under discussion, the Registrar General claimed that deaths in public institutions, including hospitals, had been redistributed to 'normal district of residence'. However, a readjustment of this kind was never undertaken for district death-rates from specific causes. The tables and maps in this article, therefore, have attempted to reduce serious misrepresentation by modifying the Registrar General's statistics in the light of data available from those hospitals which admitted large numbers of fever patients. The following points should be noted:

1851–70:   Deaths occurring in the London Fever Hospital, which was situated in Islington, have been reallocated to district of residence, following the extensive admissions data contained in Charles Murchison, *A Treatise on the Continued Fevers of Great Britain* (3rd ed., edited by W. Cayley, London, 1884), pp. 74–5.

1871–90:   Some distortion was caused by the admission of growing numbers of fever patients to hospitals administered by the Metropolitan Asylums Board in Hackney, Lambeth and Greenwich. Adjustment has been made by applying approximate case fatality rates to data contained in the regular listings of case admissions to the various hospitals in *Minutes* of the Metropolitan Asylums Board for each of the relevant years: and for 1887–90, in *Annual Reports* of the Statistical Committee of the Metropolitan Asylums Board.

1891–1900: Because of the dramatic increase in hospitalization in this period, many of the Registrar General's figures for mortality at district level are quite meaningless. It is, however, fortunate that cases of infectious disease at district level began to be recorded annually from 1890 onwards. These statistics constitute probably the most comprehensive source for disease incidence for any late nineteenth-century city, and they may be located in the pullout tables and graphs attached to the *Annual Reports* of the Statistical Committee of the Metropolitan Asylums Board, 1890–1902.

Infant mortality in nineteenth-century Bradford

Barbara Thompson

High rates of infant mortality, especially in the rapidly growing northern industrial towns, proved to be one of the most intransigent of all the public health problems of nineteenth-century England. This essay, by examining the experience of one typical boom town of the Industrial Revolution, provides an illustration of the reasons why the infant death rate was so slow to reflect the downward trend in general mortality rates during the period before 1900, and which influences were most likely to be significant in reducing the dangers to infant life after that date. Bradford, which by the mid nineteenth century 'exemplified in a superlative degree the deleterious effects on life and health of . . . rapid and intensive industrial development',[1] had one of the highest infant mortality rates in the country, and therefore makes an ideal case study.

The first part of the essay looks at the dangers to infant life in the period before 1875, when population was increasing rapidly and industrial expansion reached its peak; the second section deals with the social, economic, and locational factors which underlay the disparities in infant death rates between the various wards within the Borough in the last quarter of the century, when the town's birth rate fell rapidly and its industries entered on a new phase of gradual, but inexorable, decline.

Bradford by the 1870s had already a long-established and unenviable record of high infant mortality which reflected not only its status as an environmentally despoiled area, but also the disadvantages of its rainy and windswept Pennine location. The fact that the town was situated in 'a huge natural amphitheatre almost enclosed by high land'[2] or, in the blunter phraseology of an exasperated mid nineteenth-century railway engineer, 'in a hole', only served to exacerbate the problems created by the dramatic growth of population and industry. In 1801 the town had a mere 13,000 inhabitants; by 1881 there were over 180,000, most of whom lived and worked in the congested inner basin where housing and industry competed for the limited available space.

By the mid-1820s land in the central township of Bradford was already becoming scarce and dear.[3] This, together with the lack of control on the building of anything other than mill chimneys (which had to be above ninety feet high), before the Incorporation of the Borough in 1847, led to the erection of large quantities of high density 'back-to-back' housing. Underneath many of these dwellings were cellars, which were let separately to the poorest section of the population. Some of this accommodation was completely bereft of the most rudimentary sanitary facilities; houses were often situated close to, or incorporated, the walls of adjacent mills, stables, and even burial grounds. As Robert Baker, the Leeds surgeon who became an assistant inspector of factories, observed in 1851, 'the great object of the builders of cottages has for many years been to plant as many dwellings upon a given area as it would contain, without any reference to health, decency, or morality . . .'[4] In addition to these problems, the almost universal use of coal, to generate steam power and as a domestic fuel, gave rise to vast quantities of smoke, which was trapped by the surrounding hills so that it overhung the town. Small wonder that one visitor in the 1840s compared his entry into the town from the encircling hills with a descent into Hell![5]

The local gentry, who had once had their town houses along Kirkgate,[6] had long since departed by the middle years of the nineteenth century; and even the middle classes were rapidly deserting the inner parts of the town for the higher, more salubrious areas, 'open to fresh air and breezes'.[7] However, Bradford was a predominantly working-class town where the majority of the inhabitants, men, women, and even children, who worked long hours in the worsted mills along the beck, needed cheap housing within easy walking distance of their workplace rather than housing in healthier areas. Most of the remainder of the working-class population lived close to and worked in the local coal and iron mines which scarred the south-eastern districts of the town; or in the huge Bowling, and Low Moor ironworks situated nearby. It was on these three industries, worsted textiles, iron and coal, that the wealth and rapid expansion of the town was based, but they were also responsible, directly and indirectly, for the growing environmental and social problems which, by the 1840s, made high infant mortality almost inevitable.

I

There are no precise figures of infant mortality in Bradford before 1860. The town formed the urban core of the much larger registration district of Bradford which also included 16 other, more rural townships, and large tracts of the surrounding countryside. Nevertheless, it is clear from the figures for the registration district, and from the rising crude death rate in the Borough during the 1840s, that at least one in five, and sometimes one in four babies who were born in Bradford during this period, failed to survive the first perilous year of urban life. [8]

The decade of the 1840s was probably the most traumatic in Bradford's history. It began with the building of a barracks to house the troops drafted in to quell the riotous population, and ended, after the Chartist disturbances of 1848, and the cholera outbreak of 1849, with the vision of the model factory community at Saltaire—one man's paternalistic solution to the problems of the new urban industrial society. However, for the town of Bradford itself, the solution could not be found so easily. The old social controls and administrative structures, which had been sufficient to meet the needs of a small face-to-face community, crumbled under the strains imposed by a vast influx of newcomers; the twin economic pressures of cyclical distress and technological dislocation; and the inadequacies of the town's infrastructure. As the major hazards to infant life—dirt, destitution, and disease— proliferated, the Tory-dominated Commissioners for Lighting and Watching (a self co-opting oligarchy formed under an Act of 1803) fiercely resisted the attempts of the politically motivated Liberals to obtain a Charter of Incorporation. Disputes arose between the Commissioners and the more recently constituted Board of Surveyors over spheres of authority; and the town constables appointed by the Vestry were forced to act as reluctant arbiters whilst the workmen of a private householder undid the street repairs carried out by the Commissioners. [9]

The report produced by the Health of Towns' Commissioner, James Smith of Deanston, when he visited Bradford in 1844, provides a lurid insight into conditions prevailing in the town. He found 'the sewerage . . . defective and the supply of water for cleansing most deficient . . . the chief slaughterhouse . . . in the middle of the town . . .' and the Bradford beck so obstructed 'by the erection of mill dams and the encroachment of houses, [that] it frequently overflows the lower part of the town, causing much havoc in the cellers . . .'. In the steep narrow streets 'the drainage of the upper houses [was] falling in upon those below'; paving was almost non-existent in 'the inferior and cross streets chiefly inhabited by the working classes' but 'dung heaps', 'open privies' and 'swill tubs of the swine feeders' were to be 'seen in many directions'. In the majority of these streets the sewage flowed in 'open channels' and 'the whole sub-soil [was] saturated with sewage water'. The beck and the canal basin were the stinking receptacles of every kind of filth, giving off 'bubbles of sulphurated hydrogen', occasionally catching fire (to the delight of youthful pranksters) and having disastrous effects on the '*watch cases and other materials of silver* . . .' (my emphasis) 'in the pockets of the workmen employed near the canal'. Small wonder that Smith felt bound to pronounce Bradford 'the most filthy town' he had visited. The only hopeful signs were the ingenious, but largely abortive, efforts made by some manufacturers to reduce the smoke problem, and the formation of a joint stock company to provide an improved supply of water. At the time of Smith's visit water had to be purchased from water carriers at the cost of a halfpenny for three gallons. This, he considered, was 'most expensive . . . and forces an economy . . . [which is] . . . highly injurious to health, cleanliness, and comfort'. [10]

If dirt constituted a threat to the health of almost all babies born in Bradford, destitution was slightly more selective. Factory reformers from the late 1820s had agitated about the effects on the health and morals of the female population of their employment in factories, but the report submitted to Edwin Chadwick in 1842 by the Clerk to the Bradford Poor Law Union [11] indicates that by the 1840s it was the infants of those who remained outside the factory system who were sometimes more at risk. The most unhealthy section of Bradford's working population was the thousands of domestic based woolcombers, many of them Irish—the most recent arrivals, often already debilitated by the privations experienced in their native land. Amongst woolcombers and their families the average age at death was a mere 16 years, and almost 70 per cent of these deaths were at ages under 15, compared with 60 per cent for the rest of the working-class population. Even in full-time employment a comber could earn barely sufficient to sustain life, and the surplus of labour in this degraded craft meant long periods when work was scarce or unobtainable.

A report prepared by the woolcombers themselves in 1845, appealing to their employers for 'clean, well-ventilated shops' in which they could work, revealed that home for many combers and their families was a subterranean cellar dwelling, often barely twelve feet square. In this miserable room as many as six or seven persons might struggle to exist, amongst the filth and the fumes emitted by the 'pot o' four'. Typical of the entries in the report was the cellar in Spink's Buildings, measuring 13 ft. 9 in. by 12 ft., which was 'four feet below the surface' of the adjoining street; here 'a man, his wife, and four children, sleep in one bed composed of shavings'. In a back-to-back in Club Houses: 'Four persons work in the upper apartment, in which a man and his wife sleep. They had to cease from work a week since whilst the woman was lying-in. She now lies in bed exposed to their gaze. A dead child is laid in the same room.' [12]

The heat, the fumes, and the desperate poverty, meant that woolcombers were especially vulnerable to the twin scourges of tuberculosis and alcoholism, which together with venereal disease undermined the health of many adults and threatened the lives of their children in mid nineteenth-century urban England. In Bradford, which was a magnet for newcomers from rural areas, life was particularly harsh and brutal. Ever-increasing numbers of people were crammed into dirty, over-crowded lodging houses, where sometimes beds were shared by whole families or even total strangers. Beer-shops and brothels were to be found in every street. They offered a brief temporary escape to those men who could scrape together a few pence, but as George White, the Chartist Secretary of the Woolcombers' Sanitary Committee, and a self-confessed heavy drinker, admitted, money spent on drink usually meant even greater hardships for wives and families. [13]

Temperance campaigners, in a town which proudly claimed to have the first Temperance Association in England (formed in 1830), [14] saw to it that the evils and consequences of drink received wide publicity, but evidence about venereal disease is more difficult to obtain. Nevertheless, it was almost certainly a major factor in high infant mortality and continued to be so throughout the century. No surprise was expressed when an inquest on a baby, which had first been given an heroic dose of emetic, and then provided with a coffin by a carpenter who supplemented his income by acting as medical adviser to the poor, revealed that the child had actually died of syphilis. The carpenter–physician was warned that his combination of employments was undesirable, but no further action was taken. [15]

It seems highly probable that for this period, even those figures of infant deaths which do exist considerably understate the size of the problem. After the Registration Act of 1837 was introduced the sexton at Bradford parish church admitted that the deaths of unbaptized children were treated as still-births, even though the infant concerned might have lived for a period of days or weeks. [16] The fact that a still-born child could be buried without registration and with very little question, in a grave opened for another interment, encouraged both parents and midwives to treat peri-natal deaths as still-births. Some parents, too poor even to afford the few coppers demanded by the verger for this service, resorted to more desperate measures. In 1837, one Bradford couple were discovered late at night in the graveyard attached to the Roman Catholic church, in the process of burying a dead baby. Although the circumstances of the case aroused the suspicions of the town authorities, who ordered a post-mortem to be carried out, the couple were released when the surgeon confirmed their story that the infant had died from natural causes. [17]

In reality, unless it took a particularly blatant form, infanticide was almost impossible to detect during much of the nineteenth century. When infant deaths were a common occurrence, only the rumour-mongering of suspicious neighbours or clear evidence of deliberate murder brought any official investigation. The lurid cases reported in the Bradford press, such as the desperate servant girl who disposed of her illegitimate new-born baby in her employer's privy, the deserted mother who abandoned her infant in a communal middenstead, or the baby found drowned in a mill dam, can give no indication of the actual extent of infanticide in the town. [18] Even in the years after 1875,

Bradford's Medical Officers of Health frequently alleged that parents and midwives connived at disguising the true circumstances of infant deaths; on occasion they even hinted at more sinister arrangements; but, as with abortion, prosecutions were very rare, and the harshness of the penalties made juries reluctant to convict those accused.

In the years between 1845 and 1875 one of the aspects of infant mortality which aroused most attention amongst contemporaries was the wide disparities which existed between different parts of the country. The *Annual Reports* of the Registrar General revealed that whilst in the 1850s the national average of infant mortality was 150 per 1,000 births, in the 'healthiest districts' it was only 94 per 1,000 births, but in the 'seven principal town registration districts of Yorkshire' 187 in every 1,000 babies died within a year of birth. In the Bradford registration district 200 out of every 1,000 babies born failed to survive their first year — 33 per cent above the national average.[19]

At a national level, those most concerned with public health, especially John Simon (who became Medical Officer to the Privy Council after the dissolution of the General Board of Health in 1858) and his team of medical inspectors, were quick to point to high levels of infant deaths as an index of the general insanitary condition of many industrial towns.[20] In the locality such explanations were not always acceptable, particularly if the general death rate seemed to be falling; an improvement usually attributed by contemporaries to a reduction in the level of 'harmful miasmas' responsible for epidemic disease, consequent upon the removal of some of the most glaring environmental inadequacies. The false assumption that foul smells, especially those arising from putrefying animal or vegetable matter, or closely packed, unwashed, human bodies, gave rise to disease, led sanitary reformers, councillors, and ratepayers to expect dramatic results from very limited improvements which, in practice, were of little relevance to the most vulnerable section of the urban population, the very poor and the very young.

In Bradford, where local rates had risen steadily throughout the 1850s, as the new Town Council sought to carry out 'improvements' ranging from the municipalization of the water supply to the widening and straightening of streets (where some councillors just happened to be the owners of valuable property), such expenditure attracted much criticism. The municipal take-over of the Water Company had been the compromise solution to several years of bitter political wrangling, involving the Town Council in the acceptance of a scheme and an engineer originally chosen by the Company, and the rejection of a more ambitious scheme drawn up for the Council by one of the leading water engineers of the nineteenth century, Bateman of Manchester.[21] The result was years of delay and mounting expense so that by 1864 even the sanitary-conscious, Liberal editor of the local newspaper, William

Byles, was driven to exclaim that 'the water-works have become a nightmare . . .'.[22]

The Radicals on the Council argued against any further expenditure on facilities such as sewerage (which, unlike water supply, had little chance of ever becoming a profitable enterprise), and pointed to the ineffectiveness of a sewerage scheme in Halifax in preventing a major epidemic of scarlet fever.[23] Other ratepayers, on the other hand, including disgruntled Tory millowners and an increasingly vocal body of respectable working men, were becoming restive about the priority given to street widening when the town was still without any effective mains sewerage. The majority of the working classes in the 1840s had frequently resisted the efforts of sanitary reformers to prevent them from keeping pigs in their yards and even in their homes, preferring to risk the 'harmful miasmas' rather than sacrifice their sole remaining link with self-sufficiency. Yet by the end of the 1850s they became more resigned to the sanitary discipline necessary to civilized urban life; and, indeed, an increasingly confident aristocracy of labour was prepared to challenge the decisions taken by middle-class councillors over such matters as the need for street drains and the type of housing in which working men might choose to live. Bradford's working classes did not regard the 'back-to-back' with the same animadversion as the members of the Sanitary Committee, and resented attempts to replace this type of accommodation with 'draughty' through houses. Meanwhile, the poor, with the collusion of unscrupulous landlords, continued to evade the regulations introduced by the Council to prevent overcrowding and restrict the letting of unfit cellar dwellings—for these people even a miserable hovel was preferable to the hated workhouse, or to no home at all.[24]

Despite the predictions of Edwin Chadwick and his supporters,[25] the urban poor were the last to benefit from the public health movement of the mid nineteenth century. An increased supply of water created as many problems as it solved for those who lived in a house without a sink, in a street where the only drainage was an open channel and the subsoil was saturated with faecal matter. Although the extra privy accommodation, which the Town Council pressured slum landlords to provide, undoubtedly improved the conditions of life for some of their tenants, it brought little consolation to those whose homes had to be demolished to provide the necessary space. Even when construction of the new mains sewerage was finally commenced, in 1859, after several false starts, it was of little benefit to the majority of the working class whose houses lacked the drains to connect them to the sewers. It was flooding in the late spring of 1859, when extensive damage was caused to stocks in the cellars of the central trading area, rather than any sudden upsurge of direct concern for public health which provided the major impetus to the construction of the new sewerage.

Sometimes regulations imposed with the most public-spirited intentions could have undesirable consequences. This was true of the new bye-laws passed in 1860 to prevent the erection of any more 'back-to-back' housing in Bradford. The main housing problem was in the town centre (where the quality of any new houses was in any case of little relevance to those who could not afford to move out of the slums): here the street widening activities of the Town Council and the influx of newcomers during the Lancashire Cotton Famine only served to exacerbate existing overcrowding and to push up the level of rents. When Dr Hunter visited Bradford in 1865, as part of his national survey of housing conditions amongst the urban poor, he noted with disapproval that, whilst the Town Council was concentrating on defending controversial bye-laws to stop the building of good-quality 'back-to-backs' in the suburbs, the much more urgent problem of deteriorating conditions in the overcrowded central areas was being overlooked, and regulations were being ignored with impunity. [26]

It seems almost certain that the most significant contribution to the improvement in the health of Bradford's working classes during the 1850s and 1860s came not from the efforts of the Town Council, but from a change in the organization of the worsted industry which transferred the woolcombing process from home to factory. In the short term, the redundant hand-combers suffered intense hardship. Earlier cyclical depressions had always brought a response in the form of charitable relief schemes, to which both philanthropic and self-interested manufacturers had been major contributors, but in the 1850s, after the invention of an efficient combing machine, even those who were inspired by humanitarian motives felt that the only solution to the problem was to encourage these unwanted workers to seek employment elsewhere. [27] Many left the town, some leaving behind wives and families whose application for poor relief was often rejected by Relieving Officers convinced that the alleged desertion was merely a ruse to obtain aid from the township. Nonetheless, despite these hardships, the demise of Bradford's most unhealthy domestic-based craft and the outward migration which reduced the pressure of demand for the cheapest housing, and slowed down the rate of population growth in the 1850s to a mere 2.5 per cent, undoubtedly brought a long-term improvement in the general condition of the working population. It also gave the Town Council a breathing space in which to begin tackling the worst problems of fifty years of rapid expansion.

Changes in the employment structure of the town during the 1850s and 1860s dramatically reduced the number and proportion of men employed in the worsted textile industry, and brought an increase in the number of those engaged in skilled and semi-skilled jobs, especially in building, engineering, and transport. These shifts in occupational structure were reflected in a decline in adult deaths from pulmonary tuberculosis and typhus, and a steady increase in the membership of self-help institutions such as friendly societies. Even in the mills and mines the conditions and hours of work were generally thought to have improved considerably by 1859, when the National Association for the Promotion of Social Science (N.A.P.S.S.) chose Bradford as the venue for its third annual conference. A succession of local contributors to the meeting ranged from Robert Baker, assistant inspector of factories, to Thomas Beaumont, an ardent teetotaller, factory and sanitary reform enthusiast, who was chairman of the Bradford Town Council's Sanitary Committee, and John James, local historian and champion of the old Tory establishment; all testified to the improvement in the health and morals of the factory population since the passing of the first supervised Factory Act in 1833. When a visiting lady speaker rose to express the conventional mid nineteenth-century middle-class opinion that factory girls were promiscuous and resorted to measures such as birth control, abortion, and infanticide to avoid the consequences of their depravity, local representatives of all classes were quickly on the defensive. At the solitary evening session of the conference, to which the respectable working classes were invited, a Bradford working man vigorously refuted the slurs which had been made by outsiders on the moral character of the town's female population. [28]

Nevertheless, the undeniably excessive death rate amongst children under five in Bradford constituted a blot on the sanitary reputation of the Town Council, and an embarrassment to local delegates. When William Hudson, the Town Clerk, rose to address the Conference, he was understandably anxious to provide an explanation of this circumstance which would exonerate his employers. Therefore, like most other local contributors, he made one major reservation in his hymn of praise to the regulated factory system, with regard to its effect on infant life. Hudson alleged that 'the employment of married women having children' was a 'festering sore' which was 'sapping the stamina' of the 'rising manufacturing population' and that this had prevented the infant population of Bradford from sharing in the general downward trend in mortality rates. [29] However, Hudson's mortality rates were based on inaccurate estimates of population size and, in fact, there had been very little improvement in death rates in Bradford during the 1850s. Yet there were few persons in his middle-class audience who would have cared to challenge the validity or completeness of contemporary explanations of infant mortality which placed the responsibility squarely on the shoulders of individual mothers. Social disparities in infant deaths could also be conveniently accounted for by blaming mothers' cupidity, ignorance, indifference, or wilful neglect as causes of untimely demise of their babies.

Whilst some contemporaries agreed with Hudson that the high infant death rate endangered the 'national interest' to a sufficient extent to justify legislative intervention, others felt that, in view of the continuing high birth rate, particularly amongst the 'lower orders', the annual toll on infant life was to be welcomed as a safety valve which prevented a Malthusian crisis. William Farr, in a letter to the Registrar General, alluded to these fears in the early 1870s, when he suggested that there was no inevitable connection between a reduction in infant mortality and an increase in population because 'the birth rate may itself fall'.[30] The accuracy of this prediction was to be dramatically demonstrated in late nineteenth-century Bradford.

The 1870s saw an increase in concern at the national level about high infant mortality, which was reflected in legislation to safeguard infants put out for nursing, to prevent the adulteration of food and drink, and to tighten the regulations for the registration of births. These were essentially negative, deterrent measures, against what was still seen as a problem of deliberate individual abuse. In 1874 *The Lancet* took up the theme with an editorial which emphasized the need for the government to use 'the powers of the state' to protect infant life; a matter which had been the subject of heated discussion at the annual conference of the N.A.P.S.S. in that year.[31] Although the major upsurge of interest in preventing infant deaths came at the beginning of the twentieth century,[32] by the 1870s the emphasis in explanations of causation had gradually shifted from working mothers to the home environment.

Bradford was slow to accept this change of direction. Even the distinguished physician to the Bradford Infirmary, Dr Bridges, a positivist who in the 1870s was to become one of the Medical Inspectors to the Local Government Board (L.G.B.), seems to have retained a belief in the role of maternal employment as the *major* factor in high infant mortality. Although in 1862 Bridges was highly critical of the failure of the Town Council to deal with the continued existence of such environmental hazards to health as 'the refuse of 20,000 houses either decomposing in cess-pools, or churned by every barge in the canal' or 'the black torrents of needless smoke' (which members of the Bradford Town Council continued to argue was either essential to trade, or even beneficial to health because it provided a carbon filter to trap the germs of infectious disease), he was, nevertheless, convinced that the con-stitutions of the local population were 'damaged at or before birth by the factory system'.[33] In 1873 he was the joint compiler of a controversial report to the L.G.B. which, drawing extensively on information derived from Bradford sources, concluded that maternal and child employment in factories was the most important factor in promoting both a high level of infant mortality and a progressive degeneration in the stature, physique, and general condition of the urban population.[34]

Whilst there may well have been some truth in these conclusions, this clearly was not the whole story. Infant diarrhoea was as common and fatal amongst mining communities, where there was little opportunity of maternal employment, as it was in the textile towns. In Bradford, during the 1860s, almost 12 per cent of all infant deaths were attributed to diarrhoea, a condition which John Simon had associated with 'the habitual breathing or drinking of putrefying animal refuse'.[35] The reports of his inspectors, Dr Greenhow in 1860,[36] and Dr Hunter in 1865 when he investigated the excessive mortality amongst infants at Leeds,[37] reaffirmed the conclusion that these deaths were closely related to prevailing sanitary conditions—especially to the existence of filthy, overflowing, privy middensteads. In 1871, after the severe outbreaks of typhoid and diarrhoea during the hot summers of 1868 and 1870, it was Bradford's turn to be investigated.

John Netten Radcliffe, a celebrated epidemiologist, and one of the ablest of Simon's Medical Inspectors, arrived in Bradford in May 1871, only to find that the Town Council was unable to provide him with any 'trustworthy data upon which to found an estimate of the health condition of the population . . .'[38] This was hardly surprising since the figures included in the *Annual Reports* of the Sanitary Committee were compiled by an over-worked clerk in the office of the Borough Surveyor. The town had no Medical Officer of Health, and no one had even noticed that there was a major discrepancy between the figures contained in the Council reports and those submitted to the Registrar General by the local Superintendent Registrar. Radcliffe was unable to complete his inquiry until the following May, when further statistical information had been provided both by the Town Council and by the office of the Registrar General. Although the Sanitary Committee can hardly have been unaware of the views of the medical inspectorate on the role played by sanitary circumstances in respect to infant deaths, it was typical of local attitudes that the report which was prepared for Radcliffe on mortality amongst under-fives in Bradford during the month of January, 1872, dealt exclusively with the questions of working mothers and illegitimacy.[39] The fact that almost 70 per cent of the 172 deaths were amongst children who were neither 'minded' nor illegitimate was completely ignored, as indeed, were environmental circumstances. In particular, as Radcliffe himself noted, no mention was made of the continued existence 'in the older parts of the borough of the old-fashioned privy with middenstead in all its revolting abomination . . . of a capacity to contain many weeks or month's refuse', which was emptied at infrequent intervals 'through the agency of contractors' but was 'for the most part as offensive when empty as when full'.[40] Radcliffe's report was finally completed in July 1872, and although it was carefully worded, praising 'the Corporation of Bradford . . . for its efforts to ameliorate the sanitary condition of the population of the borough'[41] especially through the increased supply of water and the provision of the new network of mains sewers, it was nevertheless a document full of implied criticism of the town's sanitary administration.

Even the Town Council's greatest success, the municipalization and extension of the water works, did not escape unfavourable comment. He hinted that the pursuit of profit had caused the Corporation (anxious to have some revenue to offset the growing burden on the rates and to diminish ratepayer resentment) to over-extend its supply network outside the town 'somewhat at the cost of the borough itself'[42] with the result that in times of drought the supply was insufficient to meet local needs. Radcliffe made it quite plain throughout his report and in the conclusion that the Town Council could not hope to make any effective progress in respect to public health unless it immediately appointed a M.O.H. to co-ordinate its sanitary activities, and undertook a radical reform of its 'faulty method of excrement disposal'. He commented, with directness and some sarcasm, on the special problem of infant mortality:

> The inquiries of Local Authorities to this end cannot be anticipated to lead to sound practical results unless the Local Authority is aided by an efficient Medical Officer of Health ... although the general relationship of an excessive infantile mortality to the considerable employment of women in manufactories ... is doubtless well understood ... it is not yet practicable to state the proportionate influence exercised upon the mortality of infants and young children from diarrhoeal diseases by the common sanitary defects of residences and by the neglect arising from the industrial occupations of adult women. That the prevalence of these diseases in infants is governed largely by the *same* causes as determine the prevalence of like diseases among adults is unquestioned, and among these causes the *breathing or drinking of putrefying animal refuse* holds a foremost place.[43]

Although the report was generally well received in the town, even the usually sanitary-conscious editor of the *Bradford Observer*, William Byles, baulked at the thought of the expense of converting Bradford's 20,000 privies and middensteads into water closets. In any case, as the paper hinted dourly, the drainage of the town was in a far less satisfactory state than Radcliffe had been led to believe, and the work of connecting dwellings to the new sewerage would take many years.[44] There was more truth in these comments than the editor himself probably realized at the time. The 'endemic disease' of Bradford in the 1860s and 1870s, as Radcliffe had observed, was typhoid. When the first M.O.H. was appointed in 1873, his reports quickly revealed that the middle classes living in Manningham or Little Horton were almost as vulnerable as the filthy poor living in the overcrowded districts.[45] Sanitary engineering was, even by 1870, often a very rudimentary affair; plumbers were not highly regarded within the building trades; and despite Radcliffe's conclusion that 'the drinking of animal refuse' played little part 'in the development of enteric fever in the borough',[46] it seems likely that water supplies were frequently contaminated. This was especially so in the better areas of the town where badly connected water closets were to be found in the houses. The Medical Officer of Health soon discovered what the *Bradford Observer* and many Councillors were already only too well aware of: in many of the better streets of the town, to economize on materials and skilled labour, the drains which had been constructed before and during the 1850s were of permeable rubble. The network of main sewers could do little to improve the sanitary state of the town when many of the drains running into it were hardly more than 'elongated underground cesspools',[47] and when the landlords of other properties refused to pay for the work of connection. Only after the formation of the Bradford Sanitary Association,[48] a middle-class organization employing its own surveyor to inspect the sanitary arrangements of property occupied by members, did typhoid begin to be confined to the less fashionable areas of Bradford. In these circumstances, considering also the continuing shortages of water and the problems experienced by the Town council regarding the defecation of the existing sewage at the outfall,[49] the decision by the Town Council to disregard Radcliffe's recommendation for radical reform of sewage disposal methods, and to appoint a M.O.H., may well have been fortunate.

II

The dramatic reduction in death rates for all age groups in Bradford during the last five years of the 1870s was seen by most contemporaries as a belated validation of the efforts of the Town Council to improve the sanitary condition of the town since 1847. It was seen more directly as a result of the improved co-ordination of preventive measures following the appointment of a Medical Officer of Health in April 1873, but it was probably the appointment of a Public Analyst, in July 1874, which was of most immediate relevance to the safeguarding of infant life.

One of the major complaints of the pro-incorporation party, even in the early 1840s, had been the inability of the town's old authorities to prevent the offering for sale, in the market and elsewhere, of foodstuffs which were either diseased or rotten. Whilst some of the more obvious abuses had been suppressed, particularly in the 1860s when the magistrates had imposed prison sentences on unscrupulous butchers, the more subtle practice of adulteration continued largely undetected unless some scandal, such as the lozenge poisoning case of 1859,[50] drew official attention to the matter. The unqualified Nuisance Inspectors employed by the Town Council could hardly be expected to recognize contaminated milk or other foodstuffs at a glance, and it is hardly surprising, therefore, that in his first report the new Public Analyst should declare that 'thousands of our population have never tasted pure milk . . . and there can be little doubt in the mind of any person capable of reflection that the excessive infant mortality of towns is in part attributable to the deficient supply of nutriment contained in this pabulum of life as it has been supplied'.[51] Whilst the mistaken adulteration of sweets with arsenic, resulting in the deaths of 19 people in 1858, had caused a public outcry in the town, it seems likely that dozens of infants perished every year as a result of the state of the milk supply. Of the first 20 samples of milk tested by the Public Analyst, five were seriously adulterated and almost all the others had been skimmed. When, in 1878, new regulations were introduced in relation to the production and sale of milk in Bradford, and a milk inspector was appointed, he quickly discovered that in most shops the milk was sold from uncovered bowls standing on the counter. Indeed, in at least one establishment he found that the milk bowl did double duty as a bath for the shopkeeper's own baby.[52]

Whether or not, after the appointment of a Public Analyst, the milk supply in Bradford was rendered less dangerous, it seems likely that the majority of the town's working population was able to afford rather more of the 'pabulum of life' and other foodstuffs, particularly after 1875 when real wages rose markedly. After 1873 food prices fell steadily,[53] whilst the wage rises secured during the boom years of the early 1870s were largely retained, despite a series of industrial disputes in 1879, when employers in the dyeing, engineering, and iron-working trades attempted to retrieve the concessions made earlier.[54] Nevertheless, when W. E. Forster, Bradford's somewhat controversial, long-serving Liberal MP, addressed the members of the Bradford Industrial Co-operative Society at their annual meeting in 1885, he was forced to admit that, whilst the conditions of life had improved for many people—as was instanced by the rise in membership and profits of their own society— 'still there was a class, the very lowest'[55] who were little better off than before. Although Forster saw this group as a small minority, whom he described as 'a problem to themselves',[56] incapable or unwilling to take advantage of opportunities for self-help, there is ample evidence that he underestimated the scale of the problem. Even in good times life for the vast majority of the working population of Bradford was a constant struggle to avoid the abyss of poverty, into which ill-health or even short-term unemployment almost inevitably precipitated them. For every working man who was a member of the Bradford Friendly Societies' Medical Aid Association, ten went unprotected, and only a tiny fraction of the members of the Association took advantage of the family protection scheme.[57] The continuance of widespread poverty was one of the reasons why, after the initial gains of the 1870s, infants failed to share in any further improvements in general mortality rates before 1900. Another was that infants were much more vulnerable to the types of infectious disease intimately connected with environmental circumstances of all kinds. Children between the ages of one and five were the principal beneficiaries of the reduction in deaths from the common infections of early childhood—scarlet fever, diphtheria, measles, whooping cough—as better feeding increased resistance and compulsory notification of the first two diseases brought earlier and more adequate care, often in hospital.[58] Although infants shared to some extent in this improvement, with compulsory vaccination against smallpox (if not always effectively enforced) eradicating this as a major cause of infant death after 1870, the babies whose lives were thus saved frequently succumbed to other diseases, especially in the poorer parts of the town.

The borough boundaries were extended in 1882 to include some of the more salubrious areas just outside the town, and at the same time 15 wards were created for which detailed data on the causes and ages of mortality were prepared by the M.O.H., providing an insight into the variations in the social and spatial distribution of disease, and in particular of infant deaths. Figure 6.1 and tables 6.1 to 6.4 show the situation of each ward, and give a breakdown of infant mortality.

In the nine innermost wards over 60 per cent of the housing was said by the M.O.H. in the 1890s to be of the 'back-to-back' variety.[59] The other six, outer wards, contained a rather smaller proportion of this type of accommodation, which almost all nineteenth-century sanitarians regarded as inimical to health (possibly due to the continuing influence

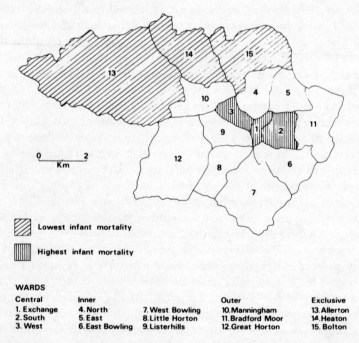

Lowest infant mortality

Highest infant mortality

WARDS

Central	Inner		Outer	Exclusive
1. Exchange	4. North	7. West Bowling	10. Manningham	13. Allerton
2. South	5. East	8. Little Horton	11. Bradford Moor	14. Heaton
3. West	6. East Bowling	9. Listerhills	12. Great Horton	15. Bolton

Figure 6.1 Location of wards with highest and lowest infant mortality, Bradford, 1882–1900

of the miasmatic theory of disease) and many more of the substantial terraces and villas which housed the town's expanding middle-class population. However, unlike some other northern industrial towns, most notably Leeds and Sheffield, Bradford had few rigidly segregated residential zones. 'The subdivided nature of the tenure'[60] (especially in the period before the bye-laws of the 1830s had attempted to prevent the erection of unsuitable cottage properties in the better parts of the town by laying down differing street width requirements for 'first, second, and third class' developments),[61] meant that contrasting types of housing had often been erected on adjoining plots. Yet, even though there was no complete homogeneity of housing or population in each ward, it is possible to generalize sufficiently to make meaningful comparisons, and the groupings used by the M.O.H. provide a useful basis for an analysis.

The nine inner wards can be further sub-divided into three central wards which contained the most disadvantaged social groups living in the worst and most overcrowded housing, notably the Irish quarters referred to in *Das Kapital*;[62] and six other wards where the more respectable working classes predominated. Here the usual type of housing was the somewhat better 'bye-law back-to-back', the compromise solution to the disputes of the 1860s. Many of these houses had been erected under the auspices of Building Societies, but there is little evidence that, in Bradford, such houses were any better than those erected by private builders or landlords during the same period for a similar type of occupant. Most houses consisted of one downstairs room, approximately fifteen feet by twelve, with a small cellar-head scullery; either one large or two smaller bedrooms above; and a part share in a back-yard (reached by means of a ground floor level passageway between each four houses) which contained two privies and one ashpit for all four properties.[63]

Surrounding the inner wards, on the upland areas overlooking the smoky valley, were the six outer wards. The three 'exclusive' wards, the most favoured in the borough, contained the houses of many of the better-off inhabitants besides the majority of Bradford's several hundred farms. These wards faced south, making the most of the available sunshine but sheltered from the prevailing winds, which helped to keep away the smog from almost a thousand factory chimneys in the valley below. These wards in the early 1880s had the lowest infant mortality rate (1,000 q_0) in the borough, 127 compared with 194 in the central wards, and 157 for the town as a whole (see tables 6.2 and 6.3). The other three wards were far less heterogeneous. Great Horton and Bradford Moor were predominantly working-class areas, expanding rapidly as a result of the opening of the tramways during the 1880s. Many of the houses were of a superior 'back-to-back' variety, the best of which had once been described by the *Bradford Observer* as 'back-to-back villas'.[64]

Table 6.1. Crude birth and death rates (in parts per thousand), Borough of Bradford, 1841–1900

	1841–50	1851–60	1861–70	1871–80	1881–90	1891–1900	Percentage change, 1841–1900
Death rate	27.5	26.5	26.6	25.3	20.4	18.9	−31.0
Birth rate	n.a.	n.a.	38.3	39.2	30.5	26.3	−31.0

Sources: Medical Officer of Health for Bradford *Annual Reports; Population Censuses of England and Wales, 1841–1901;* Registrar General's *Annual Reports, 1840–1870*

Table 6.2. Infant mortality ($1,000\ q_0$), Borough of Bradford, 1861–80

$1,000\ q_0$	1861–65	1866–70	1871–75	1876–80	Percentage change, 1861–65 to 1876–80
	200.0	207.8	203.2	167.1	−16.5

Sources: see table 6.1.

Table 6.3. Spatial variations in infant mortality (1,000 q_0),
Borough of Bradford, 1883–99*

Years	Central	Inner	Outer	Exclusive	Borough
1882–85	194	159	149	127	157
1886–90	216	171	163	128	170
1891–95	235	174	165	144	176
1896–99	227	172	161	127	172

Note: * the four districts are defined in Figure 6.1. In 1882 and 1900 there were
boundary changes, thus 1882–85 and 1896–99 refer to 4 year periods

Sources: see table 6.1.

Manningham, the other outer ward, was until the last quarter of the
nineteenth century the town's premier residential area, housing many of
the 'millocracy' and professional classes in palatial detached, semi-
detached, and terraced residences alongside Manningham Lane, the
most impressive entrance to the town. Nevertheless, Manningham had a
dark underside, for to the east of Lumb Lane were street upon street of
seamy 'back-to-backs' and, a little further along, the huge Manningham
Mills towered like an ominous giant over the mean streets which housed
many of Samuel Cunliffe Lister's enormous workforce.

The three major causes of infant deaths in Bradford during the late
nineteenth century (table 6.4) — gastro-intestinal disorders (diarrhoea,
atrophy and debility, and convulsions); respiratory infections (bronchitis, pneumonia, and pleurisy); and premature births — accounted for
well over 70 per cent of all infant deaths. The apparent stability in the
level of premature deaths, in an age before incubators were generally
available, and when registration procedures were being improved,
cannot be regarded as an outright failure of preventive measures, though
the high lead content of Bradford's high level water supply may have
been a contributory factor.[65] The other two categories of diseases, even
in the nineteenth century, were recognized as more a reflection of
temporal inadequacies than any unavoidable 'visitation of God'. Even
so, what was not so widely appreciated was the inability of many
individual mothers to overcome the environmental and social hazards
which threatened their babies' lives.[66]

The prevalence of gastro-intestinal disorders amongst babies in
Bradford during this period can be largely attributed to the glaring
inadequacies in domestic sanitary provision, to the general disregard for
hygiene prevailing at all levels, and to the practice of feeding infants
artificially, either on milk or other foods, which was allegedly on the
increase. Whilst both these influences were important, their impact was

Table 6.4. Major causes of infant mortality (1,000 q_0), Borough of Bradford, 1876–99*

Years	Gastro-intestinal infections	Respiratory infections	Prematurity	Tuberculosis, measles, whooping cough	Other causes
1876–80	72.2 (43.5)	30.1 (18.0)	19.2 (11.5)	17.8 (11.0)	26.7 (16.0)
1882–85	68.7 (44.0)	27.3 (17.5)	18.9 (12.0)	13.8 (9.0)	27.3 (17.5)
1886–90	77.4 (45.5)	29.0 (17.0)	20.1 (12.0)	17.1 (10.0)	26.3 (15.5)
1891–95	75.6 (43.0)	37.1 (21.0)	21.1 (12.0)	15.9 (9.0)	26.4 (15.0)
1896–99	75.6 (44.0)	28.6 (16.5)	19.8 (11.5)	14.3 (8.5)	33.4 (19.5)

Notes: * the figures in brackets are in percentages

Sources: see table 6.1.

not necessarily identical. Whereas water-closets were almost totally absent in the inner areas, in the outer wards where they were much more common, mothers were generally more easily able to afford to feed their babies on cow's milk or patent foods.

Even by 1900, less than 25 per cent of houses in Bradford had the use of a water-closet,[67] and the scandalous privy midden continued to be the only form of sanitary provision for those who lived in all but the best areas of the town. These 'filthy receptacles' were most dangerous to infant life in the inner parts of the borough where housing densities were highest. Worst of all were the crowded central wards where poverty and ignorance compounded the dangers from the flies breeding in the communal privies situated in noxious shared yards—a 'no-man's-land replete with every form of refuse'.[68] Yet, even in so-called respectable homes the dangers from insect carriers of disease were ever present. In 1878, an especially virulent epidemic of infant diarrhoea led to a detailed investigation of the surrounding sanitary circumstances by the M.O.H., Dr Butterfield. Somewhat to his surprise he found a higher preponderance of deaths in the 'front' houses which faced the street than in the 'back' houses which looked directly on to the privies. He concluded that the disparity was due to the reluctance of mothers in the 'front' houses to be seen carrying the slop-pail (the receptacle utilized as a domestic sanitary convenience) to the privy during the hours of daylight; whereas the mothers in the 'back' houses had a more ready and secluded access to these dubious conveniences, and, therefore, were less inclined to delay the removal of excreta and other refuse. His enquiries had also revealed that the usual repository for the slop-pail was underneath the shelf in the cellar-head scullery, which also served as a pantry and storeplace, so that baby foods such as an opened tin of condensed milk, or a jug of fresh milk were also to be found there.[69] Butterfield's findings may have been nothing more than coincidence, for a similar investigation by one of his successors, Dr W. A. Evans, in the 1890s, showed a higher proportion of deaths in the 'back' houses.[70] It seems likely that, to some extent, the conclusions of both men reflected their own outlook and prejudices. Dr Butterfield, although a frequent critic of the unsatisfactory sanitary conditions in Bradford, was a firm believer in the ethic of individual responsibility; whereas Dr Evans, a close collaborator of Fred Jowett, the first Independent Labour Party chairman of the Sanitary Committee, placed more emphasis on communal responsibility. At the time of his survey he was actively engaged in a campaign to abolish the anachronistic system of letting out the emptying of the middens to private contractors (who had a vested interest in delaying collection as long as possible) and to introduce a regular collection by direct labour.[71]

The infrequently emptied middens, however, were not the only fertile breeding ground for bacteria-carrying flies; the animal manure which in the days of horse-drawn transport was often left to rot in the badly cleansed working-class streets, was another. In hot weather, when street cleansing was likely to be suspended for lack of water, the danger was at its height; especially in the central wards, where high density building, narrow streets, and congested yards helped to ensure that the right breeding temperatures for bacteria, and bacteria-carrying organisms, were more easily sustained. In the outer wards even climatic conditions were less dangerous. These areas always had temperatures which were slightly below those of the lower lying inner wards;[72] moreover, excreta—both animal and human—was less in evidence. Even those visitors who were well acquainted with the inadequacies of urban sanitation found conditions in Bradford something of a revelation:

> In walking through a few of the many slum districts of Bradford during the week we spent there, I was at first disgusted to observe that children, even of respectable parents, were encouraged to make a convenience of the open street, if not of the kitchen floor. On closer observation of the sanitary accommodation provided, I felt there was much excuse ... I have seen without enthusiasm, both earth closets and middens where pails were used but this was my first acquaintance with the truly primitive arrangement in vogue in Bradford, and the flies that bred in and swarmed about these filthy places also settled thickly about the eyes of the babies in the wretched little houses, whose front doors opened within a few feet of these insanitary conveniences. It was remarked once or twice during the Congress that it is of no use to give people a good house until you have taught them to be clean. May I say that I think it is at least as doubtful whether a people can be civilized while they are housed worse than savages.[73]

Two main reasons underlay the reluctance of the Town Council to force property owners to replace privy midden by water-borne methods of sewage disposal in the late nineteenth century. Firstly, in the light of the economic difficulties, especially for the middle classes, there was a reluctance to impose the expense of connecting large numbers of older houses to the sewers; for many of the property owners in the town—those who did not own large units, but merely a few houses, perhaps living in one and renting out the others—the burden of repairs and improvements was a heavy one. Secondly, the property owners of Bradford were an influential pressure group. Their own association, the Property Owners' Protection Society, founded originally in the 1850s to combat the closure of cellar dwellings, in the 1890s busily fought closure of unfit property under the Housing of the Working Classes Act, which allowed for very little compensation. The building and propertied interests were also strongly represented on the Town Council, especially in the 1880s and early 1890s when John Hardaker, a local builder, was chairman of the Sanitary Committee. In 1888, they succeeded in effecting the dismissal of the abrasive but energetic M.O.H., Dr Hime, whose over-zealous exposure of malpractice and inadequacies had proved embarrassing. [74] They scored another victory in 1893 when, after the provision of water closets had been made compulsory for all new housing (due more to reasons of economic expediency than to any consideration for public health), the building lobby secured permission for the erection of inferior closets constructed on the waste water principle. These 'tipplers' were favoured by landlords because they were cheap to instal, and had an automatic mechanism which reduced the (admittedly real) risk of abuse or damage by tenants. The utilization of waste water from the sink drains to flush these closets offered the Council a partial solution to another pressing problem, that of water supply.

The continuing scarcity of water which, in 14 of the years between 1876 and 1900, resulted in supplies being discontinued or severely restricted during the dry summer months, [75] was probably the most important factor underlying the Council's reluctance to speed up the introduction of water closets. Almost certainly a water closet without water would have been just as dangerous as a privy in heavily populated areas of the town; and this chronic shortage of water must therefore be seen as one of the most serious contributory causes to the town's high infant mortality rate. Despite continual efforts to find new sources of supply, the growth in domestic demand, together with the priority frequently given to commercial consumers, meant that until the completion of the first stage of the huge Nidd Valley scheme just before the First World War Bradford never had sufficient water to meet the requirements of public and private hygiene.

Scarcity of water, particularly in the poorer areas of the town, may also have been important in rendering the hand-feeding of infants so dangerous at this time. Artificial feeding was seen by contemporary commentators as one of the primary causes of infant deaths, for which mothers who neglected to perform their 'natural' functions were generally held responsible. No doubt the increasing availability of patent foods such as tinned condensed milk, and the more plentiful and somewhat more wholesome supply of fresh cow's milk in urban areas, did tempt some mothers to abandon breast-feeding, but there seems to have been little awareness that for many malnourished and overworked working-class mothers early failure of breast milk was almost inevitable. In fact, middle-class mothers were probably the most likely to succumb to the temptation held out by advertisements in magazines and infant-care booklets, illustrating and praising the new 'modern' infant foods and feeding utensils, especially as the wet-nurse had by now become an expensive and unacceptable alternative. Ignorance about the feeding and care of infants was almost universal; even the leading medical journals contained misleading, and frequently conflicting, advice and infor-mation from editors and contributors alike. [76] In the 1890s an inquiry by the Local Government Board revealed that, in many Poor Law institutions, the Medical Officer took no interest in the welfare of the youngest inmates:[77] however, for once Bradford came out of this investigation quite well, perhaps as a result of the infiltration of the local Board of Guardians by Independent Labour Party supporters and socially conscious Liberals.

There were high risks for all hand-fed infants as the foods were all, to a greater or lesser extent, deficient in essential proteins and vitamins. In addition, the need for hygiene, especially the sterilization of feeding equipment, was only dimly perceived. As hand-fed infants were usually inadequately nourished, their resistance to infectious diseases was lowered and their chances of recovery retarded. They faced, also, an increased tendency to hypothermia from lack of protein, and to rickets from vitamin deficiencies. The vulnerability of hand-fed babies, even in the 'exclusive wards', may help to explain the upsurge of infant deaths in these areas during the generally unfavourable climatic conditions and water shortages of the early 1890s, especially during the aftermath of the epidemics of Russian 'flu in 1891, and scarlet fever in 1893. The dangers from artificial feeding for infants in poor homes were even greater. The foods were often totally unsuitable or indigestible: the cheapest variety of skimmed condensed milk, 'pobbies' (a soggy mess of bread, sugar, and water), or titbits from the plates of adults were but a few of the less bizarre offerings. In the 1870s the M.O.H. reported that some babies were fed on solid food and dosed with castor oil within hours of birth.[78] When heroic treatments were still in vogue, even those babies who received professional medical attention were liable to be literally dosed to death, and in most homes patent medicines and soothing syrups containing opiates were liberally administered. Even for the infants who escaped being dosed with purgatives or soothing syrups, the dangers from lack of hygiene connected with feeding remained. In the homes of the better-off unused milk could be thrown away; hot water was easily available for washing both baby and utensils; and bottles could be purchased without regard to durability or expense. However, in the central areas of Bradford, even after 1900, it was quite common for a bottle to remain unemptied and unwashed between feeds, and, indeed, in some notorious instances between infants.[79] Some homes had neither piped water nor drainage, while few could boast a hot water supply. Many poorer mothers favoured the long tubed bottle which was cheap, virtually unbreakable and allowed the infant to self-feed. Unfortunately it was also, according to the M.O.H., 'a seething mass of corruption'[80] which was impossible to clean and dangerous to use. After 1900, the female sanitary inspectors waged a constant battle to remove these objectionable utensils and replace them by the more fragile, but easily cleaned, glass variety. Their efforts did not always meet with success:

after the milk depot was opened in 1903, there were reports of the clean, humanized milk, which was provided in sealed bottles ready for use, being transferred into the old favourites.

In the central wards, where the most disadvantaged social groups were concentrated in cheap, poor quality housing, or in rented rooms, and the illegitimacy rate was five times higher than in the outer wards,[81] there was a much greater likelihood that mothers would have to seek work outside the home, almost inevitably leading to hand-feeding of infants. During the economic difficulties of the late 1880s, and in the 1890s when the McKinley Tariff decimated Bradford's lucrative American export markets,[82] many men, especially the unskilled and low paid, faced wage reductions, short-time and unemployment. Their wives were forced to try to supplement the inadequate family income, often by working as chars or washerwomen in the homes of the lower middle classes. For other women, widows, deserted wives, or those whose husbands were in prison, the only alternative to full-time employment was the inhospitable workhouse, out-door relief being only rarely allowed by the Guardians in such cases.[83]

Three far-sighted German Jewish philanthropists, familiar with the Elberfeld system in Germany, and recognizing with a greater per-spicacity than most of their contemporaries that for some mothers work was a vital necessity, established in the 1880s a day nursery in Wynne Street (which they coyly named 'The Nest') as a way of preserving the family unit. One unusual feature of this institution was that it opened its doors to all infants, even those whose mothers, in the opinion of the proprietors, had no need to work, because whilst the conduct of the mother might be considered reprehensible the infant was still deserving of proper care and attention. The founders of 'The Nest', Florence Moser, her husband Jacob, and her brother Bernard Cohen, hoped that their nursery would be the first of many in Bradford, and that in the long run the venture would either be self-financing, or would attract support from other charitable individuals. Their hopes were to be dashed on both these counts, but it was the example of 'The Nest' which finally gave rise to both the municipal milk depot, and to the schemes for the feeding of necessitous children in Bradford.[84] The response of working-class mothers to the nursery was very cautious. The fees charged were higher than those of the more usual 'minders' who, although not necessarily cruel or deliberately neglectful, were often too old or too young for other employment. Moreover, some mothers resented the 'starchy' nursery nurses and their instructions on regular feeds and infant hygiene, just as in the early twentieth century, they were to dislike the qualified midwives with their 'airs and graces', who wouldn't demean themselves to prepare a meal or run an errand. Thus, 'The Nest', even with the classes which it ran for young potential mothers, had only a very limited impact on infant welfare in Bradford in the short term.

Yet, despite the allegations which were frequently made to the contrary, working mothers in nineteenth-century Bradford were not the norm.[85] In the six inner wards and three outer wards, those women whose husbands had steady jobs were unlikely to seek work outside the home once they had a child to care for unless there was some co-resident female relative to provide a mother substitute. The economic and social factors surrounding infant feeding here differed considerably from those elsewhere in the borough. This, together with the improvements in living standards secured by some of the 'aristocracy of labour' and the expansion of the lower middle classes towards the end of the nineteenth century, may help to account for the relative stability of infant mortality rates in these areas during the 1890s, when they were rising in the other wards. Breast feeding, for mothers who were physically able to do so, was cheap, convenient, and believed by many to reduce the risk of another pregnancy. Moreover, although, as Dr Butterfield's investigation revealed, the cult of respectability could have undesirable side effects, it did mean that in many working-class homes cleanliness was regarded as the prime symbol of virtue. It seems certain that this generation of mothers—the first to be indoctrinated in the elementary schools on the need for discipline, orderliness, and personal hygiene; to have homes with water supply and mains drainage; and to determinedly restrict the size of their families (see table 6.5),[86] were in a better position to care for their babies than their own mothers.

The breast-fed offspring of such mothers may also have been better able to resist the upsurge in respiratory infections which were always most fatal during periods of general debility. Bradford throughout the nineteenth century suffered from climatic and locational disadvantages and, with the perpetual problem of air pollution, endured a death rate from respiratory diseases for all age groups in the population well above the national average.[87] As with other conditions, it was infants who were most vulnerable. Whilst 'each man's chimney' may have been 'his golden milestone' all too often it was also a baby's tombstone.[88] Once more, there can be little doubt that poverty was one of the most significant factors in determining the level of respiratory deaths. Lack of

Table 6.5. Average number of births per year per thousand women aged 15–44 (child:woman ratio, CWR), Borough of Bradford, 1871–1900

	1871–80	1881–90	1891–1900	Percentage change, 1871–80 to 1891–1900
CWR	146.6	116.3	87.0	−40.5

Sources: see table 6.1.

money meant bad housing conditions, poor feeding (whether by hand or by breast), exposure to the extremes of temperature, and clothing made of cheap, durable cotton, rather than warm, expensive wool. It also affected the level of domestic hygiene for, as one female sanitary inspector was to observe in 1905, 'even soap costs money', and in houses without even a sink mothers had to carry all slop water to the nearest street drain.[89] Lack of ventilation was another hazard which was not only the result of 'back-to-back' housing, or the constant rain of soot particles which made an open window a direct invitation to dirt. In many homes windows, even those in a good state of repair, were rarely opened because the poor were susceptible to cold and draughts. In cold weather the family spent their few leisure hours huddled round the fire in the single room which usually served all daytime purposes, probably with the washing suspended from a rack on the ceiling. Outside, the atmosphere was cold and smoky, inside it was hot and steamy. At night the family retired to a bedroom which was usually cold and often damp; few working-class families in nineteenth-century Bradford could afford the luxury of a bedroom fire, so a drastic change of temperature was almost inevitable. In these circumstances it is not surprising that many mothers resisted the instructions of well-meaning lady infant welfare visitors after 1900 to put the baby in a separate cot. Even if a cot was available, or could be improvised from an empty drawer, the risk from bronchitis or pneumonia during a Bradford winter was considerably greater than that from over-laying in the parental bed.

III

The fact that infant mortality, for all social groups, showed little improvement during the last quarter of the nineteenth century was not entirely due to negligence or apathy on the part of the community or of individuals. However, it did reflect a failure to recognize the greater vulnerability of malnourished babies to environmental hazards, and to realize that poverty was the most important underlying cause of social disparities in infant deaths. The prevailing emphasis was on public rather than personal health services, with only the example of a few philanthropic individuals to give an indication of what municipal welfare schemes might achieve after 1900. The apparent lethargy of the Town Council is to some extent explained by a reluctance on the part of many ratepayers (not all of whom were wealthy) to add to the already considerable burden of municipal debt incurred during the provision of a basic infrastructure of public utilities.

By the early years of the twentieth century, when the Independent Labour Party was more strongly represented on the Council, and when infant mortality was increasingly coming to be regarded as a public rather than a personal loss, new attitudes had begun to emerge. The still poor environmental conditions gradually began to improve as the Town Council took a firmer line over matters such as the provision of proper water closets, and the control of smoke from mill chimneys. [90] Of yet greater significance was the shift in the emphasis of municipal activity from public health to the provision of personal and more direct welfare services. Only then was it possible to reduce the level of infant deaths in Bradford, but even so the disparities between rich and poor remained as wide as before. [91] Only action at central government level could help to reduce the real burden of poverty; measures in the locality could only be a palliative, not a cure, for inequalities in infant mortality rates.

Health, society and environment in Victorian Manchester

Marilyn E. Pooley and Colin G. Pooley

The growth of towns in Victorian Britain not only evoked comment from contemporaries,[1] but has also stimulated a considerable volume of recent historical research into the patterns, processes and problems associated with population change and urban growth in the nineteenth century.[2] One of the most distinctive features of Victorian cities was their unhealthiness, and in particular the degree to which high rates of disease and mortality were spatially concentrated in certain areas of towns. This phenomenon was observed by contemporary medical men and government officials, but detailed investigation of the effects of disease on the quality of life in Victorian cities, and of detailed relationships between an individual's health, the environment in which he lived and the development of urban society has been relatively neglected in recent research. Existing studies have concentrated principally on three areas. First, at the national level, there have been attempts by medical historians and historical demographers to assess the relative contributions to the reduction in mortality of such factors as improvements in the standards of living, the changing nature and prevalence of specific diseases, and improved medical therapy.[3] Second, certain epidemic diseases, especially cholera, have generated detailed case studies of the development and effects of particular epidemics;[4] and third, at both national and local levels, the responses of authorities to the perceived public health crisis, through the provision of basic urban services and the increased management of the urban environment, has been investigated.[5]

Future research into the social history of disease and mortality in Victorian cities should build on these studies by focusing both on conditions in particular towns and on the relationships between the characteristics of the social, cultural, economic, political, physical and disease environments of urban areas. For instance, at the most basic level, relatively little is known of the detailed mortality experiences of the various regions, cities, towns and villages within England and Wales;[6] while the causes and effects of intra-community contrasts in levels of health have scarcely begun to be studied on a comprehensive basis.[7] Although the intervention of authorities in the management of the urban environment has been chronicled, relatively few attempts have been made fully to assess the actual contribution of such intervention to public health improvement, with regard to the effects of changes in the socio-economic profile of cities, particularly rises in real wages and improvements in standards of living;[8] yet socio-economic and environmental conditions are particularly important influences on levels of exposure to infection and on reactions to it. Lastly, as George Rosen stressed in 1973,[9] medical history must be more clearly set within its social and environmental contexts. Only by examining the relationships between the health status of populations and the social, economic, environmental and political contexts in which they were set can the true impact of disease on all aspects of Victorian life be assessed.

I

This essay analyses selected aspects of the interactions between disease, mortality, society and environment in Manchester in the mid-Victorian period. The city of Manchester was perceived by contemporaries as one of the most exciting products of the Industrial Revolution,[10] but it also achieved notoriety through the writings of Engels,[11] and was widely regarded as one of the least healthy cities in the country.[12] Manchester was not, however, untypical of other large provincial cities in Victorian Britain.

As in other towns, the scale and rapidity of population growth in Manchester from the late eighteenth century was a major factor in the creation of public health problems in the Victorian town. High levels of immigration combined with natural increase caused rates of population growth in excess of 20 per cent per decade in the registration districts of Manchester, Salford and Chorlton between 1801 and 1851 (Figure 7.1). It is probable that incoming migrants from rural areas and small towns would have had little chance to develop resistance to the endemic and epidemic diseases of large urban areas, while migrants from Ireland, who accounted for 13.1 per cent of the population of Manchester and Salford Boroughs in 1851, both were blamed for introducing disease and were themselves particularly susceptible to infection during the massive famine migration of the 1840s.[13]

The attractions of employment opportunities and the availability of relatively low-cost accommodation led many migrants to central areas

Figure 7.1 Manchester (including Prestwich), Salford and Chorlton registration districts, showing locations named in the text

of the city. There, as in many other rapidly growing towns, the supply of large decaying terraced houses had been supplemented by the mostly uncontrolled development of high-density, low-quality 'back-to-backs' and court and cellar dwellings; by the mid nineteenth century most of this housing was occupied at extremely high densities. Although decent working-class housing was being built around the edge of the city, it did not match the locational or low-cost requirements of most working-class families. Thus, over-occupation of a decaying housing stock with inadequate communal sanitation and water supply posed a major health hazard to the city, through both the lack of basic facilities for personal hygiene, and the increased chances of infection arising from greater inter-personal contact in crowded conditions.[14]

The availability and regularity of employment was of crucial importance to the level of living which could be attained in a Victorian city. A regular reasonable income would not only allow movement towards lower-density bye-law terrace suburbs, in the second half of the century, but would also enable levels of nutrition to be improved and thus resistance to disease increased. Although Manchester was less dependent on direct employment in the textile industries than many other towns in south Lancashire and west Yorkshire, and the economic structure of the town diversified considerably towards the end of the nineteenth century, no less than 30.4 per cent of the adult male population of Manchester and Salford Boroughs in 1851 were directly employed in the textile and clothing trades. As ancillary industries, such as bleaching, dyeing and machine-making, and employment in warehousing and commerce, were also closely tied to the fortunes of the cotton textile industry, a considerable proportion of the population of mid-century Manchester was affected by the cyclical fluctuations in the textile economy, so that regular employment and a predictable income were comparative rarities amongst the working-class population.[15] Opportunities for female employment, and thus an increased family income, were greater in Manchester than in non-textile towns,[16] but most of this was either poorly-paid semi-skilled factory work or home-based textile employment where wage levels tended to be even lower; and both were affected by the same cyclical fluctuations as male employment. Moreover, nineteenth-century factory employment brought its own dangers to health, through increased exposure to disease and specific occupationally-related illness.[17]

In some aspects of its health care, however, Manchester's population was more fortunately placed than that of other towns. The first of a large number of hospitals, the Royal Infirmary (established 1752) and House of Recovery (1796), only provided specialist care for a small and carefully-circumscribed minority of the sick; but the physicians and surgeons who held honorary positions within these institutions, together with those employed by the Poor Law Unions, formed the nucleus of a growing body of concerned, knowledgeable and influential medical men, who recognized the importance of disease prevention and created local and national pressure for improved sanitation, new housing developments and control of environmental pollution, as well as recognizing the structural causes of much ill-health.[18] Manchester Borough did not appoint a Medical Officer of Health until 1868, but the local authority had a long history of passing public health bye-laws often well in advance of national legislation, although like the national authorities they were reluctant to become fully involved in the comprehensive management of the urban environment. This hesitation, coupled with the medical profession's partial knowledge of disease causation and the lack of success of much therapy, inevitably limited the effectiveness of many of the public health measures which were taken in response to the crisis of health and the environmental malaise faced by Manchester in the nineteenth century.

It has been suggested by George Rosen that throughout most of the nineteenth century and into the twentieth century health workers confronted substantially similar problems. Undesirable conditions and situations like those uncovered in urban communities by the classic investigations of the 1830s and 1840s were still being explored in the 1880s and 1890s. Even the reasons for these conditions were not dissimilar. [19] In studying the relationships between socio-economic and physical environments and the health of the population in Victorian Manchester, the changing nature and extent of the public health problems may be assessed and the reasons for those changes explained. Specifically, this chapter describes, first, changes in the rates and components of mortality in Manchester between 1838 and 1900, focusing on the contribution of infectious diseases to overall mortality and on the differential mortality of particular sub-groups of the population. Second, spatial variations in the pattern of disease mortality and in selected social and environmental variables are examined; and, third, the relationships between these variables are investigated and an attempt is made to evaluate the effects of socio-economic change, environmental modification and institutional action on the mortality experience of the city between *circa* 1840 and 1900.

II

Any historical study which attempts to investigate problems such as the prevalence and impact of disease, and the quality of the urban environment, is fraught with difficulty. Although contemporary accounts and occasional diaries may provide invaluable (if possibly atypical) information on these behavioural variables, any comprehensive and comparative assessment of conditions must rely mainly on what are essentially surrogate measures. For instance, malnutrition, sickness and ill-health cannot be directly investigated on a comprehensive scale, although Poor Law and Hospital Reports provide some information: our knowledge of the impact of disease relates mainly to its effects on the mortality rate of a town. This clearly underestimates the total impact of disease on families and on society as a whole. The long-term and widespread effects of ill-health on family income and quality of life were far greater than the short-term and more limited impact caused by the death of an individual. Likewise, housing conditions can only be comprehensively measured through indices such as rates of occupancy, whilst broad occupational data must be used as a surrogate for information on individual family incomes. The rigours of living in overcrowded accommodation with little sanitation, an inadequate water supply and an irregular income were vividly described by Chadwick, Engels and others,[20] but a comprehensive spatial and temporal assessment of conditions can only be gained through the use of necessarily impersonal and inadequate measures of social and environmental conditions. These measures also lose the effects of small-scale variations in personal circumstances that would have been apparent to any resident of a Victorian city, particularly the life-cycle effects and the influence of short-term loss of personal income on family circumstances, noted by many contemporary observers.[21]

Prior to the institution of civil registration in 1837 even accurate data on mortality are hard to come by. Parish registers and Bills of Mortality provide a basic outline of mortality trends, though there are many problems in their use and interpretation, and information on cause of death is at best limited and frequently non-existent.[22] The *Annual Reports* of the Registrar General from 1838 form a sounder factual basis, providing information on actual deaths (rather than burials), and (from 1855) giving data on cause-specific mortality by registration district.[23] The use of the Registrar General's material is not, however, without problems. First, under-registration undoubtedly occurred and there is evidence that infant deaths in Manchester were significantly under-recorded even at the end of the nineteenth century.[24] Second, totals of deaths in some districts were inflated by those occurring in medical and other institutions located there; only from 1869 can institutional deaths be excluded from district totals, and such adjustments may cause a significant under-estimate of deaths in unhealthy areas with institutions. Third, even twentieth-century diagnoses of causes of death have been shown to be inaccurate, so that Victorian statistics are unlikely to be totally reliable.[25] Fourth, changes in methods of disease nomenclature and classification frequently confound comparative analysis; particularly serious was the failure until 1869 to distinguish deaths from water- or food-borne typhoid fever from those caused by vector-borne typhus.[26] Lastly, registration district boundaries rarely coincided with municipal limits or with the built-up area, posing problems for spatial analysis. Thus, the analysis in this chapter refers variously to the Boroughs of Manchester and Salford, and to the units defined by the Registrar General, depending on the availability of data.

Other information on mortality such as that available in the *Annual Reports* of Medical Officers of Health and the minute books of Local Boards of Health[27] is more spatially and temporally variable, but is none the less important in that it often provides information in more detail than that available from the Registrar General and in some cases can give information on morbidity as well as mortality. Such sources also provide details of the aspirations and operations of local authorities in the field of public health and sanitary reform. Whereas Liverpool was first in the field, appointing William Duncan as Medical Officer of Health in 1847, Manchester did not appoint John Leigh until 1868,[28] thus removing an important source of information for much of the mid nineteenth century although Leigh, a sub-district registrar, frequently contributed to the *Annual Reports* of the Registrar General from their inception. However, this deficiency is partially offset by the existence of local voluntary public health bodies, such as the Manchester and Salford Sanitary Association founded in 1852, which published weekly totals of all cases of infectious disease occurring in public medical practice and also provided a commentary on local government sanitary reforms.[29]

The social and environmental context to which these health statistics must be related is provided on a comprehensive basis by two sources, the published census volumes and, in particular, the census enumerators' books, which detail the characteristics of the entire enumerated population and should be available at decennial intervals from 1841 to 1881, although there are substantial gaps in the Manchester data for 1851. Although suffering from some problems of inconsistent recording and changing classifications, these sources are essentially easy to use and have been extensively reviewed in a number of recent works.[30] When used in conjunction with large-scale ordnance survey plans they allow the detailed spatial analysis of variations in social and environmental conditions. However, in order to give substance to these statistical profiles, and especially to attempt explanations of apparent relationships between socio-economic, environmental and health variables, the more subjective contemporary accounts and enquiries already mentioned must also be utilized. Of particular importance in Manchester were the investigations carried out under the auspices of the Manchester Statistical Society, founded in 1833, which compensate to some extent for the lack of early Medical Officers' reports. The present analysis is based mainly on data collected from reports of the Registrar General, the census enumerators' books, Medical Officer of Health reports and a range of supporting archival evidence relating to Victorian Manchester.

III

Crude and standardized mortality rates[31] have been analysed for the three registration districts of Manchester, Salford and Chorlton from the start of annual registration in 1838 to 1900. Although the problems of using the Registrar General's material already outlined must be borne in mind, Figure 7.2 and table 7.1 do provide a reasonable summary of the

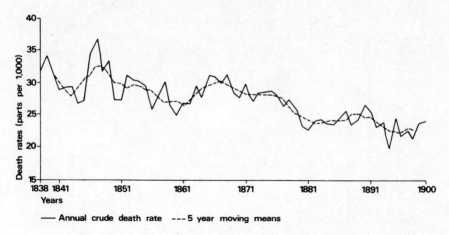

Figure 7.2 Annual crude mortality rate (in parts per 1,000), Manchester (including Prestwich), Salford and Chorlton registration districts, 1838–1900

course of mortality in the Manchester conurbation. The overall trend in mortality is clearly downwards, with standardized decadal rates for the three registration districts falling from 27.37 in 1851–60 to 23.00 per thousand in 1891–1900, but within this trend considerable fluctuations also occurred.

Major peaks in mortality can be discerned in the late 1830s and 1840s, 1852–5, 1858 and in the mid-1860s. These periods of high aggregate mortality represent known epidemics of infectious diseases and many coincide with trade depressions in the cotton textile industry which would have lowered standards of living and reduced resistance to disease. For instance, the period of high mortality in the late 1840s was coincident with an industrial recession and the influx of Irish famine migrants, and was the result of epidemics of typhus, influenza, diarrhoea and, in 1849, cholera.[32] The cyclical nature of mortality trends is emphasized by the way in which mortality was lowered after each crisis period as living standards improved and the number of susceptible individuals within the population decreased; but it is not until the late 1870s that the beginnings of a long-term decline in mortality can be discerned. Any substantial improvement in Manchester's public health did not occur until the 1880s when standardized mortality rates for the three registration districts fell from 26.13 in 1871–80 to 23.78 parts per thousand in 1881–90.

Age-specific mortality rates emphasize the high rate of infant mortality within the Manchester conurbation; 40–50 per cent of all deaths in all decades occurred among children under five years, with the bulk of these deaths being of those under one year of age (see 1,000 q_0 in

Table 7.1. Average annual crude and standardized* mortality rates per decade, Manchester, Salford and Chorlton Registration Districts, 1841–1900

	Average annual mortality per thousand population**					
	1841–50	1851–60	1861–70	1871–80	1881–90	1891–1900
Crude mortality rates						
Chorlton×	25.69	23.94	25.06	23.63	20.90	19.70
Salford	27.66	26.00	26.89	27.65	24.72	24.28
Manchester+	33.08	31.48	32.80	30.51	27.36	25.50
3 Districts	30.08	28.07	28.90	27.34	24.30	23.00
Standardized mortality rates						
Chorlton	—	23.53	24.14	22.72	20.61	19.78
Salford	—	25.11	25.56	26.07	23.98	24.09
Manchester	—	20.66	31.42	29.17	26.68	25.39
3 Districts	—	27.37	27.69	26.13	23.78	23.00

Notes: * mortality rates are standardized to the mean age structure of the study area population in 1891–1900
** decadal rates are calculated on the basis of the Registrar General's population estimates
× the whole of Barton-upon-Irwell is excluded from the calculations, although it was part of Chorlton until 1850
+ from 1871–80 figures for Manchester include both those of Manchester township and Prestwich into which it was sub-divided in 1874

Source: Registrars' General *Annual Reports* and *Decennial Supplements*

Figure 7.3). Furthermore, infant mortality rates, although declining slightly in 1851–90, increased substantially in the last decade of the century. Mortality fell most dramatically amongst those aged five to nine, but for all other groups the overall decline was relatively small and discontinuous. Calculation of the relative contribution of different age groups to the overall decline in Manchester's mortality from 1851[33] shows that despite continuing high infant mortality, more than 60 per cent of total lives saved in the period 1851–1900 were of under-fives, thus emphasizing the important demographic impact of a relatively small proportionate fall in the death rate amongst this age group. The varied mortality experiences of the different age groups also emphasize the need to examine individual components of mortality change instead of seeking macro-explanations of mortality decline.

Explanation of these varied mortality trends among different age groups can, in part, be sought in analysis of cause-specific mortality within the three registration districts (table 7.2). Unfortunately only

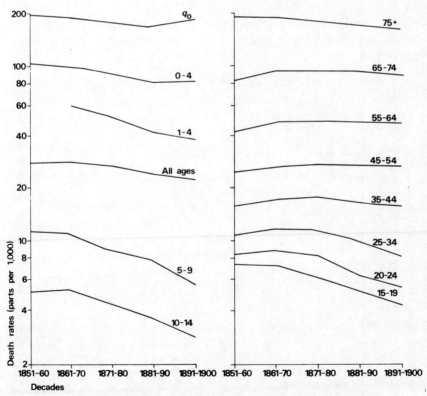

Figure 7.3 Average annual age-specific mortality rates (in parts per 1,000), Manchester (including Prestwich), Salford and Chorlton registration districts, 1851–60 to 1891–1900

Table 7.2. Average annual standardized* mortality rates from selected infectious diseases, Manchester, Salford and Chorlton Registration Districts, 1851–1900

Diseases	1851–60	1861–70	1871–80	1881–90	1891–1900
Smallpox	0.19	0.13	0.29	0.02	0.01
Measles	0.54	0.60	0.58	0.71	0.77
Scarlet fever	1.46	(1.30)	1.08 (0.98)	0.73 (0.51)	0.49 (0.27)
Diphtheria		(0.16)	(0.10)	(0.22)	(0.22)
Whooping cough	0.82	0.85	0.72	0.57	0.58
Typhus			(0.10)	(0.03)	(0.003)
Typhoid fever	1.03	1.38	0.61 (0.37)	0.36 (0.31)	0.27 (0.250)
Simple continued fever			(0.14)	(0.02)	(0.005)
Diarrhoea, dysentery and cholera	2.07	2.04	1.48	1.07	1.35
Pulmonary tuberculosis	3.26	3.10	2.97	2.40	2.02
Non-respiratory tuberculosis	0.89	0.89	0.83	0.94	0.93
Total from above	10.26	10.45	8.56	6.80	6.42
All other causes	17.11	17.24	17.57	16.98	16.58
All causes	27.37	27.69	26.13	23.78	23.00
Mean population	479,349	555,566	650,341	754,429	845,519

Note: * rates per thousand are standardized to age structure of the area in 1891–1900.

Source: see table 7.1.

thirteen causes of death can be consistently identified from the Registrar General's statistics for 1851–1900; however, although these account for less than half the total mortality during the period, they do include most of the clinically-identified infectious diseases at which Victorian urban sanitary reform was aimed. As the percentage of all deaths due to such infectious diseases fell from 37.5 in 1851–60 to 27.9 in 1891–1900, deaths from other causes fell only very slightly. It would seem that such mortality decline as did occur in the nineteenth century can be mainly attributed to a reduction in the incidence and/or virulence of infectious disease. The extent to which this was due to Victorian excursions into urban sanitary reform is assessed later.

It is not possible here to examine the detailed changes which occurred within individual infectious diseases in Victorian Manchester, but the more significant changes will be highlighted to amplify the figures in table 7.2. Pulmonary tuberculosis (phthisis) was demographically the most important disease, accounting for more than 10 per cent of all deaths in the three registration districts in all decades from 1851–1900; it also showed a significant and steady decline throughout the period, and was a disease associated almost entirely with the adult population. The tubercle bacillus is spread by droplet infection, and although not highly contagious, its transmission is favoured by the frequent and extensive exposure to an open case of tuberculosis of individuals made susceptible through low nutritional levels or lack of previous exposure.[34] It is thus associated in its most virulent form with poverty and with overcrowded and badly-ventilated workshops and homes. In investigations carried out by the General Board of Health in the 1850s its incidence and that of other lung diseases was correlated with variables such as population density, manufacturing employment and levels of pauperism.[35] It was a disease that might reasonably be expected to respond to improvements in nutrition following a rise in living standards, and to improvements in conditions at home and work resulting from attempts to reduce overcrowding and improve ventilation.[36] A more generally healthy urban population would be increasingly resistant to infection while greater segregation of cases in hospitals would have reduced exposure to the disease.

Typhus, typhoid and relapsing fever also mainly affected the adult population, but in the 1850s these diseases together accounted for less than one third of the deaths attributed to pulmonary tuberculosis. They did not decline evenly throughout the period but increased in the 1860s, probably because of typhus epidemics associated with the trade depression and the related reduction of living standards during the cotton famine, then fell sharply from the 1870s, when typhus became relatively unimportant. It is unfortunate that these three diseases were grouped together by the Registrar General until 1869, as typhoid is a food- or water-borne disease whereas typhus and relapsing fever are spread by an animal vector. Typhus, spread by the body-louse, thus affected essentially the same population as was most seriously affected by pulmonary tuberculosis—the poor living in overcrowded conditions— but the more fatal typhoid was spread through sewage-contaminated water, food and milk and thus could affect all classes.[37] Typhoid, by the 1870s, was responsible for more than 60 per cent of the deaths in this group and remained the most important of this set of diseases until the end of the nineteenth century. It is likely that improvements in housing conditions brought about both by local government action and rising living standards were responsible for the decline in typhus after the 1860s, whereas better sanitation and water supply and less contaminated food eventually contributed to a gradual reduction in mortality from typhoid fever in the last quarter of the century.

These sanitary improvements would also have been partly responsible for the sharp fall during the 1870s in mortality from the diarrhoeal group of diseases which, like typhoid, are mainly food- and water-borne. In contrast to typhoid deaths, however, more than 80 per cent of diarrhoeal fatalities throughout the second half of the nineteenth century occurred among the under-fives, despite the inclusion in this classification of deaths from cholera, which was responsible for a substantial number of adult deaths in Manchester during the epidemics of 1832, 1849, 1854 and 1866. In addition, unlike typhoid mortality, the marked decline in diarrhoeal deaths in the 1870s was offset by a rise in the 1890s, particularly among the under-fives. It is possible that the unsuitable and frequently contaminated food, blamed for the deaths of many infants among the poorer classes throughout the century, was being replaced as living standards rose by the early weaning of infants on to equally contaminated fresh or tinned milk.[38]

The other diseases of childhood—smallpox, scarlet fever, diphtheria, whooping cough and measles—were all spread by droplet infection and were particularly serious among malnourished children living in overcrowded conditions. However, in addition, scarlet fever and diphtheria were frequently transmitted in milk and thus affected children of all classes; in the 1850s the two diseases produced a mortality rate of 8.26 per thousand among children under five years. Death rates for all except measles fell between 1851 and 1900, although virulent epidemics could still occur; the increase in measles fatalities in the 1880s and 1890s was probably due to the increased exposure of a susceptible population consequent upon the crowding of children into elementary schools.[39]

The state of public health in the Manchester conurbation, as measured by mortality, thus improved during the second half of the nineteenth century, but no substantial reduction in overall mortality occurred before the eighth decade, at least 40 years after serious concern was being expressed about the unhealthiness of the city.[40] Infectious diseases were responsible for the greater part of this reduction, with the decline in pulmonary tuberculosis, especially towards the end of the century, responsible for more than one quarter of lives saved. The decline in infant mortality on the other hand, although numerically important, was proportionately much less, and deaths from certain diseases which mainly attacked infants actually increased towards the end of the century.

IV

Further explanation of mortality experiences within Manchester can be provided by examining spatial variations which occurred within the three registration districts. Figures 7.4 and 7.5 show average annual crude mortality rates per decade for the 18 sub-districts which existed in 1851. Although providing only a coarse spatial mesh they do begin to demonstrate the spatial structure of the aggregate mortality experience previously discussed. Data constraints mean that these mortality statistics cannot be standardized to the age structure of sub-districts, cause-specific mortality cannot be analysed, and, prior to 1870, institutional deaths cannot be separated from the mortality of residents of sub-districts, but with cautious interpretation the maps do provide a valuable starting point for spatial analysis.

The overwhelming impression from the first three decades is of centre-periphery contrasts—often accentuated by the presence of central institutions—but around the unhealthy city centre sub-districts of Deansgate, London Road and Market Street, the high mortality of older working-class residential districts such as Ancoats and Salford Greengate can be contrasted with the newer but still relatively central working-class residential areas of St George and Hulme, which had much lower and declining mortality rates throughout the period. Other adjacent sub-districts such as Chorlton-upon-Medlock and Ardwick had much lower mortality rates throughout the period as they grew more slowly and developed into decent middle-class suburbs, while more exclusive suburban areas such as Cheetham and Broughton had even lower rates of mortality. After 1871, when institutional mortality can be taken into account, the most unhealthy districts formed a ring around the depopulating central city; and by the end of the century sub-districts such as Greengate and Ancoats increasingly became the foci of high mortality, although a narrowing range of mortality rates demonstrates both the reduction of overall mortality and a lessening of differentials between central and suburban areas at this scale of analysis. Analysis of annual variations in mortality rates by sub-district shows that the widest fluctuations in mortality were also concentrated in the central areas of Manchester, where mortality peaks were the result of epidemics

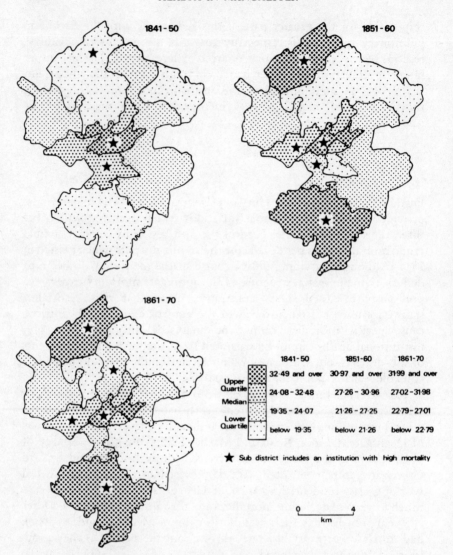

1841 - 50   1851 - 60

1861 - 70

	1841 - 50	1851 - 60	1861 - 70
Upper Quartile	32·49 and over	30·97 and over	31·99 and over
Median	24·08 - 32·48	27·26 - 30·96	27·02 - 31·98
Lower Quartile	19·35 - 24·07	21·26 - 27·25	22·79 - 27·01
	below 19·35	below 21·26	below 22·79

★ Sub district includes an institution with high mortality

0   4
km

Figure 7.4 Average annual crude mortality rates by sub-districts (in parts per 1,000), Manchester (including Prestwich), Salford and Chorlton registration districts, 1841–50 to 1861–70

often coincident with trade depressions and other crises such as the Irish famine migration.

A more detailed spatial picture of mortality variations within the city of Manchester may be examined for the periods 1861–70 and 1871–5 (Figure 7.6), using crude mortality data collected by the first Manchester Medical Officer for the census enumeration districts used in 1871. The

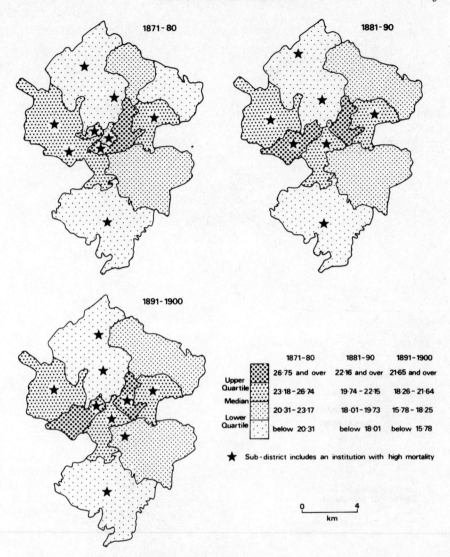

Figure 7.5 Average annual crude mortality rates by sub-districts (in parts per 1,000), Manchester (including Prestwich), Salford and Chorlton registration districts, 1871–80 to 1891–1900

basic pattern of low mortality in the central business district (C.B.D.), high mortality in the inner residential areas and low mortality around the periphery appears as before, but more localized variations are also apparent. A block of enumeration districts with crude mortality rates in excess of 34 per thousand are found in the 1860s in the pre-nineteenth-century core of the city adjacent to the C.B.D., and all the central ring

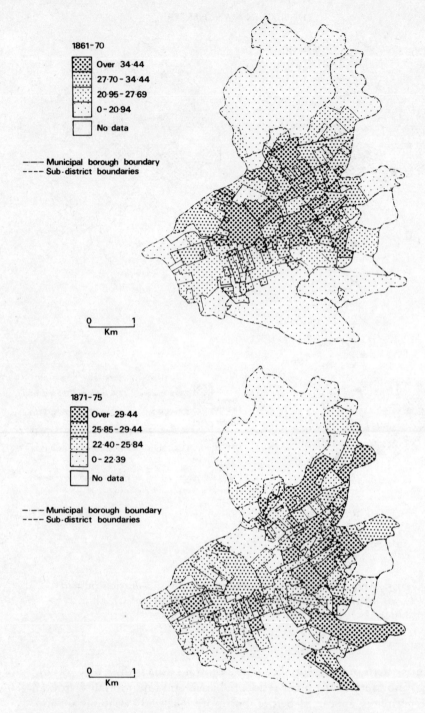

Figure 7.6 Average annual crude mortality rates by enumeration districts, Manchester Borough, 1861–75.
Source: Medical Officer of Health for Manchester, *Annual Report*, 1876

of enumeration districts had high mortality rates. Indeed, almost all of Manchester township, together with most of Hulme and parts of Chorlton-upon-Medlock and the township of Ardwick, had mortality rates in excess of 27 per thousand, in contrast to the outer suburban areas where mortality rarely exceeded 21.

By 1871–5 the range of mortality experience in Manchester had diminished a little, and the area of low central mortality had expanded considerably as central-area clearances and warehouse development had led to depopulation in previously high-mortality areas such as the older parts of Ancoats and St George sub-districts. The zone of highest mortality had moved out towards the inner working-class streets of Hulme, Chorlton and Ardwick, but death rates remained low in most of the peripheral area. Spatial variation in mortality was thus considerable and the health-profile of Manchester's population could change markedly over quite small distances.

It is unfortunate that neither the sub-district nor the enumeration district data allow calculation of age-specific and disease-specific mortality rates, but patchy data drawn from various statistical enquiries and from reports of the Medical Officer of Health allow some variations between townships to be highlighted.[41] The age-specific mortality data both confirm the massive contribution of deaths among the under-fives to total mortality and reflect the overall spatial pattern of the crude mortality statistics. In the decade 1871–80, for instance, deaths of those under five years of age accounted for more than half the total mortality of all areas of the city of Manchester except in the townships of Cheetham and Chorlton-upon-Medlock, both mainly middle-class suburbs with an older age structure, and in Market Street and Deansgate sub-districts, which were affected by the presence of institutions and central-area depopulation, giving them an ageing population.

Examination of the available cause-specific data again suggests that those areas with the highest total mortality were, in general terms, worst affected by all specified infectious diseases. There were, however, interesting exceptions. In 1840–2, for instance, while most diseases displayed distinctly different rates between central and peripheral townships (table 7.3), scarlet fever was remarkably constant in its occurrence. This may have been due to the increased consumption of infected milk in suburban areas, which offset the better environmental conditions, and to the lack of previous exposure of all children to a particularly virulent form of the disease.[42] Diseases of the respiratory and digestive tracts made the greatest contribution to total mortality in all areas, with higher rates in the central townships; but respiratory diseases took a greater proportion of this death toll in the more affluent suburbs, due both to the more elderly population structure of these areas and to the lower death rate from digestive diseases. Likewise in the 1850s, 1860s and 1870s the spatial incidence of infectious disease was

Table 7.3. Average annual crude mortality rates from specific causes, selected townships, 1840–42

Causes	Manchester		Salford and Pendleton		Chorlton-upon-Medlock Hulme and Ardwick		Cheetham, Broughton and Crumpsall		All Townships	
	Average no. of deaths per annum	Rate per 1,000 population	Average no. of deaths per annum	Rate per 1,000 population	Average no. of deaths per annum	Rate per 1,000 population	Average no. of deaths per annum	Rate per 1,000 population	Average no. of deaths per annum	Rate per 1,000 population
Smallpox	123	0.75	56	0.87	34	0.52	1	0.08	214	0.70
Measles	305	1.86	84	1.31	103	1.58	3	0.23	495	1.62
Scarlatina	194	1.19	59	0.92	74	1.14	15	1.19	342	1.12
Fever	232	1.42	54	0.84	56	0.86	4	0.32	346	1.13
Whooping Cough	209	1.28	53	0.82	80	1.23	5	0.40	347	1.13
Total from Above	1,063	6.50	306	4.76	347	5.32	28	2.22	1,744	5.70
Chest/Throat Diseases	1,652	10.08	503	7.83	556	8.52	74	5.86	2,785	9.10
Digestive Tract Diseases	1,072	6.54	456	7.10	348	5.34	35	2.77	1,911	6.25
Total from Above	3,787	23.12	1,265	19.69	1,251	19.81	137	10.85	6,400	21.05
All other Causes	1,712	10.44	650	10.12	559	8.57	84	6.66	3,005	9.82
All Causes	5,499	33.56	1,915	29.81	1,810	27.75	221	17.51	9,445	30.87
Total Population	163,856		64,232		65,224		12,621		305,933	

Source: Parliamentary Papers, P.P. 1945, xviii, pp. 114–16.

closely correlated with that of total mortality,[43] although fever mortality was especially concentrated in the poorer central areas; while diseases of childhood, including scarlet fever and measles, were more widespread in their occurrence, affecting areas like Ardwick, Pendleton and Pendlebury which had large reservoirs of young susceptible populations. Thus, there were marked spatial contrasts in both age-specific and disease-specific mortality rates which, although broadly reflecting the pattern of total mortality, also highlighted small-scale variations in the demographic structure, socio-economic characteristics and environmental conditions of townships.

V

Spatial variations, in those socio-environmental factors that contemporaries saw as important controlling mechanisms in the incidence of infectious disease, can also be examined within the same framework of sub-districts, townships and enumeration districts that were used for the analysis of mortality. In this chapter the smallest convenient framework of census enumeration districts is used, and selected indices of conditions within the Municipal Borough of Manchester and the township of Salford are presented for the two census years, 1851 and 1871 (Figures 7.7 and 7.8). [44] Detailed analysis, in the final section of the chapter, of these and other statistics allows the relationships between mortality and living conditions to be considered more closely.

Fundamental to the living conditions of the population was the state of the built environment, which can be measured through a surrogate index of housing density (Figure 7.7). Housing density varied according to the age and type of development; by no means all low-status areas had high housing densities, but crowded terraces, 'back-to-backs' and courts occupied at any density by any class of person would have provided a sub-standard living environment within the Victorian city. Central areas of Manchester had low housing densities in both 1851 and 1871, reflecting both the influx of commercial and industrial uses to the central area and the remaining stock of originally high status large terrace houses, mostly in multiple-occupancy in 1851. The highest housing densities were found in the inner ring of residential property, consisting either of old congested court and tenement dwellings crowded behind the main thoroughfares of the eighteenth-century town or of purpose-built working-class housing. The highest densities were found in those areas built prior to the 1844 bye-law which banned 'back-to-back' construction within Manchester Borough; but even after this date closely-packed working-class terraces spread out from the central areas to invade, by 1851, the northern parts of Hulme, Ardwick and Chorlton-upon-Medlock. Apart from small concentrations along main

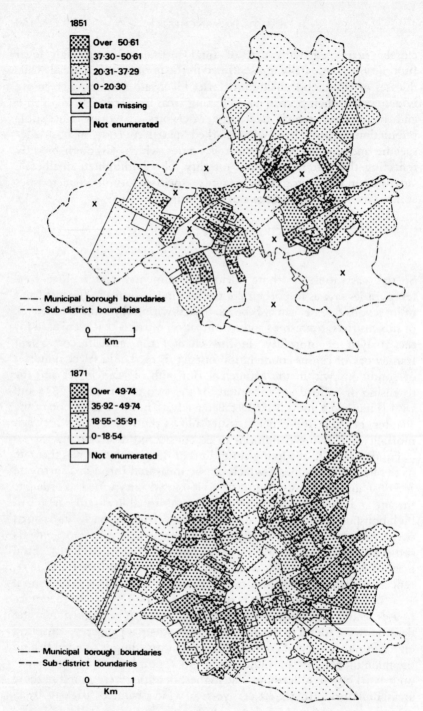

Figure 7.7 Net housing density (per acre) by enumeration districts, Manchester Borough and Salford Township, 1851 and 1871.
Source: Census enumerators' books for Manchester and Salford, 1851 and 1871

routes and in peripheral industrial townships, housing density declined fairly evenly with distance from the city centre, with uniformly low housing densities in predominantly middle-class suburbs such as outer Cheetham and Chorlton-upon-Medlock.[45]

Population density not unnaturally mirrored housing density, with a low-density core surrounded by a very high-density inner residential area thinning out into low density suburbs. It should be noted, however, that figures for the central area are misleading; although non-residential land uses have been excluded as far as possible in the calculation of densities, there is still a tendency to underestimate the extent to which the small resident population within the central area was living in closely-packed groups within certain sectors of the enumeration districts.

The extent of multiple occupancy in Manchester (Figure 7.8) provides a link between the measures of population and of housing density. Low-density housing which is occupied to a high density by several families, because of the sharing of basic facilities and greater inter-personal contact, may provide a greatly inferior living environment to that of high-density housing which is in single occupancy. The worst living conditions of all are likely to occur, of course, where high housing densities and high levels of multiple occupancy coincide to provide both a substandard built environment and a gross overcrowding of individual families. The highest rates of multiple occupancy occurred, not surprisingly, in those central areas which contained relatively large houses, some of which were occupied as common lodging houses, but several of the high density court, 'back-to-back' and terrace areas also contained substantial levels of multiple occupancy. Purpose-built, working-class bye-law terrace housing built in the second half of the century tended to be occupied mainly by single families, and most peripheral areas had relatively low rates, although changes in the definition of households between 1851 and 1871 caused the inflation of rates in some of the more respectable peripheral areas.[46] In most cases the recording of high rates of multiple occupancy in suburban areas is the result of such persons as lady companions to rich widows and high-status lodgers in professional households being treated as separate households in 1871.

Other indices such as household size, persons per house and male–female ratios can also be easily analysed from data in the summary pages of census enumerators' books; together they demonstrate that at the scale of enumeration districts Manchester had a clearly differentiated spatial structure by 1851. In 1871 this structure was more clearly defined but the basic elements of the city's social topography remained unchanged. Just as considerable spatial variations in the incidence and components of mortality existed within Victorian Manchester, other aspects of life were also spatially differentiated. Furthermore, this

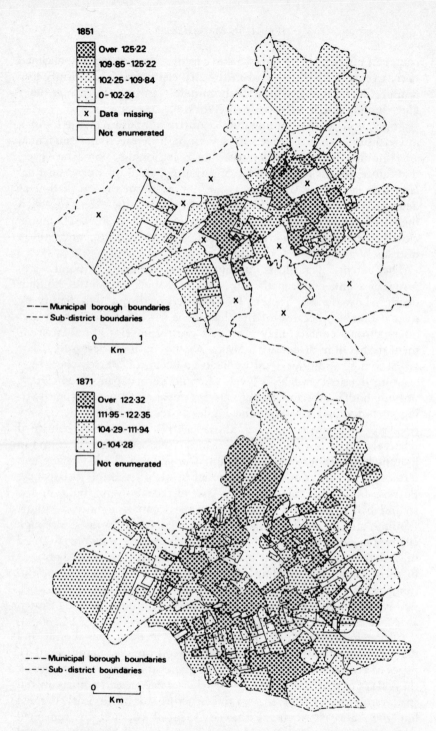

1851
Over 125·22
109·85 - 125·22
102·25 - 109·84
0 - 102·24
X Data missing
Not enumerated

Municipal borough boundaries
Sub·district boundaries

1871
Over 122·32
111·95 - 122·35
104·29 - 111·94
0 - 104·28
Not enumerated

Municipal borough boundaries
Sub·district boundaries

Figure 7.8 Multiple occupancy (households per 100 houses) by enumeration districts, Manchester Borough and Salford Township, 1851 and 1871.
Source: see Figure 7.7

statistical portrait is borne out by the comments of contemporaries, who clearly perceived not only the gross inequalities of living conditions that existed between central courts and suburban villas, but also the more subtle variations which occurred between different working-class districts of the town. [47]

VI

A superficial examination of Figures 7.4 to 7.8 suggests that there was a general association at the ecological level between areas of Manchester Borough which provided a substandard living environment, as measured by high-density housing and overcrowding, and crude mortality; especially that resulting from the infectious diseases at which most Victorian public health measures were aimed. However, statistical analysis of the data presents a less conclusive picture.

When measured within large spatial units such as registration sub-districts the statistical association is quite strong; but sub-districts obscure a great deal of internal variation and, at the more sensitive level of enumeration districts, the association is much less convincing (table 7.4). A step-wise multiple regression analysis of the enumeration district data indicated that only 25 per cent of the variance in total mortality 1871–5 could be explained by eight social and environmental indices, [48] with the best single predictor, housing density, accounting for only 17 per cent of the variance in mortality during the period. Even enumeration districts, each containing about 250 households, concealed a great deal of internal variation, and it seems reasonable to suggest that analysis at the small-group or individual level, if possible, would have revealed even weaker statistical associations between mortality and living conditions. The reasons for this low level of explanation lie in the fact that, although poor housing and environmental conditions show a general association with ill-health and mortality and may indeed have been pre-disposing factors in illness, there is not necessarily a causal relationship between living conditions and mortality. Circumstances such as life-cycle stage, family income and personal, genetic and behavioural characteristics are likely to have a much greater influence on health at the individual level; [49] and it must be remembered that the ecological data on mortality refer to deaths from all causes, and not just to those from infectious diseases most likely to be associated with socio-environmental conditions.

Contemporary Medical Officers of Health and social reformers concerned with improvements in the health of the population, however, lacked modern medical knowledge of disease causation and, not surprisingly, they seized upon the apparent ecological associations between poor living conditions and mortality to produce largely

Table 7.4. The relationship between mortality and selected socio-environmental variables, Manchester, 1841–80

Variables	Spearman rank correlations for subdistricts** Crude mortality		Product moment correlations for enumeration districts× Crude mortality	
	1841–50	1871–80	1861–70	1871–75
Net housing density:				
1851	+0.84			
1871		+0.92	+0.33	+0.40
Net population density:				
1851	+0.83			
1871		+0.91	+0.32	+0.34
Multiple occupancy:*				
1851	+0.88			
1871		+0.56	+0.13	−0.08

Notes: * defined as census schedules (households) per 100 houses. Very low correlations for 1871 are partly due to changed household definition
** all sub-districts in Manchester, Salford and Chorlton registration districts
× area defined by Manchester Municipal Borough, excluding three enumeration districts for which no mortality data are available

Sources: Census enumerators' books, Manchester, 1851 and 1871; Registrars' General *Annual Reports*, 1841–80; Medical Officer of Health for Manchester, *Annual Reports*

environmental explanations of the incidence of disease.[50] It was convenient that infectious diseases were found in their most virulent form in those areas of Manchester which were characterized by the worst housing, the highest density of occupancy and the poorest provision of sanitary facilities and water supply. Thus, it was completely logical that such public health reforms as occurred should be organized on an area basis and be spatially concentrated. Those areas identified as having the highest density housing and the worst levels of overcrowding became the focus for mid-Victorian sanitary reform in Manchester.

It is not possible here to do more than outline the course of public health reform in Manchester in the nineteenth century. One of the major obstacles to improvement was the number of authorities within the built-up area responsible for monitoring health and carrying out reforms. Outside the Manchester and Salford Municipal Boroughs there was a large number of local Boards (later Urban Sanitary Authorities) controlling sanitary administration; but the overriding impressions of their operation are of relative inactivity, because of the paramount importance of keeping down the rates, and of a positive unwillingness to co-operate with neighbouring authorities even where, as in drainage schemes, such co-operation was essential.[51] As elsewhere in this chapter, attention has been focused on Manchester Borough in the heart of the conurbation, where attempts by the local authority to intervene in the management of the urban environment fell principally into three main areas: the reduction of housing and population densities, the improvement of sanitation, and the provision of a pure water supply.

In many respects Manchester Borough Council was ahead of national legislation on housing reform, with local Acts banning the construction of 'back-to-back' housing (1844), limiting the use of cellar dwellings (1853), and giving the council powers to acquire and demolish property in order to lower densities and improve sanitary conditions (1845 and 1865) amongst other measures.[52] These powers were, however, only selectively used and for most of the nineteenth century any demolition which did occur was not followed by the construction of new working-class dwellings. Although the council from 1867 pursued a policy of compulsorily enforcing the reconditioning of houses defined as unfit, it refused to accept any direct responsibility for housing provision until 1891, preferring to rely on private redevelopment. However, builders were deterred by the very high central land values, the poor rates of return on investment and the increasingly stringent bye-laws controlling densities and type of housing.[53] Action to improve housing was, thus, concentrated in a very few parts of the worst central-city. Furthermore, it can be argued that slum clearance by the local authority and demolition for commercial and railway developments actually increased levels of overcrowding, as the failure to rebuild meant that the displaced population was simply shifted to other, equally crowded, parts

of the city. Even inspection of common lodging houses and houses let in
lodgings after 1865, to control overcrowding, had only a temporary
effect. [54]

Attempts by the local authority to improve sanitation were less half-
hearted, but were mainly directed at spatially-discrete areas of the city.
Despite improvements under the provisions of the Manchester Police
Regulation Act of 1844, 28 per cent of houses in the city had no separate
sanitation even in 1868. [55] The predominance in central areas of
infrequently-emptied privy middens with ashpits increased the risks to
health due to faecal contamination of food and water. In more suburban
areas the growing use of water closets added to the problems of river
pollution caused by manufacturing and street drainage with no
intercepting sewers. [56] In the 1870s, the council adopted a policy of
progressive removal of cesspits and the introduction of the Dolly
Varden pail closet; [57] but not until the 1890s was a waterborne system of
sewage disposal and treatment put into operation in Manchester, [58] and
even in 1902 only 37 per cent of the much-expanded city's privies were
water closets. [59]

Although the City Council took direct control of Manchester's water
supply in 1851, and the completion of reservoir schemes in Longdendale
in the 1850s and Thirlmere in the 1890s should have improved the
quality and regularity of supply, [60] the distribution of pure water
remained distinctly uneven throughout the nineteenth century. Despite
exhortations from public health reformers about the importance of
water provision to working-class districts, most of the central-city
courts and terraces did not have their own in-house water supply, but
relied on a standpipe in the yard or at the end of the street for much of the
period. Thus, although water supplied by the Corporation was
relatively pure and was readily available in middle-class suburban areas,
most working-class districts were forced to endure an inadequate
supply. This form of provision, not surprisingly, both increased the
possibility of infection as water collected from a standpipe stood around
in the house for several hours, and also encouraged the use of less pure
alternative supplies of water that may have been closer to hand. [61]

Thus, it can be suggested that the measures taken by Manchester
Corporation to lower rates of mortality and improve the health of the
city's population in the nineteenth century were unlikely to succeed, for
two principal reasons. First, the premises on which most of the measures
were based were largely unfounded. A necessarily incomplete and
inaccurate knowledge of disease causation, coupled with misinterpre-
tation of the apparent spatial associations between preventable mortality
and poor housing and overcrowding, led to measures which, with
hindsight, could never have been more than partially successful. The
traditional elements of sanitary reform could only control levels of
exposure to food- and water-borne diseases, which were responsible for
a minority of deaths, and they had no effect on susceptibility to these or

other diseases. Second, even within their own terms of reference, these schemes were doomed to failure. Attempts to improve sanitation were patchy and still kept sewage in the heart of densely populated areas for long periods. The provision of pure water was frustrated by inadequate distribution to those areas most in need, while attempts to lower housing densities actually worsened the situation by increasing levels of crowding elsewhere. Thus, those most at risk were not greatly helped.

Objectively, the health of the population of Manchester did improve during the nineteenth century, as mortality rates from most infectious diseases declined during the period under study. However, it can be suggested that much of this decline was due to the fortuitous effects of public health reforms and, more particularly, to social, economic and environmental changes outside the control of Manchester Corporation and those concerned with public health reform. Undoubtedly, improvements in sanitation, water supply and levels of crowding, together with controls on food and milk quality, did begin to reduce the incidence of disease by the last quarter of the century, through reducing exposure to infection. In addition, improvements in hospital provision from the 1870s, in particular the development of isolation hospitals, had a considerable impact. Yet the virulence of most infectious diseases would also have declined, in response to improvements in nutrition and general changes in standards of living, associated with the rise in real wages towards the end of the century, which reduced both susceptibility to infection and fatality rates among sufferers.[62] It can be suggested that these external factors, for most of the nineteenth century, were at least as important as the activities of Manchester Corporation in lowering the level of infectious disease mortality.[63]

Analysis of the relationships between disease, mortality and socio-environmental conditions in Victorian Manchester leads, therefore, to the conclusion that Rosen was substantially correct in suggesting that the components and circumstances of urban disease remained largely unchanged for most of the nineteenth century.[64] Not only did many of the most influential Victorian public health reformers fail to appreciate fully the significance, for the incidence and virulence of disease, of individual variability and behaviour within a population, but more importantly they relegated, to a position of secondary importance, essentially structural causes which lay behind the spatial concentration of mortality which they correctly observed. The acute poverty of many Victorian city dwellers, resulting from an unpredictable urban labour market and low wages in conditions of labour surplus, led inevitably to malnutrition and inadequate accommodation which progressively reduced resistance and increased exposure to disease. Not until this cycle of structural poverty began to be broken, and not until medical knowledge improved in the late nineteenth century, did the structure of urban disease and mortality fundamentally change and the health of the working-class urban population substantially improve.[65]

Mortality and sanitary conditions in late nineteenth–century Birmingham

Robert Woods

Much of the current debate on the reasons for British population growth in the industrial era has been concerned with the role of medical and environmental changes in the nineteenth century and their respective influences on the reduction in disease mortality. The aim of this discussion will be to re-examine a number of these supposed associations in the light of conditions in an English city, Birmingham, in the late Victorian and Edwardian periods.

McKeown and Record argued in the early 1960s that 'the specific changes introduced by the sanitary reformers were responsible for about a quarter of the total decline of mortality in the second half of the nineteenth century'.[1] Their assertion rests, as we have seen in Chapter 1, on an analysis of the specific causes of death, and their relative decline. Cholera, dysentery and diarrhoea, the bowel infections, accounted for about eight per cent of the reduction of mortality in the 1850–1900 period. With the exception of cholera, 'there is little doubt about the main reasons for the rapid reduction of mortality from the bowel infections. . . . These diseases are spread mainly by infected water and food and their decline began in the eighth decade (of the nineteenth century) when substantial improvements in hygienic conditions also began . . . reduction of mortality attributable to the decline of bowel infection resulted from the specific measures introduced under the sanitary revolution.'[2] Typhoid, typhus, enteric and simple continued fever accounted for some 22 per cent of the mortality decline over the half century. For typhoid, 'The spread of the disease is due to the defective sanitary arrangements, and the rapid reduction of mortality during the last third of the nineteenth century can be attributed confidently to the specific measures—particularly the improved water supply—introduced at the time.'[3] Typhus and the fevers were similarly influenced, McKeown and Record maintain, by improved hygienic standards and to some extent by better diet, but also perhaps by a changing relationship between host and parasite.

The remainder of the mortality decline was largely attributable to tuberculosis, both respiratory and non-respiratory, which seems to have been most susceptible to improvements in diet and overcrowding. Scarlet fever accounted for a further 19 per cent of the decline and here changes in the nature of the infection independent of environmental factors seem to have been most significant.

Despite recent revision of these estimates[4] water- and food-borne diseases are still claimed to account for a third of the death rate decline from 1848–54 to 1901 and 16 per cent from 1901 to 1971. McKeown and Record's estimate that a quarter of the mortality decline in the 1850–1900 period was due to sanitary improvements need not therefore be revised. Such an assertion raises a number of questions. Firstly, given that some of the diseases, especially typhoid and the other fevers, declined in importance, may it be demonstrated that it was specifically improved sanitary conditions or hygiene which led to that decline, or may it not be merely a further consequence of rising living standards? In other words, can one put forward the same causal explanation to which McKeown and Record attributed the decline in the influence of the air-borne diseases? Secondly, if sanitary reform is the prime mover in this context in what ways were the improvements made? Did they influence all classes and areas uniformly or, as with birth control, may sanitary improvements, and by implication mortality decline, be thought to have diffused down a social hierarchy or even spatially?[5]

I

By the 1880s Birmingham was claimed to be the 'Best governed city in the world',[6] at least by strangers if not by its natives. The age of Chamberlain the mayor had passed in the 1870s, the town council had been reorganized and governing interest in efficient administration and public well-being demonstrated in the water, gas and central improvement ventures. The last mentioned involved the construction of Corporation Street[7] through one of the borough's worst slums (St Mary's ward) which, together with the building of New Street and Snow Hill stations earlier in the century and the Victoria Law Courts later, effectively removed the central area population to the newer courts of the surrounding wards. It was widely believed[8] that Birmingham was as healthy as a large town could be and certainly the annual league tables of death rates showed this to be the case. To a large extent Birmingham's 400,000 population did benefit from an advantageous geography, in a medical sense, for their distance from the ports and situation on easily drained ground made them marginally less susceptible to imported infection or water-borne disease than the inhabitants of Newcastle-upon-Tyne or Liverpool, or even the miserable workers of Manchester.[9] Birmingham did not suffer, as Nottingham did,[10] from rapid release of building land adjacent to an enclosed site, and much of the housing in the 1880s was above average for the time in terms of access and ventilation: for instance, there are supposed to have been no cellar dwellings. Even in 1841 a committee of doctors, when reporting on the sanitary condition of the borough, maintained that 'this construction ("back to back" housing in courts) does not admit of that thorough ventilation of the houses which would exist if there were an outlet behind; but if the rooms are sufficiently large and lofty, if they have chimneys in them, and if the windows and doors are of good size, . . . we are not aware of any particular evils that can arise from this construction'.[11]

To a large extent this picture is misleading, for standards have changed markedly in the past hundred years, particularly in sensitivity to relative differences between housing classes and areas. In Birmingham there always has been a significant difference between the inner areas and the suburbs.[12] In the late nineteenth century this was a distinction between the greater part of the borough and Edgbaston, with small areas of Bordesley Green and Rotton Park. The very worst courts were removed by the commercialization of the urban core, but particularly bad areas still remained in the gun and jewellery quarters.[13] Edgbaston was developed in stages, but always with rigid control and to the highest standards, because it was owned as trust land while much of the rest of the borough was built-up 'on spec'.[14]

If Birmingham was well-governed and relatively well-housed, on average, were its half a million souls the recipients of any additional benefits? In terms of employment the area was one of expansion and relative diversity in metal working and engineering. Work was not seasonal, it was skilled or·semi-skilled and it was, all things considered, regular. Unlike the East End of London, where Stedman Jones[15] has shown the consequences of day hiring and service employment for the population, or the north-west, where textile manufacture had passed its boom period, Birmingham was prosperous and expansive. One might then expect the standard of living to be marginally higher than average and such components as diet to be better.

By 1872 Birmingham had a Medical Officer of Health, Dr Alfred Hill, whose duty it was to supervise and report on the public health conditions of the borough. From 1875 these reports were made to a Public Health Committee of the Borough Council. As public analyst, a post which Dr Hill held from its inception in 1860, he was obliged to examine food and milk for contamination and to consider the quality of the drinking water. From 1873 it is possible to gain a reasonably detailed picture of the changing sanitary state of the borough and the condition of its population from the Medical Officers' *Annual Reports.* Before that time only scattered information exists from an 1841 survey and local references in national compendia, the most famous of which was Chadwick's of 1842.[16] These annual reports enable one to consider the changing demography and medical geography of the borough and, comparing trends with those of other substantial urban areas established by their own M.O.H.s, and England and Wales as a whole as indicated by the Registrar General, to substantiate or otherwise the relationships that have been proposed to explain population growth.

Birmingham presents itself as an ideal candidate for study for a number of reasons. Firstly, as has been shown above, it was relatively well-administered from the 1870s onwards by a caucus of reasonably enlightened Liberals. Secondly, a vigorous and a highly respected Medical Officer of Health made extensive enquiries into the health of the borough from that time. Thirdly, the size of the town and its large population allow patterns of spatial differentiation to appear which may be related to varying degrees of sanitary condition.

Watts[17] has shown that by the end of the 1870s Birmingham had two extensive hospital complexes, the General and Queen's, as well as a number of more specialized institutions—a lunatic asylum, sewage processing plant, water supply sources (albeit inadequate), and a municipal cemetery. A further major development occurred during the 1870s and 1880s. This was the designation, subsequent expansion and growing use of isolation hospitals for infectious diseases. Of the reported cases of infectious diseases (mainly smallpox and scarlet fever) 14 per cent entered hospital in 1882–5, 70 per cent in 1886–9, and 83 per cent in 1890–3.[18] Bearing in mind McKeown and Brown, and McKeown and Record's[19] warnings about over-enthusiastic views of hospitalization before the twentieth century this development may be regarded with some ambivalence.[20] But it would seem that at least for scarlet fever there was a substantial difference between in-hospital (6.4 per cent) and at-home case fatalities (9.7 per cent),[21] although there may have been other reasons for this discrepancy. McKeown[22] showed the reduction in scarlet fever and diphtheria to have accounted for some 12 per cent in 1848–54 to 1901, and four per cent in 1901 to 1971 of the mortality decline.

More generally the 1870s and 1880s saw other great developments. Domestic cleanliness was enforced, zymotic diseases attacked, and the death rate, which had been 25.2 per 1,000 for the years 1871–5, 3.2 per cent above the national rate, was reduced to 20.7 per 1,000 for the years 1881–5, only 1.3 per cent above the national rate.[23] 'Their achievement (the sanitarians) was the great one, considering all the circumstances, of preventing the cities from becoming even more lethal than they already were.'[24]

Some of the major developments in the administration of Birmingham in the period, and the suggested reasons for the decline in mortality in England and Wales as a whole in the last half of the nineteenth century, have been outlined above. We may now turn to a consideration of the demographic structure of the borough, and especially the role of disease mortality in controlling that structure, together with a discussion of the relationship between sanitary conditions and infectious diseases in the spatial context. This will be tackled at two levels. Firstly, a more general review will be made of the pattern of cause-specific mortality for the Birmingham population for the period 1870–1910. Secondly, a detailed analysis will be carried out of the temporal and spatial impact of mortality in Birmingham in the eighth decade of the nineteenth century—a period of considerable significance according to McKeown and Record,[25] and one offering vital statistics and survey material of adequate detail.

II

There are always considerable difficulties in establishing a time series of mortality statistics. Firstly, definitions change from time to time and there are additions and subtractions to the list of notifiable diseases. For instance, the Registrar's *Decennial Statistical Reviews for England and Wales* used cause of death classifications which only included some 17 or 18 per cent of deaths in the 'other causes' category in the last three decades of the nineteenth century. In the first decade of the twentieth century some 46 per cent were in this grouping. Little more than 30 per cent of deaths were included in consistent categories for the whole 40-year period. Secondly, changing boundary lines make time series analysis impractical in many cases, but the inconsistency of geographical, administrative and statistical units may pose an equally insoluble problem. Cause of death statistics are reported by registration districts, but these rarely conform to administrative areas. Birmingham is a good example of this. Whilst the boundary and the population of the registration district remained constant in this period, the latter being about 235–245,000, the administrative area grew from Borough to City and County Borough with successive territorial enlargements. In the 1871 census the borough had a population of 343,787; in the 1911 census the much enlarged County Borough included 525,833 persons.

The consequence of these two difficulties is that any study of mortality in Birmingham will need to employ the registration district, which always contained considerably fewer persons than the local authority area. Further, the categories of cause of death used will have to be less than ideal because of the changes that were instituted in official tabulations.

Table 8.1 shows the number of deaths and the death rates by cause for Birmingham registration district, 1871–1910. The 13 causes specified are

Table 8.1. Cause-specific death rates (per thousand), Birmingham Registration District, 1871–1910

Cause of death	1871–80		1881–90		1891–1900		1901–10	
	Number	D.R.	Number	D.R.	Number	D.R.	Number	D.R.
Smallpox	1,042	0.44	204	0.08	253	0.10	1	—
Measles	1,055	0.44	1,476	0.60	1,284	0.52	1,258	0.53
Scarlet fever	2,672	1.12	1,030	0.42	743	0.30	556	0.24
Diphtheria	532	0.22	379	0.15	743	0.30	717	0.30
Whooping cough	2,141	0.90	1,634	0.66	1,441	0.59	1,277	0.54
Typhus	57	0.02	5	—	2	—	—	—
Typhoid	788	0.33	436	0.18	592	0.25	351	0.15
Diarrhoea and dysentery	4,396	1.84	3,114	1.27	3,121	1.27	2,810	1.19
Cancer tubes	1,176	0.49	1,778	0.72	2,255	0.92	2,630	1.11
Mesenterica	496	0.21	700	0.28	583	0.24	172	0.07
Phthisis	5,913	2.48	5,232	2.15	4,887	1.99	3,036	1.29
Childbirth and puerperal fever	397	0.17	364	0.14	398	0.16	314	0.13
Violence	3,319	1.39	2,950	1.20	2,917	1.19	2,720	1.15
All other causes	37,651	15.77	37,251	15.15	39,919	16.27	36,506	15.47
All causes	61,635	25.82	56,553	23.00	59,138	24.10	52,348	22.18

the only ones that appear in all four of the Registrar General's *Decennial Reviews* although they do not account for even a third of all deaths. A number of major points are obvious, even allowing for this drawback. Smallpox had become unimportant by the 1901–10 decade. Scarlet fever was less influential as were whooping cough, typhoid (enteric fever), diarrhoea and dysentery although they were all still very important causes of death. Another childhood disease, measles, had actually increased in importance whilst mortality at the older ages was still dominated by tuberculous diseases (phthisis being a representative in table 8.1), but cancer was becoming even more significant as a major killer. Diseases like cholera and typhus had ceased to be of any importance.

It is difficult to take the interpretation of table 8.1 any further without knowing age-specific death rates. These are shown in table 8.2. Despite the decline in many childhood diseases, infant mortality remained relatively stable, even allowing for the higher value for the 1890s, but there was a marked decline in the mortality of the early childhood age group. Other age groups exhibit little significant change.

Tables 8.1 and 8.2 raise as many problems as they solve for, although a few major killer diseases can be shown to have declined in importance, age-specific death rates remained relatively stable. It is within this

Table 8.2. Age-specific death rates, Birmingham Registration District, 1871–1910

Age groups	Age-specific death rates (per thousand)			
	1871–80	1881–90	1890–1900	1901–10
0	179*	174*	200*	175*
1–4	45	37	36	33
5–9	8	6	6	6
10–14	4	3	3	3
15–19	5	4	4	4
20–24	7	6	6	5
25–34	11	9	9	8
35–44	17	16	18	15
45–54	25	24	27	24
55–64	44	43	47	42
65–74	85	84	84	79
75 +	181	167	165	159

Note: * Infant mortality is expressed by the ratio of deaths to children under one year of age in a year to the number of births in that year

context that one may approach a more detailed consideration of the spatio-temporal pattern of disease mortality and its relation to improvements in sanitary conditions.

III

A change in the level of detail also permits a change of scale. One may now deal with the actual Borough of Birmingham rather than the registration district, because of the Medical Officer of Health's mortality statistics. By the 1880s both birth and death registration were relatively accurate,[26] although one can imagine that there were under-counts particularly in the urban areas with rapid population turnover. Census data provide the means of estimating mid-year populations and here some difficulty is encountered with inter-censal years. The annual reports of the Medical Officer of Health give birth, death and marriage rates as well as the actual numbers of births, deaths and marriages, without stating the mid-year estimates from which the rates were derived. Table 8.3 shows these in column (2), but it should be noted that these are applicable to the death rates and that different values result when one divides births by birth rates. New mid-year estimates may be derived by adding in births, subtracting deaths and making some adjustment for net migration. An adequate estimate of the mid-year population in 1881 would seem to be 402,331, given a census figure of 400,774 for the 3rd/4th April. Local government reorganization in 1891 made the City of Birmingham a much enlarged place and for this reason the natural increase in the first half of 1881 will be used to represent that of 1891. The natural increase for 1881–91 was therefore 58,676 (143,735 births less 85,059 deaths) while actual inter-censal population growth for the area of the 1838 borough was 28,394 and net migration would therefore have to be placed at 30,282. Net migration removed roughly 48 per cent of natural increase. If one assumes that the net migration rate is constant over the decade then one can deduce successive mid-year estimates from July to June births less deaths reduced by a factor of 0.4839. The results of this exercise are shown in table 8.3 column (3) whilst adjusted birth and death rates appear in columns (7) and (9) respectively. It is particularly towards the end of the decade, when the death rate seemed to fall, that this adjustment has its most significant influence. The same may also be said for the birth rate (Figure 8.1).

Table 8.3 also shows the death rates for four other large English towns. Birmingham appears most closely comparable with Bristol, whilst Liverpool, Manchester and Sheffield always have higher rates, apart from one year. This would tend to confirm the reports of contemporaries that, for the time, Birmingham was a 'healthy town'.

The overall population structure of Birmingham is somewhat more

Table 8.3. Population and vital rates of the Borough of Birmingham and four other large English towns, 1880–91

Year	Census (1)	M.O.H. estimate (2)	New estimate (3)	Births (4)	Deaths (5)	M.O.H. birth rate (6)	New birth rate (7)	M.O.H. death rate (8)	New death rate (9)	Liverpool death rate (10)	Manchester death rate (11)	Sheffield death rate (12)	Bristol death rate (13)
1880		394,729	398,819	15,111	8,088	38.28	37.89	20.49	20.28	27.3	25.4	21.1	20.1
1881	400,774	402,331	402,331	14,869	7,938	36.96	36.96	19.73	19.73	26.7	25.5	21.1	19.6
1882		408,584	405,840	14,866	8,425	36.38	36.63	20.62	20.76	26.5	26.8	21.7	19.2
1883		414,755	408,957	14,701	8,714	35.45	35.95	21.01	21.31	26.6	27.6	22.9	17.8
1884		429,392	412,105	14,991	9,043	34.91	36.38	21.06	21.94	25.1	26.3	22.3	18.3
1885		427,687	414,948	14,383	8,156	33.63	34.66	19.07	19.66	25.6	26.4	21.0	20.1
1886		434,287	418,134	14,282	8,499	32.89	34.14	19.57	20.33	26.1	26.3	20.1	19.8
1887		441,137	421,124	13,893	8,536	31.49	32.99	19.35	20.27	26.4	28.7	22.0	21.0
1888		447,970	423,873	13,673	7,835	30.52	32.26	17.49	18.48	23.1	26.1	21.1	17.5
1889		454,902	426,990	14,001	8,352	30.78	32.79	18.36	19.55	24.9	26.7	21.5	18.3
1890		470,753	429,548	14,076	9,561	29.92	32.77	20.31	22.26	27.5	30.5	25.9	20.5
1891	429,168	429,949	431,770	14,623	9,317	34.01	33.87	21.67	21.58	26.9	26.5	23.8	20.8

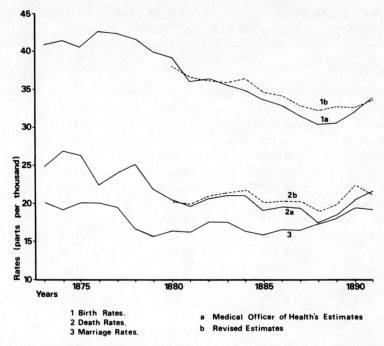

1 Birth Rates.
2 Death Rates.
3 Marriage Rates.

a Medical Officer of Health's Estimates
b Revised Estimates

Figure 8.1 Crude birth, death and marriage rates, Birmingham Borough, 1873–91

difficult to establish, but estimates of an 'average stable condition' may be derived from model life tables. Keyfitz and Flieger[27] give the life expectancy at birth (e_0) of males as 44.19 and 47.38 for females in 1881 with 41.94 and 45.64 in 1891 for England and Wales. (However, Case[28] gives the equivalent e_0 for 1881–5 as 43.19 and 46.37, with 43.92 and 47.21 for 1886–91.) The equivalent birth and death rates would be respectively 33.92 and 18.88 for 1881, with 34.42 and 20.21 for 1891. For Birmingham 1880–9 they would be 35.03 and 20.22, thus reducing the life expectancy slightly. Infant mortality over the decade was 165.44 per thousand live births (compared with 174 in table 8.2). With such estimates to hand it is possible to reconstruct the average population of the Borough of Birmingham in the 1880s. Coale and Demeny's regional model life tables[29] may be employed for this purpose. West Level 11 gives a male e_0 of 42.12 and a female e_0 of 45.00 which would seem most appropriate given the above rates. The appropriate gross reproduction rate (GRR) would be 2.25 having a growth rate of 14.28 (Birmingham 1880–9 has a 14.80 rate). Given this selection procedure one may decompose Birmingham's average 1880s male and female populations into age groups and this is shown in table 8.4. Once this estimate of age

Table 8.4. Stable age structure from West Model Life Table, Level 11, GRR 2.25, Birmingham Borough, 1880s

Age groups	Males	Females	Total
0	6,470	6,321	12,791
1–4	21,945	21,617	43,562
5–9	24,500	24,146	48,646
10–14	22,295	21,928	44,223
15–19	20,276	19,918	40,194
20–24	18,277	17,949	36,226
25–29	16,340	16,063	32,403
30–34	14,527	14,322	28,849
35–39	12,816	12,684	25,500
40–44	11,189	11,171	22,360
45–49	9,602	9,782	19,384
50–54	8,077	8,435	16,512
55–59	6,573	7,109	13,682
60–64	5,110	5,741	10,851
65–69	3,688	4,332	8,020
70–74	2,390	2,984	5,374
75–79	1,298	1,741	3,039
80 +	680	1,016	1,696
Total	206,053	207,259	413,312

structure has been made one may turn to a consideration of the varying levels of age-specific mortality and the various causes of death.

Firstly, then, table 8.5 presents average age-specific mortality rates for 1880–9 based on the model age structure and reported deaths. Further, the maximum and minimum deaths for each of the six age groups over the ten-year series are given and their corresponding crude death rates calculated. Extreme statistical occurrences could mean the difference between crude death rates of 22.76 and 17.57 whereas the average is 20.22.

The possibility presents itself that part of the decline in mortality in the nineteenth and twentieth centuries was in fact the result of a reduction in the frequency of extremely high mortality occurrences. If one considers the fluctuations in the number of weekly deaths over the 1880–9 period by age groups then one may be able to elaborate this point. Figure 8.2 presents these detailed curves. If one recalls that nearly 46 per cent of deaths were to children under the age of five and then examines the violent fluctuations in the 'under one year' curve one may

Table 8.5. Age-specific mortality rates, Birmingham Borough, 1880–9

Age groups	Model population	Deaths	Death rate	Minimum deaths	Minimum death rate	Maximum deaths	Maximum death rate
0	12,791	2,395 (28.65)	187.24	2,105 (28.99)	164.57	2,611 (27.75)	204.13
1–4	43,562	1,422 (17.01)	32.64	1,155 (15.91)	26.51	1,704 (18.11)	39.12
5–19	133,063	528 (6.32)	3.97	444 (6.11)	3.34	688 (7.31)	5.17
20–39	122,978	1,002 (11.98)	8.15	925 (12.74)	7.52	1,115 (11.85)	9.07
40–59	71,938	1,389 (16.61)	19.31	1,235 (17.01)	17.17	1,510 (16.05)	20.99
60+	28,980	1,624 (19.43)	56.04	1,397 (19.24)	48.21	1,780 (18.92)	61.42
Total	413,312	8,360 (100.00)	20.22	7,261 (100.00)	17.57	9,408 (100.00)	22.76

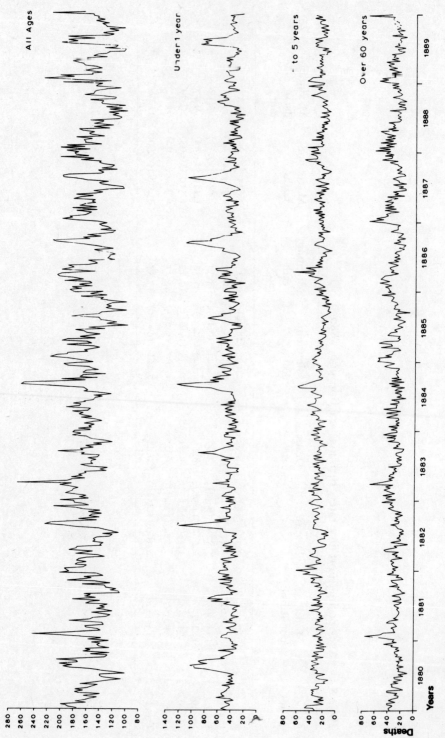

Figure 8.2 Weekly deaths by age, Birmingham Borough, 1880–89

appreciate the contributions of these peaks to the overall death rate. However, this procedure may be somewhat deceptive. If one removes the exceptional peaks which occur in the summer months of each year and replaces them with an average number of deaths operative throughout the rest of the year then the crude death rate may be reduced from 20.22, but only to 19.67, whilst the infant death rate (ie not deaths under one year to births, but the former to an estimate of the population under one year of age) declines from 187.24 to 166.81. The much less marked winter peaks in the 'over 60s deaths' curve may also be removed, but the results of this would be even less spectacular. It would seem therefore that reducing the peak mortality experiences does not have a marked overall effect on death rates by itself. One must look to a general decline in mortality for specific ages, diseases or throughout the year or, indeed, any combination of these three potential factors.

Table 8.6 considers specific diseases and their potential contribution to mortality decline. Nearly 43 per cent of deaths came from seven diseases: measles, scarlet fever, whooping cough, typhoid fever, diarrhoea, phthisis (consumption) and respiratory infections. The minimum crude death rate from these diseases would be 6.58 and the maximum 11.10 so that the corresponding general death rates would be 18.14 and 22.66. Removing all seven diseases completely would give a death rate of 11.50, a level not reached in Birmingham until the 1950s. The removal of deaths from diarrhoea and phthisis would alone reduce the death rate to 17.20 and a removal of all except respiratory diseases would give a death rate of 15.60 (table 8.7 shows the individual contribution of each disease).

Table 8.6 may be supplemented by Figures 8.3 and 8.4 which show the weekly fluctuations in deaths from the seven diseases. The most straightforward is typhoid which at that stage lacked seasonality and was responsible for, on average, only 78 deaths a year. Whooping cough and measles are most significant in the winter months, but not every winter and not only in the winter. Both are particularly infectious air-borne diseases. The former began to decline in significance from the 1880s (table 8.1) whilst decline was not apparent for the latter until after 1910.[30] The pattern of scarlet fever deaths in Figure 8.3 raises more considerable problems of interpretation. Between 1885 and 1888 there was a significant drop in the deaths from this disease in Birmingham. This one might attribute to the increased degree of hospitalization, but since the streptococcus responsible for the disease was not isolated until the early 1880s and therapy was ineffective until after 1935 it is difficult to see how hospital treatment could have helped apart from minimizing the contagious effects and perhaps providing better care than would be available in many poor home environments.

It was the water- and food-borne diseases causing bowel disorders which were responsible for the seasonally high levels of infant mortality.

Table 8.6. Deaths from seven diseases, Birmingham Borough, 1880-9

Year	Measles (1)	Scarlet fever (2)	Whooping cough (3)	Typhoid fever (4)	Diarrhoea (5)	Phthisis (6)	Respiratory diseases (7)
1880	63	123	217	83	777	733	1,761
1881	132	164	362	65	341	690	1,792
1882	150	256	317	87	533	776	1,684
1883	155	325	176	81	412	763	1,861
1884	333	134	289	84	736	771	1,656
1885	119	31	253	77	338	734	1,706
1886	383	39	94	65	729	695	1,540
1887	237	23	379	78	550	708	1,614
1888	191	40	235	64	305	654	1,620
1889	197	156	279	44	465	690	1,585

Year	Total of above 7 (8)	Total deaths (9)	Per cent of total (10)	Total population (11)	Death rate from above 7 (12)	Total death rate (13)	Difference (13)−(12)
1880	3,757	8,088	46.45	398,819	9.42	20.28	10.86
1881	3,546	7,938	44.67	402,331	8.81	19.73	10.92
1882	3,803	8,425	45.14	405,840	9.37	20.76	11.39
1883	3,773	8,714	43.30	408,957	9.23	21.31	12.08
1884	4,003	9,043	44.27	412,105	9.71	21.94	12.23
1885	3,258	8,156	39.95	414,948	7.85	19.66	11.81
1886	3,545	8,499	41.71	418,134	8.48	20.33	11.85
1887	3,589	8,536	42.05	421,124	8.52	20.27	11.75
1888	3,109	7,835	39.68	423,873	7.33	18.48	11.15
1889	3,416	8,352	40.90	426,990	8.00	19.55	11.55
Total	35,709	83,586	43.82		8.66	20.22	11.56

Table 8.7. Death rates from individual diseases, Birmingham Borough, 1880–9

Disease	Average annual deaths	Disease death rate (per 1,000)	Death rate resulting from removal of disease
Measles	196	0.474	19.748
Scarlet fever	129	0.312	19.912
Whooping cough	260	0.629	19.592
Typhoid fever	73	0.177	20.048
Diarrhoea	519	1.256	18.959
Phthisis	721	1.744	18.466
Respiratory diseases	1,682	4.070	16.124

Figure 8.3 shows the deaths from diarrhoea which, over the decade, represented nearly as many as those due to measles, scarlet fever and whooping cough in combination. It was these deaths in August and early September that created the peaks in deaths 'under one year' shown in Figure 8.2. Beaver[31] has argued that it was the reduction in the contamination of food, and particularly milk, which, by working through a diminution in deaths from bowel infections, dramatically reduced infant mortality after the turn of the century. Deaths from respiratory diseases also have a marked seasonality (Figure 8.4) with a winter peak and summer trough, but in exceptional winters (in this series 1880–1 and 1888–9) there was an additional peak. Phthisis (consumption or tuberculosis), on the other hand, lacks seasonality and keeps up a fairly uniform average of 720 deaths a year.

In addition, Figure 8.5 shows the incidence of smallpox in the 1870s and 1880s by dealing not only with the number of reported cases, but also the number of fatalities from the disease. Although the outbreak in the early 1870s was clearly important—there were for example 607 deaths in 1874—by the 1880s there were relatively fewer occurrences of a disease which could so readily be vaccinated against.[32]

The population of Birmingham in the 1880s had a life expectancy at birth of about 43 years; 45 per cent of deaths were to children under five years of age and 43 per cent of deaths were attributable to seven major groups of air-, water- and food-borne diseases. This situation could have been changed in a number of ways. Seasonal mortality peaks might have diminished (this seems to have only a marginal effect when applied to deaths under one year). Certain specific diseases might decline. If all the seven diseases had been removed one would have been left with a death rate equivalent to post-Second World War levels whilst removal of all but respiratory diseases would produce a rate equivalent to 1930s levels.

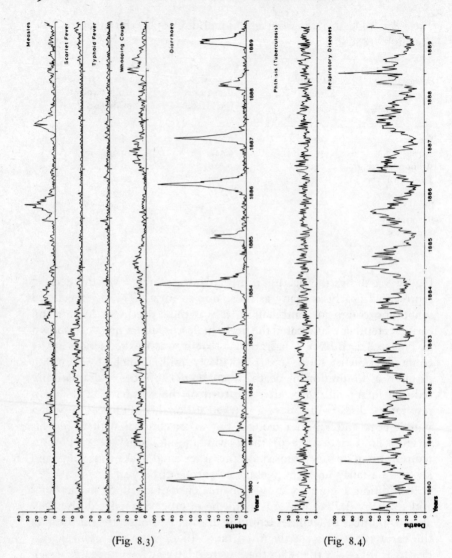

(Fig. 8.3)   (Fig. 8.4)

Figure 8.3. Weekly deaths from five diseases, Birmingham Borough, 1880–89

Figure 8.4 Weekly deaths from two diseases, Birmingham Borough,
1880–89

However, many of these diseases were spatially biased to particular parts
of the borough in their influence, to the extent that averages expressed in
the foregoing obscure gross inequalities in morbidity, mortality and
medical geography.

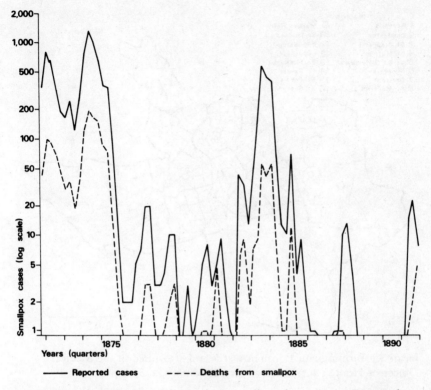

Figure 8.5 Reported cases of deaths from smallpox by quarters, Birmingham Borough, 1871–91

IV

Following Dr Snow's pioneering attempt in 1855 to identify the cause of cholera by mapping the addresses of persons dying from that disease, Medical Officers of Health in the late nineteenth century often followed the same approach. In Birmingham Dr Hill had maps drawn of the distribution of persons dying from measles, scarlet fever and typhoid for each year during the 1880s. Unfortunately, it was not until 1891 that the place of usual residence of the deceased was plotted. Up until that time deaths in hospital, the workhouse or the jail gave certain areas a disproportionately large number of deaths. Figure 8.6 shows the boundaries of the 16 wards into which the borough was divided in the 1880s and a set of 170 smaller areas used in the collection of data for a 'sanitary conditions' survey of 1885. Figure 8.7 shows the location of the borough hospitals, the jail and the workhouse. Information on disease

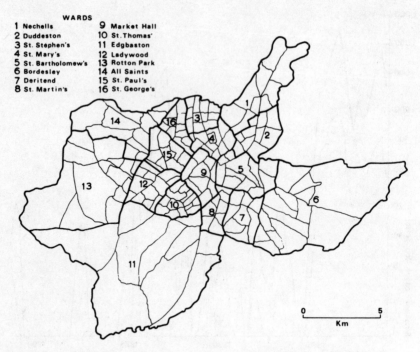

Figure 8.6 Birmingham Borough wards and areas used in the Medical
Officer of Health's survey of sanitary conditions, 1885

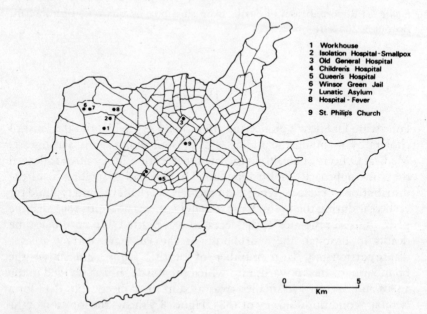

Figure 8.7 Location of the principal hospitals, the jail and the workhouse,
Birmingham Borough, 1880s

mortalities may be converted from dot maps to the 170 areas so that eventually mortality may be contrasted with sanitary conditions.

One further problem remains, namely the difficulty of comparing actual numbers of deaths without taking population size into account. This has been inadequately solved by the use of location quotients. The proportion of the total borough deaths from, say, measles that occur in area A is expressed as a ratio of the proportion of the total number of households occurring in area A. The latter proportion was obtained from the 1885 survey of sanitary conditions and for this reason disease mortalities have been taken for a period of nine years centred on that year. It would have been possible to convert the number of households to an estimate of the population (Dr Hill himself used 5.2 as an average household size), but it is almost certain that there were in fact considerable variations within the borough (Laslett[33] gives a mean household size of 4.768 with 4.61 for 1881 and 4.73 for 1891, England and Wales).

Figure 8.8 shows the mortality from measles (1881–9) in terms of a location quotient (the five areas with hospitals or similar large institutions having been excluded). The town centre, Edgbaston, much of Rotton Park and Bordesley stand out as areas of low mortality from this disease. This may be due partly to the low population density of

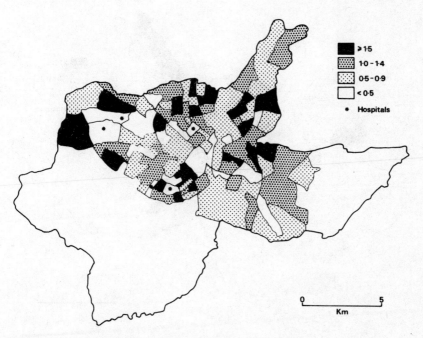

Figure 8.8 Measles deaths location quotients, Birmingham Borough, 1881–89

these areas,[34] but it may also be the result, except in the town centre, of the concentration of the borough's wealthy classes in them. Whilst measles as an illness may be no respecter of class as a killer disease amongst children, diet and living conditions may prove crucial. The worst areas for measles mortality were St Thomas's, St Bartholomew's, Duddeston, St Stephen's and Rotton Park (Winson Green).

If one turns to consider deaths from scarlet fever (Figure 8.9) then there appears to be a specific directional bias to the disease. Nechells, Duddeston and St Bartholomew's are the worst affected areas, all of which lie to the north east of the town centre. Many of the worst areas of the borough escape a high concentration of the disease. McKeown and Record maintain that 'changes in the behaviour of scarlet fever appear to be largely independent of the environmental changes . . ., and there is no reason to differ from the general opinion that they have resulted from a change in the nature of the disease. This change was probably due mainly to variation in the virulence of the haemolytic streptococcus rather than to modification of man's response to it.'[35] Despite this there still appear to be certain areas with a higher mortality from scarlet fever than one would expect from the 'no environmental association' argument. Further, one cannot explain away the area association in terms of a single extreme outbreak in one year.

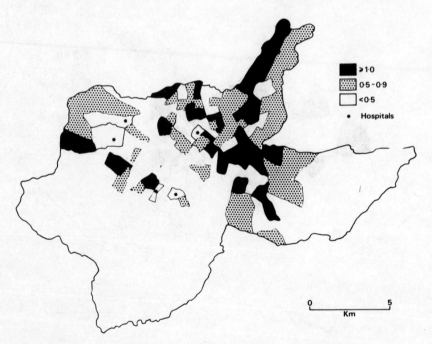

Figure 8.9 Scarlet fever deaths location quotients, Birmingham Borough, 1881–89

Typhoid fever mortality is shown in Figure 8.10. It is this infectious disease, perhaps above all others, that is associated with poor water supply and inadequate sanitary conditions. Generally Figures 8.10 and 8.8 are quite similar, but for two important exceptions. Typhoid mortality is also concentrated in Ladywood and St Martin's—north east Edgbaston. The former one might expect, but the latter requires special attention. One possible clue to this concentration is provided by Figure 8.11 which shows the distribution of wells in 1885. Most of these wells were privately owned and supplied particular households. Their use declined rapidly with the introduction of mains water supply.

Although the elimination of measles, scarlet fever and typhoid deaths would only have reduced Birmingham's crude death rate to 19.25, nonetheless the three diseases illustrate a number of important points and create several problems in the process. Even for very contagious diseases environment seems to have played a role in affecting the level of mortality. Where the diminution of the virulence of the disease can only be attributed to changes in the nature of that disease it is still possible for the populations of particular areas to be especially prone to its ravages. Further, because of the removal of the five institutional areas there may be slight distortion shown in Figures 8.8, 8.9 and 8.10.

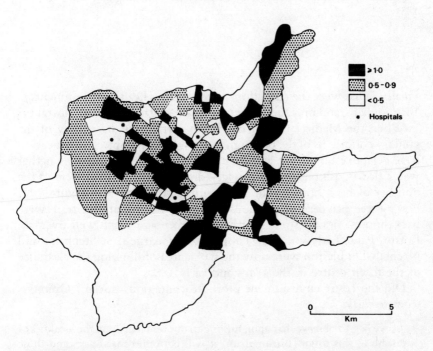

Figure 8.10 Typhoid fever deaths location quotients, Birmingham Borough, 1881–89

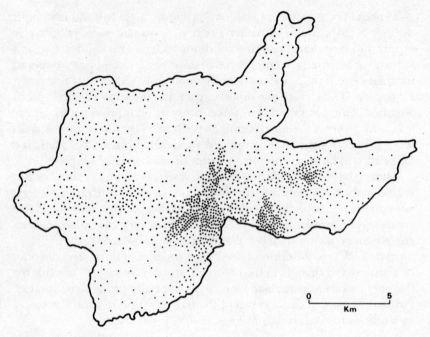

Figure 8.11 Location of wells (one dot per well), Birmingham Borough,
1885

V

Finally, what were the conditions of the various health environments in
Birmingham, and may they be related to the degree of disease mortality?

When the Medical Officer of Health carried out his survey of the
sanitary conditions of the borough in 1885, his main objective appears to
have been to establish the level of provision of toilet facilities — whether
water closets, ash pits or pan privies — and to make an assessment of the
number of back houses. The last mentioned is shown in Figure 8.12.
Forty-three per cent of the houses in Birmingham at that time were
back houses, but in some wards the percentage went well over 50.
Rotton Park, Ladywood, St Thomas's, St George's, St Stephen's and
Nechells-Duddeston were now the worst areas, following the clearance
of the town centre in the 1870s and early 1880s.

Did the court environment promote contagious disease? Opinions
seem to vary:

> ... we beg to observe that upon turning to our remarks upon the localities of
> disease in this town (Birmingham) it will be found that fevers and those
> forms of disease which are by many believed to arise from a confined and
> impure atmosphere, do not prevail in one situation or one kind of house

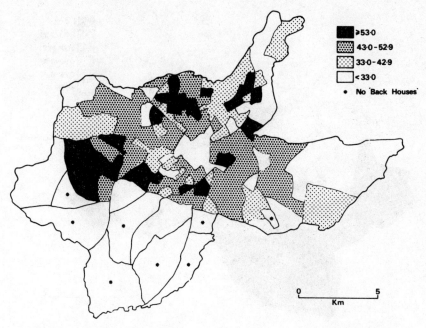

Figure 8.12 Percentage of houses that were 'back houses', Birmingham Borough, 1885

more than in another; and that contagious disorders are quite as frequent in houses of a different construction, in the front houses in the streets and in airy situations as in the dwellings in the courts which are built as we have described. The mode of erecting houses for the poor is very economical, and if not adopted, the poor inhabitants of a large town, where land is very expensive, could not obtain his house except at a much higher rent than he pays at present, by which his means for providing the other necessaries of life would be diminished.[36]

However, because the poorest population tends to live in the worst housing conditions, have the worst diet and generally consist of the least healthy members of society, there is a considerable confounding of variables in the multiple link between disease mortality and sanitary conditions. Figure 8.13 shows the location quotient for the distribution of water closets—the most advanced form of sanitary provision of the time. Most of the populous parts of the borough fall into the lowest category creating a 'cordon insanitaire' round the town centre and separating it from the well-provided suburbs to the south-west.

How may disease mortality variables be related to those for sanitary conditions? One attempt is represented by the matrix of product moment correlation coefficients in table 8.8. The strongest relationship is that between measles (variable 5) and percentage back houses (1) with

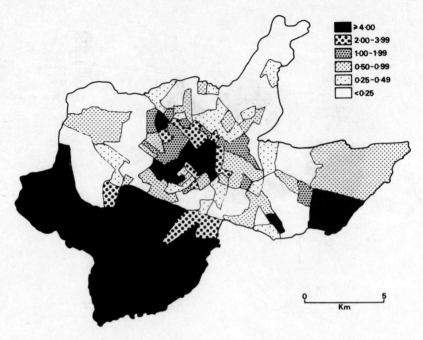

Figure 8.13 Water closets location quotients, Birmingham Borough, 1885

a coefficient of determination ($r^2 \times 100$) of 59.4. The second highest relationship is found between measles (5) and ash pit privies (4), but here the association is negative with a coefficient of determination of 46.6. All other relationships, apart from (4) with (1), are lower, but significant, apart from (7) with (3). Taken at its face value table 8.8 would tend to show that there is generally a positive and significant association between disease mortality and sanitary conditions, but that the correlation is low. Each of the three disease variables (5, 6 and 7) are most closely associated with the percentage of 'back houses' (1) rather than the level of sanitary provision in the strict sense. This applies to typhoid (7), a disease traditionally linked with poor water supply and infected food, as much as the other two variables (5 and 6). Table 8.8 is clearly subject to a considerable number of restrictions. It deals not with death rates but location quotients and not with individuals but with the characteristics of areas. It portrays a set of relationships specific to one point in time whereas what one would wish to analyze in the ideal case would be the continuing impact of sanitary improvements on mortality. However, this having been said, the degree of association between sanitary condition and mortality variables is lower than one might expect if an improvement in the former were in fact capable of influencing the latter to any marked degree.

Table 8.8. Relationship between disease mortality (1880–9) and sanitary variables (1885), Birmingham Borough

Independent variables (X)	Dependent variables (Y)						
	1	2	3	4	5	6	7
1 Per cent back houses	—	−0.532[a]	0.286[c]	−0.691[d]	0.771[b]	0.489[b]	0.419[b]
2 Water closet—L.Q.		—	−0.246[c]	0.497[a]	−0.461[c]	−0.454[b]	−0.364[b]
3 Pan privies—L.Q.			—	−0.423[d]	0.544[b]	0.238[b]	−0.133 n.s.
4 Ash pit privies—L.Q.				—	−0.683[c]	−0.353[c]	−0.231[c]
5 Measles deaths—L.Q.					—	0.487[b]	0.341[b]
6 Scarlet fever deaths—L.Q.						—	0.292[b]
7 Typhoid fever deaths—L.Q.							—

Notes: Calculated over 165 areas shown in Figure 8.6, the five hospital areas were excluded

Product moment correlation coefficients (r)

[a] — arith X, arith Y

[b] — log X, log Y

[c] — arith X, log Y

[d] — log X, arith Y

n.s. — not significant at 95 per cent level

VI

A number of explanations are possible for this, the proof of which would require further investigation. Firstly, the low association between disease mortality and sanitary conditions may be the result of a growing number of sick people being cared for in isolation hospitals. The relationships between disease morbidity and environment could in fact be quite high. If this were true then improvements in sanitary conditions need to be coupled with developments in hospital provision, in order to create a fuller account of the decline in death rates during the nineteenth century. Secondly, one is faced with the possibility that it is the poor in the new courts of the outer wards who are most susceptible to high death rates and that the level of sanitary provision is no more than a side issue.[37] If this is the case it casts some doubt on McKeown's attempt to attribute a quarter of the mortality decline in the late nineteenth century to sanitary improvements.[38] It does not detract from the obvious need to quantify the relationships identified in Figure 1.1, for example, but it does serve to reiterate, as has this entire volume, the difficulties involved and the complexity of the associations at work.

Notes

Chapter 1

1 As introductions to this topic see, for example, M. Dobb, *Studies in the Development of Capitalism* (London, 1946); G. A. Cohen, *Karl Marx's Theory of History: A Defence* (Oxford, 1978); P. N. Junankar, *Marx's Economics* (Oxford, 1982); T. Carver, *Marx's Social Theory* (Oxford, 1982); A. Maddison, *Phases of Capitalist Development* (Oxford, 1982)

2 See G. Stedman Jones, *Outcast London* (London, 1971); C. G. Pooley, 'Residential mobility in the Victorian City', *Transactions, Institute of British Geographers*, New Series 4(2) (1979), pp. 258–77, and other contributions to that issue

3 This argument is fully developed in E. A. Wrigley and R. S. Schofield, *The Population History of England, 1541–1871: A Reconstruction* (London, 1981); See also M. W. Flinn, 'The population history of England, 1541–1871', *Economic History Review*, 2nd Series, 35 (1982), pp. 443–57, and the contributions to T. Barker and M. Drake (eds), *Population and Society in Britain, 1850–1980* (London, 1982)

4 R. Lawton, 'Rural depopulation in nineteenth-century England', in R. W. Steel and R. Lawton (eds), *Liverpool Essays in Geography*, pp. 227–55 (London, 1967); 'Population changes in England and Wales in the later nineteenth century: an analysis of trends by registration districts', *Transactions, Institute of British Geographers*, 44 (1968), pp. 55–74; 'An age of great cities', *Town Planning Review*, 43 (1972), pp. 199–224; 'Population and society, 1730–1900', in R. A. Dodgshon and R. A. Butlin (eds), *An Historical Geography of England and Wales*, pp. 313–66 (London, 1978); 'Regional population trends in England and Wales, 1750–1971', in J. Hobcraft and P. H. Rees (eds), *Regional Demographic Development*, pp. 20–70 (London, 1980); J. Saville, *Rural Depopulation in England and Wales* (London, 1957)

5 C. M. Law, 'The growth of urban population in England and Wales, 1801–1911', *Transactions, Institute of British Geographers*, 41 (1967), pp. 123–43. On the nature of urban society see, for example, H. J. Dyos and M. Wolff (eds), *The Victorian City* (2 vols) (London, 1973); Asa Briggs, *Victorian Cities* (London, 1963); M. Anderson, *Family Structure in Nineteenth-Century Lancashire* (Cambridge, 1971); W. A. Armstrong, *Stability and Change in an English County Town: A Social Study of York, 1801–51* (Cambridge, 1974); Dennis Smith, *Conflict and Compromise: Class Formation in English Society, 1830–1914, A Comparative Study of Birmingham and Sheffield* (London, 1982)

6 Edwin Chadwick's report of 1842 still provides a valuable introduction. M. W. Flinn (ed), *Report on the Sanitary Condition of the Labouring Population of Great Britain by Edwin Chadwick, 1842* (Edinburgh, 1965). Enid Gauldie, *Cruel Habitations: A History of Working-Class Housing,*

1780–1918 (London, 1974) and John Nelson Tarn, *Five Per Cent Philanthropy: An Account of Housing in Urban Areas Between 1840 and 1914* (Cambridge, 1973) provide accounts of urban housing conditions whilst F. B. Smith, *The People's Health, 1830–1910* (London, 1979) describes the general background to health care and J. H. Treble, *Urban Poverty in Britain, 1830–1914* (London, 1979) outlines the economic and social conditions of the new urban era. Much useful information on the individuals involved in the sanitary movement and the conditions they had to face is provided in R. A. Lewis, *Edwin Chadwick and the Public Health Movement, 1832–1854* (London, 1952); S. E. Finer, *The Life and Times of Sir Edwin Chadwick* (London, 1952); R. S. Lambert, *Sir John Simon and English Social Administration, 1816–1904* (London, 1963). Anthony Wohl, *Endangered Lives: Public Health in Victorian Britain* (London, 1983) provides the most up-to-date survey

7 The notation employed by demographers to relate to the functions of the life table are: the number alive and aged x, l_x; the probability of dying between age x and age $x+n$, $_nq_x$; the life expectation at age x, e_x. Thus infant mortality is q_0 and life expectation at birth is e_0. (See also 'Note on demographic notation', p. 17.)

8 See J. Cullen, *The Statistical Movement in Early Victorian Britain: The Foundation of Empirical Social Science* (New York, 1975); E. A. Wrigley (ed), *Nineteenth-Century Society* (Cambridge, 1972); R. Lawton (ed), *The Census and Social Structure* (London, 1978); W. Farr, *Vital Statistics* (London, 1885); D. V. Glass, *Numbering the People: The Eighteenth-Century Population Controversy and the Development of Census and Vital Statistics in Britain* (Farnborough, 1973); M. W. Flinn, *British Population Growth, 1700–1850* (London, 1970); R. Mitchison, *British Population Change since 1860* (London, 1977); M. W. Flinn, et al., *Scottish Population History: From the Seventeenth Century to the 1930s* (Cambridge, 1977)

9 W. A. Armstrong, 'The trend of mortality in Carlisle between the 1780s and the 1840s: a demographic contribution to the standard of living debate', *Economic History Review*, 2nd Series, 34 (1981) pp. 94–114; W. Farr (1885) op. cit.

10 Wrigley and Schofield (1981) op. cit. p. 230 suggest that e_0 in England increased from about 35 in the 1750s to 40 in the 1850s. See Chapter 2 especially Figure 2.1 for the post vital registration trends in England and Wales

11 A. Sharlin, 'Natural decrease in early modern cities: a reconsideration', *Past and Present*, 79 (1978) pp. 126–38; R. A. P. Finlay, 'Natural change in early modern cities', *Past and Present*, 92 (1981), pp. 169–80

12 A simulation model of this form has yet to be fully developed, but see D. J. Loschky, 'Urbanization and England's eighteenth century crude birth and death rates', *Journal of European Economic History*, 1 (1972), pp. 697–712. Wrigley and Schofield (1981) op. cit., pp. 466–84 employ the mortality increasing effect of urbanization in their demographic systems

13 W. Farr (1885) op. cit.; D. V. Glass, 'Some indicators of differences between urban and rural mortality', *Population Studies*, 17 (1964), pp. 263–8

14 Estimated from Armstrong (1981) op. cit.

15 Charles Booth, *Life and Labour of the People in London*, (17 vols) (London, 1902–4)

16 The poverty data from which Figure 1.3 was constructed are to be found in Booth (1902–4) op. cit. *First Series: Poverty*, vol. 2 (1902), Appendix tables II and III see also *Final Volume: Notes on Social Influences and Conclusion*, vol. 17 (1902), pp. 16–31. The coefficient of determination ($r^2 \times 100$) is 46.83 and $q_0 = 0.1085 + 1.3069 \, PI$; r is the correlation coefficient, q_0 is infant mortality and PI is Booth's estimate of the percentage in poverty. (Only 29 observations are used, registration district 12 has been excluded)

17 This particular example is taken from Chapter 8, but many others are to be found from London (Figure 5.4) and Manchester (Figures 7.4 to 7.8)

18 The original source for this observation is Dr Lee the Medical Officer of Health for Manchester; it was used by Joseph Chamberlain in a speech to the Sanitary Conference held in Birmingham on 14 January 1875. It was also cited by Frederick Engels and included by him in the third German edition of Marx's *Capital*. See K. Marx, *Capital*, vol. 1 (London, 1976, Penguin edition), p. 795

19 In a stationary population the birth rate and the death rate are equal (they also equal e_0^{-1}), but the population represented in table 1.2 are likely to be growing, in which case e_0 will be higher than the mean age at death

20 Henry Ratcliffe, *Observations on the Rate of Mortality and Sickness* (Manchester, 1850) reprinted in R. Wall (ed), *Mortality in Mid-Nineteenth Century Britain* (Farnborough, 1974)

21 These estimates are derived from the West family of model life tables in A. J. Coale and P. Demeny, *Regional Model Life Tables and Stable Populations* (Princeton, 1966)

22 See C. W. Smith, *Class and the Decline of Fertility in Nineteenth-Century England*, Unpublished Ph.D thesis, University of Sheffield, 1982; R. Woods and C. W. Smith, 'The decline of marital fertility in the late nineteenth century: the case of England and Wales', *Population Studies*, 37 (1983), pp. 207–25, see table 5. In their recent review of living standards during the Industrial Revolution P. H. Lindert and J. G. Williamson, 'English workers' living standards during the Industrial Revolution: a new look', *Economic History Review*, 2nd Series, 36 (1983), pp. 20–21 argue that occupational differences in mortality levels in the early part of the nineteenth century were far smaller than spatial differences. The evidence for this view appears dubious in the pre-vital registration era whilst in the 1860s it is contradicted by table 1.4 and Figure 2.4. Williamson has also developed his ideas further in J. G. Williamson, 'Earnings inequality in nineteenth-century Britain', *Journal of Economic History*, 40 (1980), pp. 457–75; 'The structure of pay in Britain, 1710–1911', in P. Uselding (ed.), *Research in Economic History*, 7 (1982), pp. 1–54 (Greenwich, Conn.) and particularly on the urban standard of living and 'disamenities' in, 'Urban disamenities, dark satanic mills, and the British standard of living debate', *Journal of Economic History*, 41 (1981), pp. 75–83 (see also Sidney Pollard's comments and Williamson's reply pp. 902–7); 'Was the Industrial Revolution worth it? Disamenities and death in 19th century British towns', *Explorations in Economic History*, 19 (1982), pp. 221–45

23 Many of these views are summarized in Thomas McKeown, *The Modern Rise of Population* (London, 1976), but they are also to be found in T. McKeown and R. G. Brown, 'Medical evidence related to English population changes in the eighteenth century', *Population Studies*, 9 (1955), pp. 119–41; T. McKeown and R. G. Record, 'Reasons for the decline of mortality in England and Wales during the nineteenth century', *Population Studies*, 16 (1962), pp. 94–122; T. McKeown, R. G. Brown and R. G. Record, 'An interpretation of the modern rise of population in Europe', *Population Studies*, 26 (1972), pp. 345–82; T. McKeown, R. G. Record and R. D. Turner, 'An interpretation of the decline of mortality in England and Wales during the twentieth century', *Population Studies*, 29 (1975), pp. 391–422

24 Chapter 4 takes up this theme in detail

25 Chapter 5 provides a detailed discussion of the changed impact of typhoid and typhus. The literature on cholera is voluminous, but see, for example, Charles Creighton, *A History of Epidemics in Britain* (2 vols) (2nd edn, London, 1965); Asa Briggs, 'Cholera and society in the nineteenth century', *Past and Present*, 19 (1961), pp. 76–96; C. E. Rosenberg, 'Cholera in nineteenth-century Europe: a tool for social and economic analysis', *Comparative Studies in Society and History*, 8 (1966), pp. 452–63; P. E. Brown, 'John Snow—the autumn loiterer', *Bulletin of the History of Medicine*, 25 (1961), pp. 519–28; J. M. Eyler, 'William Farr on the cholera: the sanitarian's disease theory and the statistician's method', *Journal of the History of Medicine*, 28 (1973), pp. 79–100 and *Victorian Social Medicine: The Ideas and Methods of William Farr* (Baltimore, 1979); R. J. Morris, *Cholera, 1832* (London, 1976); Margaret Pelling, *Cholera, Fever and English Medicine, 1825–65* (Oxford, 1978); M. Durey, *The Return of the Plague: British Society and the Cholera, 1831–2* (Dublin, 1979). On Cholera in France see Louis Chevalier (ed.), *Le Choléra. La Première Épidémie du XIX^8 Siècle*, Bibliotheque de la Revolution de 1848, Tome XX (La Roche-sur-Yon, 1958); P. Bourdelais and J.-Y. Raulot, 'La marche du choléra en France: 1832 à 1854', *Annales: E.S.C.*, 33 (1978), pp. 125–42; in Russia see R. E. McGrew, *Russia and the Cholera, 1823–32* (Madison, 1965); and in the USA see, C. E. Rosenberg, *The Cholera Years. The United States in 1832, 1849 and 1866* (Chicago, 1962); G. Pyle, 'Diffusion of Cholera in the United States', *Geographical Analysis*, 1 (1969), pp. 59–75

26 loc. cit. note 23, especially McKeown and Record (1962)

27 These issues are dealt with in Chapter 3, but see also J. H. Woodward, *To Do The Sick No Harm* (London, 1974); M. Jeanne Peterson, *The Medical Profession in Mid-Victorian London* (Berkeley, 1978); G. Rosen, 'Disease, debility, and death', in H. J. Dyos and M. Wolff (eds), *The Victorian City*, vol. 2, pp. 625–67 (London, 1973); Eyler (1979) op. cit.; Pelling (1978) op. cit.

28 These issues have been summarized in A. J. Taylor (ed.), *The Standard of Living in Britain in the Industrial Revolution* (London, 1975), pp. xi–lv.

Valuable background material is also to be found in E. H. Hunt, *British Labour History, 1815–1914* (London, 1981), pp. 57–116; François Crouzet, *The Victorian Economy* (London, 1982), also M. W. Flinn, 'Trends in real wages, 1750–1850', *Economic History Review*, 2nd Series, 27 (1974), pp. 395–413; G. N. von Tunzelmann, 'Trends in real wages, 1750–1850, revisited', *Economic History Review*, 2nd Series, 32 (1979), pp. 33–49. The most recent statement on these issues in Lindert and Williamson (1983) op. cit., argues forcefully that although there may have been little change in *real wages* before 1810–14, 'There was general real wage improvement between 1810 and 1815, and a decline between 1815 and 1819, after which there was continuous growth. After prolonged wage stagnation, real wages, . . ., nearly doubled between 1820 and 1850' (p. 11). However, the rate of increase did vary markedly between social classes (Figure 1, p. 12 and table 7, p. 24). 'Quality of Life', as opposed to 'real wages', may require more careful consideration in future evaluations, they remark

29 Armstrong (1981) op. cit.

30 Much valuable material on the matter of long-term changes in real wage rates is to be found in H. Phelps Brown and S. V. Hopkins, *A Perspective on Wages and Prices* (London, 1981). See also R. A. Church, *The Great Victorian Boom, 1850–1873* (London, 1975); E. H. Hunt, *Regional Wage Variations in Britain, 1850–1914* (Oxford, 1973). Changes in diet and food supply are outlined in J. Burnett, *Plenty and Want* (London, 1966); D. Oddy and D. Miller (eds), *The Making of the Modern British Diet* (London, 1976); W. L. Langer, 'Europe's initial population explosion', *American Historial Review*, 69 (1963), pp. 1–17, 'American foods and Europe's population growth, 1750–1850', *Journal of Social History* (Winter, 1975), pp. 51–66

31 Woods and Smith (1983) op. cit.; J. A. Banks, *Prosperity and Parenthood* (London, 1954), and, *Victorian Values* (London, 1981)

32 See especially, S. H. Preston, *Mortality Patterns in National Populations* (New York, 1976), 'The changing relation between mortality and level of economic development', *Population Studies*, 29 (1975), pp. 231–48; S. H. Preston and V. E. Nelson, 'Structure and change in causes of death: an international summary', *Population Studies*, 28 (1974), pp. 19–51, for discussions of contemporary international patterns

33 Several recent American studies have taken up this theme, most are critical of the McKeown thesis; see, for example, E. Meeker, 'The improving health of the United States, 1850–1915', *Explorations in Economic History*, 9 (1972), pp. 353–73; R. Higgs, 'Cycles and trends in mortality in 18 large American cities, 1871–1900', *Explorations in Economic History*, 16 (1979), pp. 381–408; G. A. Condran and E. Crimmins-Gardner, 'Public health measures and mortality in U.S. cities in the late nineteenth century', *Human Ecology*, 6(2) (1978), pp. 27–54; G. A. Condran and R. A. Cheney, 'Mortality trends in Philadelphia: age- and cause-specific death rates, 1870–1930', *Demography*, 19 (1982), pp. 97–123

34 McKeown and Record (1962) op. cit., p. 120. This theme is examined more closely in Chapter 8

35 G. Rosen, 'Social variables and health in an urban environment: the case of the Victorian city', *Clio Medica*, 8 (1973), pp. 1–17

Chapter 2

1 See W. Farr, *Vital Statistics* (London, 1885); *Vital Statistics of Health, Sickness, Disease and Death*, reprinted in R. Wall (ed), *Mortality in Mid-Nineteenth Century Britain* (Farnborough, 1974), and R. A. M. Case et al., *Chester Beatty Research Institute Serial Abridged Life Tables, England and Wales, 1841–1960* (London, 1962)

2 The symbols employed by demographers denote life expectation at age x by e_x, with e_0 as life expectancy at birth. The probability of dying between ages x and $x+n$ is $_nq_x$, with q_0 as infant mortality. See also 'Note on demographic notation' (p. 17) and R. Woods, *Population Analysis in Geography* (London, 1979), pp. 37–61

3 On mortality variations in the United States see: G. A. Condran and R. A. Cheney, 'Mortality trends in Philadelphia: age- and cause-specific death rates, 1870–1930', *Demography* 19 (1982), pp. 92–123; G. A. Condran and E. Crimmins, 'Mortality differentials between rural and urban areas of States in the northeastern United States, 1890–1900', *Journal of Historical Geography* 6 (1980), pp. 179–202; M. R. Haines, 'Mortality in nineteenth-century America: estimates from New York and Pennsylvania census data, 1865 and 1900', *Demography* 14 (1977), pp. 311–32 and, 'The use of model life tables to estimate mortality for the United States in the late nineteenth century', *Demography* 16 (1979), pp. 289–312; R. Higgs, 'Cycles and trends in mortality in 18 large American cities, 1871–1900', *Explorations in Economic History* 16 (1979), pp. 381–408; M. A. Vinovskis, 'Mortality rates and trends in Massachusetts before 1860', *Journal of Economic History* 32 (1972), pp. 184–213. On France see: E. van de Walle, 'La mortalité des départements français ruraux au XIX^c siècle', in J. Dupâquier (ed), *Hommage à Marcel Reinhard*, pp. 581–89 (Paris, 1973); and in general N. Keyfitz and W. Flieger, *World Population: Analysis of Vital Data* (Chicago, 1968)

4 T. H. Hollingsworth, *The Demography of the British Peerage*, Supplement to *Population Studies* (1964), pp. 56–7 and, 'Mortality in the British peerage families since 1600', *Population* (Special Number) 23 (1977), pp. 323–52

5 Roger Schofield and E. A. Wrigley, 'Infant and child mortality in England in the late Tudor and early Stuart period', in Charles Webster (ed), *Health, Medicine and Mortality in the Sixteenth Century* (Cambridge, 1979), pp. 61–95; E. A. Wrigley, 'Mortality in pre-industrial England: the example of Colyton, Devon, over three centuries', in D. V. Glass and R. Revelle (eds), *Population and Social Change* (London, 1972), pp. 243–73; E. A. Wrigley and R. S. Schofield, *The Population History of England 1541–1871: A Reconstruction* (London, 1981). Wrigley and Schofield (1981) op. cit., table 7.15, p. 230 estimate that life expectation at birth (sexes combined) in England was as follows:

Year	e_0	Year	e_0	Year	e_0
1551	38.0	1801	35.9	1851	39.5
1601	38.1	1811	37.6	1861	41.2
1651	37.8	1821	39.2	1871	41.3
1701	37.1	1831	40.8		
1751	36.6	1841	40.3		

6 F. B. Smith, *The People's Health, 1830–1910* (London, 1979) deals with the experience of each age group in turn

7 T. McKeown and R. G. Record, 'Reasons for the decline in mortality in England and Wales during the nineteenth century', *Population Studies* 16 (1962), pp. 94–122; T. McKeown, R. G. Brown and R. G. Record, 'An interpretation of the modern rise of population in Europe', *Population Studies* 26 (1972), pp. 94–122; T. McKeown, R. G. Record and R. D. Turner, 'An interpretation of the decline in mortality in England and Wales during the twentieth century', *Population Studies* 29 (1975), pp. 391–422; T. McKeown, *The Modern Rise of Population* (London, 1976)

8 D. V. Glass, 'Some indicators of differences between urban and rural mortality', *Population Studies* 17 (1964), pp. 263–8; T. Ferguson and B. Benjamin et al., *Public Health and Urban Growth* (Centre for Urban Studies, University College, London, 1964)

9 One suspects that this was because of Dr William Farr's own interests. See J. M. Eyler, *Victorian Social Medicine: The Ideas and Methods of William Farr* (Baltimore, 1979)

10 The age groups used here are: 0, 1–4, 5–9, 10–14, 15–19, 20–24, 25–34, 35–44, 45–54, 55–64, 65–74, 75–84 and over 85. Deaths to those aged 1, 2, 3 and 4 are also reported

11 After 1911 vital statistics were collected for the new local authority areas

12 D. V. Glass, 'A note on the under-registration of births in Britain in the nineteenth century', *Population Studies* 5 (1951), pp. 70–88; M. S. Teitelbaum, 'Birth under-registration in the constituent counties of England and Wales, 1841–1910', *Population Studies* 28 (1974), pp. 329–43

13 M. Anderson, 'The study of family structure', in E. A. Wrigley (ed), *Nineteenth-Century Society* (Cambridge, 1972), p. 64

14 See, for example, N. Keyfitz, *Introduction to the Mathematics of Population* (Reading, Mass., 1968); N. Keyfitz and W. Flieger, *Population: Facts and Methods of Demography* (San Francisco, 1971); H. S. Shryock and J. S. Siegel, *The Methods and Materials of Demography* (New York, 1976)

15 The relevant techniques are described in R. Woods (1979) op. cit., pp. 48–54

16 It has been necessary to combine a small number of registration districts in order to allow comparability with other time periods. Most of these amalgamations affect West Yorkshire, the Wirral and South Wales

17 The coefficient of determination ($r^2 \times 100$; where r is the Pearson product moment correlation coefficient) is 78.67

18 In this case the coefficient of determination is 60.25

19 See S. H. Preston (ed), *The Effects of Infant and Child Mortality on Fertility* (New York, 1978). For a recent review of the 'replacement effect' see J. E. Knodel, 'Child mortality and reproductive behaviour in German village populations in the past: a micro-level analysis of the replacement effect', *Population Studies* 36 (1982), pp. 177–200

20 The indirect standardization technique is described in R. Woods (1979), op. cit. table 5.8, p. 116; it is also to be found in D. V. Glass, 'Changes in fertility in England and Wales, 1851–1931', in L. Hogben (ed), *Political Arithmetic* (London, 1938), pp. 161–212. The control of fertility in nineteenth-century England and Wales is considered in R. Woods, *Theoretical Population Geography* (London, 1982), pp. 102–30; R. Woods and C. W. Smith, 'The decline of marital fertility in the late nineteenth century: the case of England and Wales', *Population Studies* 37 (1983), pp. 207–25. The constants used here for the age-specific fertility (female births only) in the seven 5-year age groups 15–19 to 45–49 are as follows:

15–19	20–24	25–29	30–34	35–39	40–44	45–49
0.064	0.138	0.141	0.113	0.079	0.034	0.011

21 Coale's fertility indices are defined in A. J. Coale, 'Factors associated with the development of low fertility: an historic summary', *Proceedings of the World Population Conference, 1965*, vol. 2 (New York, 1967), pp. 205–9. The index of marital fertility (I_g) is a measure indirectly standardized on the age-specific marital fertility schedule of a population with 'natural fertility', that is fertility within marriage is not restricted in a parity-specific way. I_g not only measures marital fertility, but it also gives an impression of the extent to which fertility within marriage is being controlled. I_g values >0.6 suggest natural fertility. See R. Woods (1979) op. cit., pp. 118–21

22 The graph shown in Figure 2.12 is an amended form of the system used by Wrigley and Schofield (1981) op. cit., Figure 7.10, p. 239. In their version both the GRR and e_0 axes are logged so that the r isolines may be plotted as straight parallel lines at equal distances apart. The intrinsic rate of natural increase (r) was first defined by A. J. Lotka, see R. Woods (1979) op. cit., pp. 202–8 and A. J. Coale, *The Growth and Structure of Human Populations* (Princeton, 1972)

23 See Edwin Chadwick, *Report on the Sanitary Condition of the Labouring Population of Great Britain in 1842* (ed M. W. Flinn) (Edinburgh, 1965); R. Wall (ed), *Mortality in Mid-Nineteenth Century Britain* (London, 1974); W. Farr (1885) op. cit.

24 Louis Wirth, 'Urbanism as a way of life', *American Journal of Sociology* 44 (1938), pp. 1–24. These issues are discussed in the context of nineteenth-century urbanization by A. F. Weber, *The Growth of Cities in the Nineteenth Century* (New York, 1899) and specifically with respect to England and Wales by C. M. Law, 'The growth of urban population in England and Wales, 1801–1911', *Transactions, Institute of British Geographers* 41 (1967), pp. 125–43; B. T. Robson, *Urban Growth: An Approach* (London, 1973)

25 T. A. Welton, 'The growth of population in England and Wales and its progress in the period of ninety years from 1801–91', *Journal of the Royal Statistical Society* 63 (1900), pp. 527–89; T. A. Welton, *England's Recent Progress: An Investigation of the Statistics of Migrations, Mortality etc. in the Twenty Years from 1881 to 1901* (London, 1911); A. L. Bowley, 'Rural populations in England and Wales. A study of the changes of density, occupations and ages', *Journal of the Royal Statistical Society* 77 (1914), pp. 597–652; see also R. Lawton (ed), *The Census and Social Structure* (London, 1978), p. 115

26 The following percentages of the total population of England and Wales lived in registration districts with population densities of 1,000 persons per sq. km. and above, 30.90 per cent; 400–999, 13.29 per cent; 100–399, 23.03 per cent; and less than 100 per sq. km., 32.78 per cent in 1861. See R. Lawton, 'Population changes in England and Wales in the later nineteenth century: an analysis of trends by registration districts', *Transactions, Institute of British Geographers* 44 (1968), pp. 55–74; 'Rural depopulation in nineteenth-century England', in R. W. Steel and R. Lawton (eds), *Liverpool Essays in Geography* (London, 1967), pp. 227–55; 'Population and society, 1730–1900', in R. A. Dodgshon and R. A. Butlin (eds), *An Historical Geography of England and Wales* (London, 1978), pp. 313–66; 'Regional population trends in England and Wales, 1750–1971', in J. Hobcraft and P. Rees (eds), *Regional Demographic Development* (London, 1980), pp. 29–70 for other examples of the use of registration district data

27 The coefficient of determination is 53.34 per cent ($r = -0.73$) and $Y = 55.99 - 5.12 \log X$ (where Y is e_0 for males and X is population density in persons per sq. km.)

28 The coefficient of determination is only 24.80 per cent in this case ($r = 0.498$) and $Y = 0.104 + 0.020 \log X$ (where Y is male q_0 and X is population density in persons per sq. km.)

29 Useful summaries of these methods are provided by Dennis Child, *The Essentials of Factor Analysis* (London, 1970), and R. J. Johnston *Multivariate Statistical Analysis in Geography* (London, 1978). The use of factor analysis on age-specific mortality rates is exemplified in A. J. Coale and P. Demeny, *Regional Model Life Tables and Stable Populations* (Princeton, 1966). In the case discussed here the varimax rotation was employed

30 Correlation coefficients (r) greater than $+0.1$ or less than -0.1 may be regarded as statistically significant

31 Eigenvalues are the sums of the squared factor loadings (the associations between variables and factors) and give a numerical expression of the importance of each factor. By convention only factors with eigenvalues greater or equal to 1.0 are considered important enough for subsequent use. The percentage variance is found from (eigenvalue/number of variables) $\times$ 100

32 R. Woods (1979) op. cit., table 3.10, p. 59

33 In 1970–72 e_0 for males in Social Class I was about 71 whilst that for males in Class V was 65 in 1921–23 the corresponding figures were probably 64 and 53, see R. Woods (1979) op. cit., table 3.12, p. 61

Chapter 3

1 *The Times*, 8 October 1868

2 Henry E. Sigerist, 'The history of medicine and the history of science', *Bulletin of the History of Medicine* 4 (1936), p. 6

3 George Rosen, 'Health, history and the social sciences', *Social Science and Medicine* 7 (1973), p. 7. It is not the intention of this section to enter the complexities of the concepts of health and disease and of illness behaviour. For an introduction to the literature and to its possible use in an historical framework see John Woodward and David Richards, 'Towards a social history of medicine', in John Woodward and David Richards (eds), *Health Care and Popular Medicine in Nineteenth-Century England* (London, 1977), pp. 15–55. The most recent history of public health is Anthony Wohl, *Endangered Lives: Public Health in Victorian Britain* (London, 1983)

4 See Chapters 1 and 2 for more detail and R. Woods and C. W. Smith, 'The control of marital fertility in the late nineteenth century: the case of England and Wales', *Population Studies* 37 (1983), pp. 207–25

5 The experience of individual age groups is dealt with in Figure 2.2 and in more detail by F. B. Smith, *The People's Health, 1830–1910* (London, 1979)

6 Period e_0s are shown in Figure 2.1

7 See especially T. McKeown, *The Modern Rise of Population* (London, 1976); also Chapter 1, especially Figures 1.4 and 1.5

8 M. W. Flinn et al., *Scottish Population History from the Seventeenth Century to the 1930s* (Cambridge, 1977)

9 P. E. Razzell, *The Conquest of Smallpox* (Firle, Sussex, 1977)

10 For an important discussion of the course of these diseases during the nineteenth century and the ideas surrounding then see George Rosen, 'Disease, debility and death', in H. J. Dyos and M. Wolff (eds), *The Victorian City* (London, 1973), pp. 625–67

11 D. J. Oddy, 'The health of the people', in T. C. Barker and M. Drake (eds), *Population and Society in Britain, 1850–1980* (London, 1982), pp. 121–39, especially tables 1, 2 and 3

12 See M. W. Beaver, 'Population, infant mortality and milk', *Population Studies* 27 (1973), pp. 243–54; Carol Dyhouse, 'Working-class mothers and infant mortality in England, 1895–1914', *Journal of Social History* 12 (1978), pp. 248–97, reprinted in, Charles Webster (ed), *Biology, Medicine and Society, 1840–1940* (Cambridge, 1981), pp. 73–98

13 N. D. Jewson, 'Medical knowledge and the patronage system in 18th century England', *Sociology* 8 (1974), p. 376

14 ibid., pp. 376–7

15 For a full discussion of the role of French medicine and the work in the Paris hospitals see Ivan Waddington, 'The role of the hospital in the development of modern medicine: a sociological analysis', *Sociology* 7 (1973), pp. 211–23

16 The modern National Health Service regards 1:2,000 as an ideal

17 Jeanne Peterson, *The Medical Profession in Mid-Victorian London* (Berkeley, 1978)

18 There are 5 new pence in an old shilling; 3 shillings is given by 3s. and 3s. 6d. means 3 shillings and 6 old pence ($17\frac{1}{2}$ new pence)

19 Sir Arthur Conan Doyle, *The Stark Munro Letters* (London, 1895)

20 For a further discussion of the piece-meal development of medical posts available through central and local government departments see David Richards, 'Medical men and the State, 1830–1920: Widening opportunities for State employment of the medical profession', in David Richards and John Woodward (eds), *Health Professions and the State in Modern Britain* (London, 1984)

21 On the eighteenth century see T. McKeown and R. G. Brown, 'Medical evidence related to English population changes in the eighteenth century', *Population Studies* 9 (1955), pp. 119–41, and for the nineteenth century, T. McKeown and R. G. Record, 'Reasons for the decline in mortality in England and Wales during the nineteenth century', *Population Studies* 16 (1962), pp. 94–122

22 These figures are derived from R. Pinker, *English Hospital Statistics, 1861–1938* (London, 1966). The history of the voluntary hospitals has been dealt with at some length in John Woodward, *To Do the Sick No Harm: A Study of the British Voluntary Hospital System to 1875* (London, 1974) and 'The British voluntary hospital movement—success or disaster?', *Annales Cisalpines d'Histoire Sociale*, Série 1, 4 (1973), pp. 233–54.

23 S. Cherry, 'The hospitals and population growth: The voluntary general hospitals, mortality and local populations in the English provinces in the eighteenth and nineteenth centuries', *Population Studies* 34 (1980), pp. 59–75 and 251–65, and 'The role of a provincial hospital: the Norfolk and Norwich Hospital, 1771–1880', *Population Studies* 26 (1972), pp. 291–306. On special hospitals, the London Fever Hospital for example, see W. F. Bynum, 'Hospital, disease and community: the London Fever Hospital, 1801–1850', in Charles E. Rosenberg (ed), *Healing and History: Essays for George Rosen* (New York, 1979) and on hospitals in general, B. Abel-Smith, *The Hospitals, 1800–1948* (London, 1964). Charles Webster, 'The crisis of the hospitals during the industrial revolution', in E. G. Forbes (ed), *Human Implications of Scientific Advance* (Edinburgh, 1978), pp. 214–22 provides a perceptive account of the problems faced by hospitals and medical care in general during the phase of rapid industrialization and urbanization. On asylums see, Andrew Scull, *Museums of Madness. The Social Organization of Insanity* (London, 1979) and for contemporary, yet far from parallel, developments in an American hospital system see, D. Rosner, *A Once Charitable Enterprise: Hospitals and Health Care in Brooklyn and New York, 1885–1915* (Cambridge, 1982)

24 E. M. Sigsworth, 'A provincial hospital in the early eighteenth and nineteenth centuries', *College of General Practitioners, Yorkshire Faculty Journal* (June, 1966), pp. 31–6, 'Gateways to death? Medicine, science and society, 1700–1850', in P. Mathias (ed), *Science and Society, 1600–1900* (London, 1972), pp. 97–110

25 Woodward (1973, 1974), op. cit., and, 'Before bacteriology-deaths in hospitals', *College of General Practitioners, Yorkshire Faculty Journal* (Autumn 1969), pp. 1–12

26 Woodward (1973), op. cit., p. 254

27 Woodward (1974), op. cit., p. 142

28 Cherry (1980) op. cit. The hospitals were Bristol Royal, Worcester General, Manchester Royal, Leeds General, Addenbrookes (Cambridge), Leicester Royal, and Norfolk and Norwich

29 Cherry (1980) op. cit., p. 265

30 David Hamilton, 'The nineteenth-century surgical revolution — antisepsis or better nutrition?', *Bulletin of the History of Medicine* 56 (1982), pp. 30–40; also, David Hamilton and Margaret Lamb, 'Surgeons and surgery', in Olive Checkland and Margaret Lamb (eds), *Health Care as Social History: The Glasgow Case* (Aberdeen, 1982), pp. 74–85

31 These changes should not be over-emphasized. Hamilton (1982) op. cit., p. 33 shows that there were on average 1,592 surgical operations carried out each year at the Glasgow Royal Infirmary in 1896–99; 403 in 1871–75; and only 188 in 1846–50. See Hamilton and Lamb (1982) op. cit., pp. 78–9 for an analysis of mortality from amputation of the leg or lower leg and from compound fractures of the leg which 'may have been affected by external causes'. The most sensible approach to these arguments, in the absence of strong evidence for substantial improvements in nutrition, would be to regard antisepsis and improving living conditions as complementary

32 Carolyn I. Pennington, 'Mortality and medical care in nineteenth-century Glasgow', *Medical History* 23 (1979), pp. 442–50, and, 'Tuberculosis', in Olive Checkland and Margaret Lamb (eds), *Health Care as Social History: The Glasgow Case* (Aberdeen, 1982), pp. 86–99

33 For a discussion of this shift in emphasis see, M. A. Crowther, *The Workhouse System, 1834–1929* (London, 1981)

34 See, for example, Woodward (1973, 1974) op. cit.

35 I. S. L. Loudon, 'The origins and growth of the dispensary movement in England', *Bulletin of the History of Medicine* 55 (1981), p. 322

36 I. S. L. Loudon, 'Historical importance of out-patients', *British Medical Journal* 1 (1978), pp. 974–77

37 M. Foucault, *The Birth of the Clinic* (London, 1973), p. 35

38 For a discussion of state intervention in health see, John Woodward, 'State intervention in health: from public health to personal well-being, 1830–1920', in Richards and Woodward (1984), op. cit.

39 T. McKeown, R. G. Record and R. D. Turner, 'An interpretation of the decline in mortality in England and Wales during the twentieth century', *Population Studies* 29 (1975), pp. 391–422 do not see matters quite in this light

40 Jeanne L. Brand, *Doctors and the State: The British Medical Profession and Government Action in Public Health, 1870–1912* (Baltimore, 1965), p. 165

41 For a critical analysis of these factors see, J. R. Hay, *The Origins of the Liberal Welfare Reforms, 1906–1914* (London, 1975), p. 27

42 B. Semmel, *Imperialism and Social Reform* (London, 1960), p. 246; see also G. R. Searle, *The Quest for National Efficiency* (Oxford, 1971)

43 Arnold White, *Efficiency and Empire* (London, 1901) claimed that 60 per cent of potential army recruits in Manchester in 1899 were physically unfit for active service. B. S. Rowntree, *Poverty: A Study of Town Life* (London, 1901), Charles Booth, *Life and Labour of the People in London* (17 vols) (London, 1902–04)

44 B. B. Gilbert, 'Health and politics: the British Physical Deterioration Report of 1904', *Bulletin of the History of Medicine* 39 (1965), pp. 143–53

45 Brand (1965) op. cit., p. 172. These advances were reinforced in 1905 with the appointment of the Royal Commission on the Poor Laws and the Relief of Distress. See the report on *Medical Relief* P.P. 1909, Cd. 4573, and, Sidney and Beatrice Webb, *English Poor Law Society* (London, 1910). On the general background to these health reforms see Sir George Newman, *The Building of a Nation's Health* (London, 1937)

46 See p. 44 above and Figure 2.2, also Chapter 6

47 See C. Hardyment, *Dream Babies: Child Care from Locke to Spock* (London, 1983) for a recent review also Edward Shorter, *A History of Women's Bodies* (London, 1983)

48 See Dyhouse (1978) op. cit. and, 'Good wives and little mothers: social anxieties and the schoolgirl's curriculum, 1890–1920', *Oxford Review of Education* 2 (1) (1977); also P. Branca, *Silent Sisterhood: Middle Class Women in the Victorian Home* (London, 1975); Anna Davin, 'Imperialism and motherhood', *History Workshop* 5 (1978), pp. 9–65; A. Oakley, 'Wise woman and medicine man: changes in the management of childbirth', in A. Oakley and J. Mitchell (eds), *The Rights and Wrongs of Women* (London, 1976). The decline in the birth rate from the 1860s and 1870s via family limitation probably helped to reduce infant mortality in the long-term, but see Figures 2.11 and 2.12 for the 1860s and Woods and Smith (1983) op. cit. See R. A. Soloway, *Birth Control and the Population Question in England, 1877–1930* (Chapel Hill, 1982) for a recent discussion of the background to the falling birth rate controversy

49 Jean Donnison, *Midwives and Medical Men* (London, 1977) and more recently, Edward Shorter, *A History of Women's Bodies* (London, 1983) trace developments in obstetrics and gynaecology during this period

50 See Newman (1937) op. cit. and his *Infant Mortality: A Social Problem* (London, 1906)

51 Sir George Newman, *An Outline of the Practice of Preventive Medicine* (London, 1919), p. 123

52 The author wishes to express his thanks to his fellow editor who came to his aid at a critical point in the writing of this chapter

Chapter 4

1 Arnold Rice Rich, *The Pathogenesis of Tuberculosis* (Oxford, 1951, 2 edn), pp. 56–61

2 Jay Arthur Myers with Paul A. Geissler, *Tuberculosis Among Children* (London, 1930), p. 151. Geissler remarks, 'More causes of surgical tuberculosis are reported as bovine in the younger children and this number steadily decreases as the age increases' (p. 102). See also John Bowes McDougall, *Tuberculosis: A Global Study in Social Pathology* (Edinburgh, 1949), pp. 376–82

3 *Lancet* 2 (17 September 1898), pp. 733–7

4 Study by J. B. Blacklock, cited in McDougall (1949) op. cit., p. 377

5 P. J. Atkins, 'The retail milk trade in London, c. 1740–1914', *Economic History Review*, 2nd Series 33 (1980), pp. 534–5

6 Godias J. Drolet, 'Epidemiology of tuberculosis', in Benjamin Goldberg (ed), *Clinical Tuberculosis*, vol. 1 (Philadelphia, 1935), p. A14

7 H. H. Scott, *Tuberculosis in Man and Lower Animals*, Medical Research Council, Special Report Series, No. 149 (London, 1930), p. 9

8 The relative degree of importance of natural and acquired resistance has been a matter of extensive, if inconclusive, debate. See, for example, Rich (1951) op. cit., and McDougall (1949) op. cit.

9 For example, Dr Robert Boyde, *Lancet* 1 (15 June 1844), p. 380; Sir Thomas Watson, *Lectures on the Principles and Practice of Physic*, vol. 2 (London, 1843), pp. 200–1 and fifth edition, vol. 2 (London, 1871), pp. 234–5; Dr Theophilus Thompson, *Lancet* 2 (22 November 1851), p. 480; Dr John Syer Bristowe, *A Treatise on the Theory and Practice of Medicine* (London, 1876), p. 442

10 For example, Dr H. Timbrell Bulstrode, *Lancet* 2 (8 August 1903), p. 363; Dr Arthur Latham, *Lancet* 2 (28 December 1901), p. 1781; Dr Arthur Newsholme, *Lancet* 1 (30 January 1904), p. 282

11 Another explanation, that there was a change in the nature of the disease itself, is very unlikely. As Thomas McKeown and R. G. Record, 'Reasons for the decline in mortality in England and Wales during the nineteenth century', *Population Studies* 16 (1962), p. 115, remark, '... there is reason to believe that there has been no significant variation in the tubercle bacillus'.

12 Rene Jules and Jean Dubos, *The White Plague: Tuberculosis, Man and Society* (London, 1953), Chapter xiii

13 In 1911, it was estimated that 5,500 beds were available for tuberculosis patients. Sir Arthur Newsholme, *International Studies on the Relation Between the Private and Official Practice of Medicine*, vol. III, Milbank Memorial Fund (New York, 1931), p. 219. According to my calculations, this would have been about a quarter the number of beds needed to allow each sufferer a period of treatment lasting one month. See G. Cronjé, *Tuberculosis in England and Wales 1851–1910: A Study of Social and Economic Conditions with Special Reference to Housing*, unpublished Ph.D. Thesis, University of London (forthcoming)

14 The following passages on the treatment of tuberculosis are based on opinions and reports published in the *Lancet* in the period 1840–1910. Medical textbooks, dictionaries and monographs of the period have also been used

15 For example, *Lancet* 2 (5 August 1854), p. 97. Bristowe (1876) op. cit.,

p. 444 comments that 'There is little doubt on the part of practical physicians, none on the part of the public of the great value' of cod-liver oil in the treatment of tuberculosis

16 The statistical information in this chapter is based on data contained in the *Annual Reports* and *Decennial Supplements* of the Registrar General of Births, Deaths and Marriages

17 The tuberculosis death rates have been age-standardized. This procedure involves an adjustment in the crude rates to allow for distortions caused by variations in sex and age structure. The calculation has been done for England and Wales for each decade, and for each of the 45 registration counties. This renders the death rates comparable spatially and over time (see Figure 2.3)

18 For example, Rich (1951) op. cit., p. 189

19 More details on urban and rural tuberculosis rates will be found in my thesis. The differences between tuberculosis death rates in urban and rural registration counties are discussed below, pp. 91–97. Spatial variation in the overall level of mortality are considered in Chapter 2

20 For a detailed discussion of this problem, see Gillian Burke and Peter Richardson, 'The profits of death: a comparative study of miners' phthisis in Cornwall and the Transvaal, 1876–1918', *Journal of South African Studies* 4 (1978), pp. 147–71

21 Registrar General's *Decennial Supplement*, 1891–1900, Part I, p. ix

22 To enable a consistent group of counties to be identified, Glamorgan and the rest of South Wales, which appear in the Registrar General's classification, have been excluded

23 For example, Registrar General's *Decennial Supplement*, 1881–90, Part I, p. xlii

24 John Burnett, *Plenty and Want: A Social History of Diet in England from 1815 to the Present Day* (London, 1968), pp. 202 and 318

25 Agricultural wages are used here to indicate general wage levels. The accuracy of this indicator must clearly have varied according to area. See E. H. Hunt, *Regional Wage Variations in Britain, 1850–1914* (London, 1973). He comments, '. . . farm labourers' earnings are probably the most useful single guide to wage levels in different parts of Britain' (p. 4)

26 In this decade, data are available for the 0–4 age group

27 B. R. Mitchell and Phyllis Deane, *Abstract of British Historical Statistics* (Cambridge, 1976), pp. 298 and 300. These are measures of value, not of volume. Mitchell and Deane, commenting on the inexactness of official statistics as volume indicators, nevertheless remark, 'For many purposes the official values provide a good enough guide to volume' (p. 277)

28 *Sixth Report of the Medical Officer of the Privy Council, 1863. Appendix No. 6: Report by Dr Edward Smith on the Food of the Poorer Labouring Classes in England*, British Parliamentary Papers, vol. XXVIII, 1864

29 Burnett (1968) op. cit., pp. 159–60, 161–2 and 185. Maud Pember Reeves, *Round About a Pound a Week* (London, 1979, reprint of 1913 edition), p. 97 and Chapter X

30 Tyneside Papers, No. 11, *Tuberculosis on Tyneside* (Newcastle-upon-Tyne, February 1928), p. 3

31 *Report to the Health Committee by the Medical Officer of Health on the Prevalence of Tuberculosis in South Shields* (South Shields, 1930), p. 10

32 See, for example, Maud Pember Reeves (1979) op. cit

33 Gareth Stedman Jones, *Outcast London: A Study in the Relationship Between Classes in Victorian Society* (London, 1971), pp. 174–8

34 A. Bradford Hill, 'The recent trend in England and Wales of mortality from phthisis at young adult ages', *Journal of the Royal Statistical Society* 49 (1936), pp. 264–7. McDougall (1949), op. cit., p. 168

35 Bradford Hill (1936) op. cit., pp. 271–8

36 John Saville, *Rural Depopulation in England and Wales, 1851–1951* (London, 1957), pp. 135–6 and on fertility variations see R. Woods and C. W. Smith, 'The decline of marital fertility in the late nineteenth century: the case of England and Wales', *Population Studies* 37 (1983), pp. 207–25

37 A statistical study of tuberculosis trends in the decades following the First World War stressed the influence of housing. See Philip Montagu D'Arcy Hart and George Payling Wright, *Tuberculosis and Social Conditions in England With Special Reference to Young Adults: A Statistical Study*, National Association for the Prevention of Tuberculosis (London, 1939)

38 The author wishes to express her thanks to Dr E. H. Hunt, Mr Walter Stern and W. G. Huff for their comments on an earlier draft of this chapter

Chapter 5

1 For a classic 'biography' of typhus by a great medical scientist see H. Zinsser, *Rats, Lice and History* (London, 1935). There is also valuable information in K. F. Helleiner, 'The population of Europe from the Black Death to the eve of the vital revolution', *Cambridge Economic History of Europe*, vol. IV (Cambridge, 1967), pp. 1–95; C. Creighton, *A History of Epidemics in Britain*, vol. 2 (London, 1965, revised edition); and J. D. Chambers, *Population, Economy and Society in Pre-Industrial England* (London, 1972). There is no comparable secondary work on typhoid but the reader can derive a basic framework from Creighton

2 M. W. Flinn, 'The stabilization of mortality in pre-industrial Europe', *Journal of European Economic History* 3 (1974), pp. 285–318; and, 'Plague in Europe and the Mediterranean countries', *Journal of European Economic History* 8 (1979), pp. 131–48

3 Michel Foucault dominates the historiography in this field. See, in particular, *The Birth of the Clinic: An Archaeology of Medical Perception* (London, 1973, trans. A. M. Sheridan). On asylums and prisons in Britain see A. Scull, *Museums of Madness: The Social Origins of Insanity in Nineteenth-Century England* (London, 1979) and M. Ignatieff, *A Just Measure of Pain: The Penitentiary in the Industrial Revolution, 1750–1850* (New York, 1978)

4 There are no systematic studies of the impact of typhoid on urban or rural communities during the late eighteenth and early nineteenth centuries. But one notorious 'closed community', Millbank Prison, was repeatedly afflicted during the early nineteenth century. For a full and revealing account see *Rivers Pollution Commissioners, 6th report: Domestic Water Supply of Great Britain*, P.P., 1874, (Cd. 1112), pp. 165–6 and 495

5 C. Creighton (1965) op. cit., p. 160 passim.

6 The demographic dimension is clearly set out in T. McKeown, *The Modern Rise of Population* (London, 1976). See also Chapter 1

7 Medical information on typhus has been drawn principally from E. S. Murphy, 'Typhus fever group', in P. D. Hoeprich (ed), *Infectious Diseases* (London, 1972), pp. 791–99 and J. C. Snyder, 'The typhus fevers', in T. M. Rivers (ed), *Vital and Rickettsial Infections of Man* (London, 1952, 2 edn), pp. 578–610

8 This estimate is based on E. W. Goodall, *A Short History of the Infectious Epidemic Diseases* (London, 1934), p. 88; *Fifth Annual Report of the Poor Law Commission*, 1839, P.P. (Cd. 239), Appendix C2, p. 113; *Minutes, Metropolitan Asylums Board*, 2 November 1872, pp. 408–9; and *Minutes, Association of Medical Officers of Health*, 19 March 1864. The epidemiological significance of the relative stability of the case fatality rate during this period is discussed on p. 115

9 Medical material on typhoid has been derived from F. S. Stewart, *Bigger's Handbook of Bacteriology* (London, 1962, 8 edn), pp. 328–50 and A. Patrick, *The Enteric Fevers* (London, 1955)

10 This estimate is based on data in the unnumbered pull-out tables in the *Annual Reports* of the Statistical Committee of the Metropolitan Asylums Board between 1890 and 1902; *Report of the Medical Officer of Health to the London County Council, 1910*, p. 44; and C. Murchison, *A Treatise on the Continued Fevers of Great Britain* (London, 1884, third edition by W. Cayley), p. 604. See also references to typhoid disease in Chapter 8

11 R. Thorne, *The Progress of Medicine During the Victorian Era, 1837–87* (London, 1888), p. 26

12 G. B. Longstaff, 'The seasonal prevalence of continued fever in London', *Transactions of the Epidemiological Society of London* (1884–5), p. 72, and Murchison (1873, 2 edn) op. cit., p. 682

13 J. N. Radcliffe, 'Reports on epidemics', *Transactions of the Epidemiological Society of London* (1863), p. 411 and C. Creighton (1965) op. cit., p. 201

14 Murchison (1884) op. cit., p. 52

15 *Minutes of Committees*, Metropolitan Asylums Board, 6 November 1869 and 23 April 1870

16 *Report of the MOH: Hackney 1864*, p. 13 and *idem, 1878*, p. 4; A. Hill, 'Diphtheria and typhoid and their concomitant conditions in Birmingham', *Transactions of the Society of Medical Officer of Health* (1879–80), p. 70 (MOH will be used for Medical Officer of Health)

17 *Report of the MOH: Shoreditch 1862*, p. 19; *Report of the MOH: Strand 1859*, p. 11; and *Report of the MOH: Holborn 1866*, pp. 53–4

18 M. Greenwood, *Epidemics and Crowd Diseases* (London, 1935), p. 158

19 Metropolitan Association of Medical Officers of Health, *Memorandum concerning the Present Prevalence of Typhus Fever in London*, 21 November 1863; *Report of the MOH: Whitechapel, First Quarter, 1862*, p. 5; *Report of the MOH: Shoreditch, 1862*, pp. 19–20

20 Creighton (1965) op. cit., p. 215

21 G. Rosen, 'Disease, debility, and death', in H. J. Dyos and M. Wolff (eds), *The Victorian City* (London, 1973), pp. 633–4; and, *A History of Public Health* (New York, 1958), pp. 339–40

22 T. McKeown and R. G. Record, 'Reasons for the decline of mortality in England and Wales during the nineteenth century', *Population Studies* 16 (1962), pp. 94–122. See also Chapter 1 and especially Figure 1.4

23 W. R. Baldwin-Wiseman, 'The increase in the national consumption of water', *Journal of the Royal Statistical Society* 122 (1909), pp. 282–90

24 ibid., p. 282

25 This calculation is based on data in *Rivers Pollution Commissioners, 6th Report: Domestic Water Supply of Great Britain*, P.P., 1874, (Cd. 1112), p. 622; *Report of Epidemic Cholera in England 1866*, P.P., 1867–8, (4072), Table 33 and p. 374; *Report of the General Board of Health on the Supply of Water to the Metropolis*, P.P., 1850 (1140), p. 6; and population statistics in the relevant *Annual* and *Supplementary Reports* of the Registrar General

26 *Royal Commission on the Water Supply of the Metropolis, 1893–4*, P.P., (Cd. 7172-II), p. 16; *Report of the Medical Officer of Health to the London County Council, 1892*, p. 42

27 For a comparative statement of the work completed at district level see *Metropolitan Sanitary and Street Improvements*, P.P., 1872 (298), pp. 585–654

28 There are trenchant comments on each of these epidemics in R. Lambert, *Sir John Simon, 1816–1904, and English Social Administration* (London, 1963), pp. 123–31, 202–8 and 377–80. On water transmission during the second half of the nineteenth century see W. Luckin, 'The final catastrophe: cholera in London, 1866', *Medical History* 21 (1977), pp. 32–42

29 An environmental process of this kind was perceptively identified by W. D. Scott-Moncrieff, 'River pollution: its ethics, aesthetics and hygiene', *Journal of the Royal Sanitary Institute* 30 (1909), pp. 165–72

30 The connexion between overcrowding and typhus was noted by numerous contemporary medical men. See, for example, *Report of the MOH: Bethnal Green, 1864*, p. 4; *Report of the MOH: St George-in-the-East, 1865*, p. 27; and idem, 1868, p. 19. The literature by historians emphasizing the 'crisis of the inner city' in the 1860s, and thereafter, includes G. Stedman Jones, *Outcast London* (London, 1971), Part 2; H. J. Dyos, 'Railways and housing in Victorian London', *Journal of Transport History* 2 (1955), pp. 11–21 and, 'Some social costs of railway building in London', *Journal of Transport History* 3 (1957–8), pp. 23–30. Housing indices have been authoritatively examined by A. S. Wohl in S. D. Chapman (ed), *The History of Working-Class Housing: A Symposium* (London, 1971), pp. 15–54 and *The Eternal Slum: Housing and Social Policy in Victorian London* (London, 1977)

31 *Minutes*, Metropolitan Association of Medical Officers of Health, 19 March 1864; *Report of the MOH: Whitechapel: Second Quarter, 1862*, p. 5; and idem, *Quarter ending 28th December 1867*, p. 8

32 S. B. Saul, *The Myth of the Great Depression* (London, 1969), pp. 30–4

33 See the cautious assessments of J. C. Snyder (1952), op. cit., p. 596; A. B. Appleby, 'Nutrition and disease: the case of London, 1550–1750', *Journal of Interdisciplinary History* 6 (1975), pp. 2 and 13; and T. McKeown, R. G. Brown and R. G. Record, 'An interpretation of the modern rise of population in Europe', *Population Studies* 26 (1972), p. 356

34 A means of testing such an association is available in the table of London bread prices compiled by B. R. Mitchell and P. Deane, *Abstract of British Historical Statistics* (Cambridge, 1962), pp. 497–8

35 The statistical material for Scotland requires separate consideration

36 I have attempted to summarize the position of those who argue in terms of 'autonomous' changes in the behaviour of the great historical infections in, 'Death and survival in the city: approaches to the history of disease', *Urban History Yearbook* (1980), pp. 53–63

37 See note 8 above

38 McKeown and Record (1962) op. cit., pp. 120–1

39 There is no evidence to suggest that there was any development of the milder, endemic Brill-Zinsser variant identified among immigrants to the United States. From a now large literature see the pioneering H. Zinsser, 'Varieties of typhus virus and the epidemiology of the American form of European typhus fever (Brill's disease)', *American Journal of Hygiene* 20 (1934), pp. 513–32

40 For a stimulating analysis of theoretically possible modifications for a different infection see A. B. Appleby, 'The disappearance of the plague', *Economic History Review*, 2nd Series, 33 (1980), pp. 161–73

41 On the general topic of typhus and migration see J. W. D. Megaw, 'Typhus fevers and other rickettsial fevers', in *The British Encyclopaedia of Medical Practice*, Vol. XII (London, 1952), p. 393. For London see *Report of the MOH: Mile End Old Town, 1861*, p. 6. For relatively high and continuing rates of migration from Ireland to the north-west and the north-east during this period see C. Creighton (1965) op. cit., pp. 215–17 and J. W. House, *North Eastern England: Population Movements and the Landscape since the Early Nineteenth Century* (London, 1954), pp. 51–62

42 B. Thomas, *Migration and Economic Growth: Great Britain and the Atlantic Economy* (Cambridge, 1954), p. 73

43 L. H. Lees, *Exiles of Erin: Irish Migrants in Victorian London* (Manchester, 1979), p. 47. Some of these arguments are also examined in the American context in R. Higgs, 'Cycles and trends in mortality in 18 large American cities, 1871–1900', *Explorations in Economic History* 16 (1979), pp. 381–408

44 The general epidemiological context has been meticulously described by M. Pelling, *Cholera, Fever and English Medicine, 1825–1865* (Oxford, 1978). Specific accounts of typhoid outbreaks are to be found in *Report of the MOH: Kensington, 1873*, pp. 69–70; *Report of the MOH: Hackney, 1882*, p. 6; and *Report of the MOH: St Pancras, 1891*, pp. 17–18

45 On milk transmission see G. P. Gladstone, 'Pathogenicity and virulence of microorganisms', in H. Florey (ed), *General Pathology* (London, 1970, 4 edn), p. 840, and J. Ritchie, 'Enteric fever', *British Medical Journal* 30 (2) (1937), p. 166. Important milk-borne epidemics in the capital are described in *Supplementary Report of the Medical Officer to the Privy Council and Local Government Board*, 1874, P.P., (Cd. 1066), Appendix 6; *Report of the MOH: St Pancras, 1883*, pp. 15–18; and *Report of the MOH: Islington, 1883*, pp. 54–6

46 See A. Newsholme, *Fifty Years in Public Health* (London, 1935), pp. 205–6; *Report of the MOH: Lambeth, 1894*, pp. 4–36; *Report of the MOH: Fulham, 1899*, pp. 18–19; and *Report of the MOH: St Pancras, 1900*, pp. 39–41

47 The discovery is usually attributed to Karl Wilhelm Drigalski in 1903. See C. Singer and E. A. Underwood, *A Short History of Medicine* (London, 1962, 2nd ed.), pp. 407–9

48 *Royal Commission on the Water Supply of the Metropolis*, 1893–4, P.P. (Cd. 7172–II), Appendix C 17, pp. 220 and 227

49 ibid., p. 224; Charles Booth, *Life and Labour of the People in London*, 17 Volumes (London, 1902–04)

50 For the continuing phenomenon of small-scale outbreaks in middle-class homes compare *Report of the MOH: Hackney, 1862*, pp. 13–14 and *Report of the MOH: St George, Hanover Square, 1890*, pp. 109–10

51 This figure has been computed from data contained in the tables of the *Annual Reports* of the Statistical Committee of the Metropolitan Asylums Board from 1890 to 1902. Aggregate statistics from this source have been checked against returns in the *Annual Reports* of the Registrar General

52 G. M. Ayers, *England's First State Hospitals and the Metropolitan Asylums Board, 1867–1930* (London, 1971), pp. 89–90

53 The case rate per thousand of population in London declined from 0.78 in 1891–95 to 0.52 in 1901–05. See S. Davies, 'Twenty years advance in preventive medicine', *Public Health* 21 (1908), p. 116. For a similar interpretation see G. M. Ayers (1971) op. cit., p. 106. See also Chapter 2

54 *Report of the MOH: St Giles, 1898–9*, pp. 101–4. On occasion, however, vestries could be penny-pinching in their attitude towards this novel institution. See *St Luke Vestry: Annual Report, 1899*, p. 63

55 Frankland was repeatedly assailed by a group of chemists and public health specialists, who were generally sympathetic towards the water companies, and who disagreed with his methodology for assessing the safety or otherwise of drinking water. The most persistent protagonists were Henry Letheby, J. A. Wanklyn and C. M. Tidy. From a wide-ranging and important literature see *Royal Commission on Water Supply, Minutes of Evidence*, 1868–9, P.P. (4169), qs. 5418–22; *Select Committee on Metropolitan Water Supply (No. 2)*, 1871, P.P. (381), q. 1,277; and *Minutes* of the Metropolitan Association of Medical Officers of Health, 18 January 1878

56 See, for example, his 'over-cautious' evidence to the *Royal Commission on Water Supply. Minutes of Evidence*, 1868–9, P.P. (4169), q. 6,401 and

6,418 and *Rivers Pollution Commission: 6th Report: The Domestic Water Supply of Great Britain*, 1874, P.P. (Cd. 1112), p. 768

57 On the influence of the Metropolitan Association of Medical Officers of Health see *Public Health: Jubilee Number* (1906) and A. S. Wohl, 'Unfit for human habitation', in H. J. Dyos and M. Wolff (eds) (1973) op. cit., pp. 603–24

58 One informal means of contact may have been the 'X' Club of which Frankland was a prominent member. See R. M. MacLeod, 'The X-Club: a social network of science in Victorian England', *Notes and Records of the Royal Society* 24 (1970), pp. 305–22 and J. Vernon Jensen, 'The X-Club: fraternity of Victorian scientists', *British Journal for the History of Science* 5 (1970–1), pp. 63–72. The pivotal importance of William Farr has recently been explored in J. M. Eyler, *Victorian Social Medicine: The Ideas and Methods of William Farr* (Baltimore, 1979)

59 The author wishes to thank Professor Christopher Wilcox of Harvard University for his advice and criticism on an earlier draft of this chapter

Chapter 6

1 Dr J. Buchan, *Annual Report of the Medical Officer of Health, 1919* (Bradford, 1920), p. 5

2 C. Richardson, *A Geography of Bradford* (University of Bradford, Bradford, 1976), p. 1

3 *Diary of Dr John Simpson*, Manuscript in the Archive Collection, Bradford Central Library (B.C.L.). Dr Simpson was one of the founders of the Bradford Dispensary and an entry in his diary for 1825 contains a complaint that the price of land in Darley Street (where the new Dispensary was to be built) had risen from five shillings a year in 1821, to 21 shillings a year by 1825

4 Robert Baker, *The Present Condition of the Working Classes* (Bradford, 1851), p. 43. (Pamphlet in B.C.L. Dickons Collection, JND 197)

5 George Weerth, *Collected works*, 3 vols (Bruno Kaiser, Berlin, 1956) unpub. *Selected Extracts* trans. A. Farmer, 1976, vol. 3, p. 164. (typescript in B.C.L.)

6 William Cudworth, *Historical Notes on the Bradford Corporation* (Thos Brear, Bradford, 1881), pp. 13–14

7 PP. 1842 XXVI (House of Lords) *Report on the Sanitary Condition of the Labouring Population of Great Britain*, later known as the Chadwick Report, Reprint Edinburgh, 1965, with introduction by M. Flinn, p. 263. The information on Bradford was supplied to Chadwick by Robert Baker

8 PP. 1839 to 1859, *Annual Reports* of the Registrars' General, in the early 1840s infant mortality in the registration district of Bradford, ranged from 177 to 200 per thousand births, between 1850 and 1859 it averaged 200

9 J. A. Cooper, *The Corporation Question* (John Dale, Bradford, 1845), p. 15 (copy in B.C.L.) See also A. Elliott, *Establishment of Municipal Government in Bradford*, unpub. Ph.D. thesis, University of Bradford, 1976

10 PP. 1845 XVIII *Second Report of the Commissioners Inquiring Into the State of Large Towns and Populous Districts*, Appendix Part 2, reprinted by I.U.P., *Health of Towns* (vol. 6), pp. 314–16, *Report on the Condition of the Town of Bradford*, James Smith of Deanston, 1845. See also evidence to the Select Committee on the Health of Towns, PP. 1840, vol. XI, evidence of Joseph Ellison of Bradford, pub. in *Bradford Observer* 7 May 1840

11 Facsimile of this return supplied by Mr J. Reynolds, of the University of Bradford, to whom I am indebted for his untiring assistance

12 *Report of the Bradford Sanitary Committee* (Bradford, 1845), pp. 3–6, Hailstone Collection, York Minster Library (copy available B.C.L.)

13 George White, *Drunkenness, Its Causes and Remedy, A Rhyme* (E. Smith, Bradford, 1860) (copy in B.C.L. Empsall Box 1–64)

14 *Leeds Mercury* 9 June 1830

15 Weerth (1956) op. cit., vol. 2, trans. Farmer p. 17, also *Bradford Observer* 27 July 1843. John Simon, PP. 1868–9 XXXII *Eleventh Report of the Medical Officer to the Privy Council*, p. 15, thought the amount of venereal disease amongst the working classes to be vastly over-estimated

16 *Bradford Observer* 14 September 1837; 12 October 1837, The sexton considered that only those babies who had been baptised required an official burial

17 *Bradford Observer* 12 October 1837; 19 October 1837

18 *Bradford Observer* 26 January 1837; 19 October 1865; 9 June 1866, see also C. Duanne, 'Infanticide: the Worth of an Infant', *Medical History* 22 (1978), pp. 1–24

19 J. Netten Radcliffe, 'Report on certain defects in the sanitary administration of Bradford (Yorkshire) and on the prevalence in the borough of enteric fever and other diarrhoeal diseases', 17 July 1872, in *Harvester Reprints of Reports to the Local Government Board, 1869–1908* (Copy in B.C.L.), pp. 3–4

20 J. Simon, *Papers Relating to the Sanitary State of the People of England* (London, 1858), p. xl

21 Bob West, *Worstedopolis and the Waterworks*, unpub. B.A. dissertation, University of Bradford, 1980. (Typescript in B.C.L.)

22 *Bradford Observer* 24 March 1864

23 *Bradford Observer* 17 February 1859

24 Correspondence between Bradford Town Council and the Local Government Act Office, PRO MH13/28.292758. Owners denied the acceptance of rent for cellar dwellings as separate properties, tenants declared that the cellars were part of a shared house

25 Chadwick (1965) op. cit., p. 422

26 PP 1866 *Eighth Report of the Medical Officer to the Privy Council*, Appendix II, H. J. Hunter, 'On the housing of the poorer part of the population in towns'

27 *Bradford Observer* 1 June 1854 for activities of the Woolcombers' Aid Society, in *Bradford Observer* 15 June 1854 it was estimated that only about

3,000 of the original 10,000 plus woolcombers were still practising their craft in Bradford

28 *Bradford Observer* 13 October 1859 contains a very full report of the proceedings and transcripts of many of the papers presented to the Conference

29 W. Hudson, *The Health of Bradford* (Bradford, 1859), p. 15 (copy in B.C.L.)

30 William Farr Esq. MD, FRS, DCL, 'Letter to the Registrar General on the mortality in the Registration Districts of England during the years 1861 to 1870' in C1155–11, PP. 1875 vol. XVIII *Decennial Supplement* to the *Reports of the Registrar General*, p. 16. Farr was also worried that the survival of 'weakly' individuals who lived to 'marry and propagate' would lead to a progressive degeneration of the population

31 *The Lancet* 17 October 1864

32 Anna Davin, 'Imperialism and motherhood', *History Workshop* 5 (1978), pp. 9–65

33 Dr J. H. Bridges, *Health with Remarks on the Death Rate in Bradford and Other Towns, a Lecture*, 17 November 1862 (James Hanson, Bradford, 1862), pp. 7–8. Bridges did not, however, place the responsibility on mothers but on the organisation of society, and on 'the industrial system' which made such maternal employment necessary, pp. 28–32

34 J. H. Bridges and T. Holmes, 'On the death of women, children and young persons engaged in textile manufactures with special reference to hours and ages of employment', PP 1873 LV I.U.P. *Industrial Revolution Factories*, vol. 28, pp. 47–78. For reaction to the report's findings see *The Lancet* 14 June 1873

35 Simon (1858) op. cit., p. XL

36 E. H. Greenhow, 'Reports on the prevalence and causes of diarrhoea at various towns', PP XXLX 1860 *Second Report of the Medical Officer to the Privy Council*; also E. H. Greenhow, 'On the circumstances under which there is an excessive mortality of young children in certain manufacturing populations', PP. XXLL, 1862, *Fourth Report of the Medical Officer to the Privy Council*

37 R. J. Hunter (1866) op. cit.

38 Netten Radcliffe (1972) op. cit., p. 2

39 Sanitary Committee of the Borough of Bradford, *Analysis of Infant Mortality in the Borough During the Month of January, 1872* (M. Field, Bradford, 1872) (copy in B.C.L.)

40 Netten Radcliffe (1972) op. cit., p. 6

41 ibid. p. 2

42 ibid. p. 6

43 ibid. p. 5

44 *Bradford Observer* 19 August 1872, for other comments on the Report see *The Lancet* 7 September 1872

45 Dr Harris Butterfield, *Annual Report of the Medical Officer of Health for 1881* (Bradford, 1882) shows that of the 26 deaths from typhoid in Bradford in 1881, 31 per cent took place in institutions; 27 per cent in lower middle-class streets; 25 per cent in select middle-class streets; and 19 per cent in working-class streets, but probably more of the institutional deaths originated in these areas

46 Netten Radcliffe (1872) op. cit., p. 5

47 *Report of the Street and Drainage Committee*, in *Reports of Committees to Council* (Bradford, 1853), p. 8

48 The Pamphlet Collection at B.C.L. contains the text of a lecture to the Bradford Sanitary Association, just after its formation in 1881, by Fleming Jenkin Esq. FRS, Professor of Engineering at the University of Edinburgh, in which he stressed the responsibility of the individual for ensuring that polluted and unpolluted water were strictly segregated whilst on his property, and gave a detailed and accurate account of the way in which typhoid could be passed on from one infected individual by means of the water supply

49 For details of this, and of other problems connected with the sewerage, see *Bradford Sewage Disposal: The Esholt Scheme* (Town Council of Bradford, 1922)

50 *Bradford Observer* 4 November 1858; 11 November 1858; *The Lancet* 1 (1859), p. 151

51 *Report of the Borough Analyst*, *Reports of Committees to Council* (Bradford, 1874), p. 25; see also F. W. Richardson, 'Adulteration ancient and modern', in *Proofs of Papers to the 21st Congress of the Sanitary Institute*, held at Bradford 7–11 July 1903 (copies in B.C.L.)

52 Dr McClintock, *Annual Report of the Medical Officer of Health for 1888* (Bradford, 1889), p. 29

53 *Annual Reports of the Bradford Infirmary*, 1868–1900, give the average cost of keeping a patient in food and other necessaries per day, for each of these years; from this I have compiled an index of changes in the level of prices which, taking 1868 as 100, rose to a peak of 132 in 1873, but after that fell off rapidly to 93 by 1881. and 70, the lowest point, by 1887. Other sources confirm this trend

54 *Bradford Observer* 15 March 1879; 12 April 1879; 26 April 1879; see also D. F. Garne, *Radical City in a Liberal Age*, unpub. M.Sc. thesis, University of Bradford, 1976

55 Joseph Bennett and John Baldwin, *City of Bradford Co-operative Society Ltd, Jubilee History, 1860 to 1910* (Wm Byles & Son, Bradford, 1911), p. 152; profits had risen from £33 2s. 5d. in 1860, to £14,018 17s. 8d. by 1885; membership from 201 to 6952; dividend at the end of the 1890s was around 3 shillings in the pound

56 ibid. p. 152; see also *Bradford Observer* 31 January 1885

57 *Annual Report of the Bradford Friendly Societies Medical Aid Association*, for year ending 31 December 1888; the association was formed in 1873 and by 1888 had 3,380 members, subscriptions were one penny per week, only about 10 per cent were family members. (Pamphlet 91–96 B.C.L.)

58 Bradford Fever Hospital was opened 2 March 1872, as a charity, and taken over by the Bradford Town Council in August 1887. During the 1880s when over half of all cases of scarlet fever were admitted to the hospital the case fatality rate was much lower for hospital-treated than for home-treated cases; probably as a result of the more adequate food and nursing because the treatments were unlikely to have been effective

59 W. Arnold Evans, MD, 'Back-to-back houses', *Transactions of the Epidemiological Society of London*, New Series 16 (1896), pp. 87–99. The building of back-to-backs went on in Bradford until 1894. Evans was M.O.H. for Bradford

60 *Report of the Streets and Drainage Committee, in Reports of Committees to Council* (Bradford, 1853), p. 9; see also M. J.Mortimore, 'Landownership and urban growth in Bradford and its environs in the W. Riding conurbation, 1850–1950', *Transactions, Institute of British Geographers* 46 (1969), pp. 105–19

61 *Bradford Observer* 16 February 1854; 16 March 1854; for debates on the building bye-laws and comments of councillors

62 Karl Marx, *Das Kapital* (4 edn ed. F. Engels, 1891), pp. 662–79, the sources Marx was using were the evidence of Dr Bell of Bradford to the Hunter inquiry of 1866, and the *Hunter Report* itself, and refers to the worst areas in Bradford; Engels had visited Bradford in the 1840s and been unfavourably impressed; for more information on the Irish in Bradford see C. Richardson, 'The Irish in Victorian Bradford', *Bradford Antiquary* 11, pp. 294–316

63 The plans for houses built in Bradford after 1850 are in the Archives Department of the B.C.L.

64 *Bradford Observer Budget* 14 and 21 July 1888, see also Evans (1896) op. cit. for comments on 'superior' back-to-backs

65 Dr McClintock, *Annual Report of the Medical Officer of Health, for 1888* (Bradford, 1889), pp. 30–31; *Report of the Waterworks Committee, Reports of Committees to Council* (Bradford, 1892)

66 A. Newsholme, *Fifty-Years in Public Health* (London, 1935), pp. 321–46 contains a discussion of the problems which resulted in high infant mortality during the nineteenth century, and the gradual awakening of those in authority as to the social and economic factors involved. Newsholme came from Haworth, near Bradford, and began his medical career in Bradford, before going on to eventually becoming Medical Officer to the Local Government Board in 1908

67 *Report of the Waterworks Committee, Reports of Committees to Council* (Bradford, 1900), p. 165; there were only 16,552 water closets in Bradford at that date, not all of them in private houses, at the *Population Census* of 1901, there were in 64,616 houses

68 *Report of the Female Sanitary Inspector* (Bradford, 1901), p. 3

69 Dr Butterfield, *Annual Report of the Medical Officer of Health for 1878* (Bradford, 1879); also cited in Evans (1896) op. cit. p. 98; and *Bradford Observer Budget* 28 July 1888

70 Evans (1896) op. cit., p. 98

71 Garne (1976) op. cit., pp. 253–75; also *Reports of the Sanitary Committee, Reports of Committees to Council* (Bradford, 1891–99); the contract system was finally ended on 15 July 1898

72 Richardson (1976) op. cit., p. 12; the range of altitudes between highest and lowest parts of Bradford was 900 ft, temperatures could vary up to three degrees

73 *Sanitary Record*, 23 July 1903. The writer had been a delegate to the Congress of the Sanitary Institute held at Bradford 7–11 July 1903

74 *Bradford Observer Budget* June–July 1888 contained details of the dismissal

75 *Reports of the Waterworks Committee, Reports of Committees to Council* (Bradford, 1875 to 1900)

76 *The Lancet* 4 September to 20 November 1886 provides one example of this type of controversy, see also Ann E. Roberts, *Feeding and Mortality in the Early Months of Life: Changes in Medical Opinion and Popular Practice, 1850–1900*, unpub. Ph.D. thesis, University of Hull, 1973

77 *Medical Inspector Reports* to the Local Government Board, P.R.O. MH32–107, *Local and National Reports on the Feeding of Infants in Poor Law Institutions*

78 *The Lancet* 21 March 1874; also *Annual Report of the Medical Officer of Health for 1875* (Bradford, 1876), p. 9, Dr Butterfield considered that 'it was to be marvelled at that so many survive than that so large a number die'

79 *Reports of the Female Sanitary Inspectors* (Bradford, March 1908), p. 5

80 *ibid.*, March 1905, p. 6

81 Illegitimacy in 1892: Exchange ward 10.9 per cent of births; Allerton ward 1.9 per cent; borough 5.5 per cent. The illegitimate birth rate fell even faster than the legitimate birth rate in Bradford between 1881 and 1901

82 D. Ross, *Bradford Politics, 1880–1906*, unpub. Ph.D. thesis, University of Bradford, 1977, p. 10

83 *Bradford Poor Law Union Year Book* (Bradford, 1899) standing orders were that outdoor relief was not to be given to the mothers of illegitimate children, whether or not they were married; nor to deserted wives; and to widows only where 'character (will) bear the strictest investigation' and on certain conditions

84 'The Nest', *Annual Reports*, 1886 and 1905 (pamphlet collection B.C.L. Fed. 194-1-235) also Joanna Scott, *Bradford Women: An Organization*, unpub. M.Sc. thesis, University of Bradford, 1970

85 In the *Population Census* of 1901, 18 per cent of all ever-married women (including widows) were recorded as in paid employment, only a proportion of these would be mothers of young children

86 G. A. Gaskell, *Social Control of the Birth Rate and the Endowment of Mothers* (London, 1890) discusses the need for family limitation amongst working-class families and the means available to them. Gaskell was a Bradford man, who in the 1870s campaigned in the town on behalf of the Malthusian League, and found that he was well received in many homes, and in some that his message had preceded him. Table 6.5 shows the decline in the child-woman ratio between 1871–80 and 1891–1900 in Bradford. D. V. Glass, *Population Movements in England and Wales* (London, 1940, reprinted 1967), p. 37

87 Respiratory deaths in 1900; Bradford, 3.95 per thousand population; England and Wales, 2.74 per thousand

88 Bradford Council for Social Service, *The Texture of Welfare* (P. S. King & Son, London, 1923), p. 32

89 *Reports of the Female Sanitary Inspectors* (Bradford, March 1905), p. 4

90 The minimum penalty for smoke control offences was raised from 10 shilling to £5 for a first offence in 1903, for a third offence the new penalty was £50; by 1913 73 per cent of houses in Bradford had the use of a water closet, either 'tippler' or 'flush'

91 The following infant mortality rates $(1,000q_0)$ were recorded in Bradford before and after the First World War: 1906–10, exclusive wards—102, central wards—192. 1926–30, exclusive wards—72, central wards—124

Chapter 7

1 See for example R. Vaughan, *The Age of Great Cities* (1843, Irish University Press, Shannon, 1972 edn)

2 Reviewed annually in the *Urban History Year Book* pub. by Leicester University Press. See also J. H. Johnson and C. G. Pooley (eds), *The Structure of Nineteenth-Century Cities* (London, 1982), pp. 3–35

3 For example, T. McKeown, *The Modern Rise of Population* (London, 1976); H. J. Habakkuk, 'English population in the eighteenth century', *Economic History Review*, 2nd Series 6 (1953), pp. 117–33; J. Woodward, *To Do the Sick No Harm: A Study of the British Voluntary Hospital System to 1875* (London, 1974); P. E. Razzell, 'An interpretation of the modern rise of population in Europe: a critique', *Population Studies*, 28 (1974), pp. 5–18

4 R. J. Morris, *Cholera, 1832* (London, 1976); M. Durey, *The Return of the Plague: British Society and the Cholera, 1831–2* (Dublin, 1979); W. Luckin, 'The final catastrophe: cholera in London, 1866', *Medical History* 21 (1977), pp. 32–42

5 For example, W. M. Frazer, *A History of English Public Health* (London, 1950); R. Lambert, *Sir John Simon, 1816–1904, and English Social Administration* (London, 1963); R. A. Lewis, *Edwin Chadwick and the Public Health Movement* (London, 1952); A. S. Wohl, *The Eternal Slum* (London, 1977); E. P. Hennock, *Fit and Proper Persons: Ideal and Reality in Nineteenth-Century Government* (London, 1973); M. Pelling, *Cholera, Fever and English Medicine, 1825–65* (Oxford, 1978)

6 But see R. Lawton, 'Population trends in England and Wales in the later nineteenth century: an analysis of trends by registration district', *Transactions, Institute of British Geographers* 44 (1968), pp. 55–74; G. M. Howe, *Man. Environment and Disease in Britain* (Newton Abbot, 1972); and Chapter 2

7 L. Chevalier, *Labouring Classes and Dangerous Classes in Paris during the First Half of the Nineteenth Century* (London, 1973); I. C. Taylor, '*Black spot on the Mersey': Environment and Society in Eighteenth- and Nineteenth-Century Liverpool*, unpub. Ph.D. thesis, University of Liverpool, 1976. See also Chapter 8 on Birmingham

8 See A. Sutcliffe, 'The growth of public intervention in the British urban environment during the nineteenth century: a structural approach', in Johnson and Pooley (eds) (1982) op. cit., pp. 107–24

9 G. Rosen, 'Social variables and health in an urban environment: the case of the Victorian city', *Clio Medica* 8 (1973), pp. 1–17. See also Chapter 1

10 For example, see J. G. Kohl, *England and Wales* (1844, Cass, London, 1968 edn), pp. 106–7. For a summary of such views see A. Briggs, *Victorian Cities* (London, 1963), pp. 88–138

11 F. Engels, *The Condition of the Working Class in England* (1845, Panther, London, 1969 edn); S. Marcus, *Engels, Manchester and the Working Class* (London, 1974)

12 The Registrar General's *Annual Reports* and contemporary comments stress throughout the nineteenth and early-twentieth centuries that only Liverpool rivalled Manchester and Salford's appalling urban health record. For example, *Seventh Annual Report of the Registrar General for 1843 and 1844* (London, 1846), p. 329; *Twenty-Ninth Annual Report of the Registrar General for 1866*, PP. 1867–8, XIX, p. xxxvii

13 J. Werly, 'The Irish in Manchester', *Irish Historical Studies* 18 (1973), pp. 345–58; D. Noble, 'On certain fallacies concerning the production of epidemic disease', *Transactions of the Manchester Statistical Society* (1859–60), p. 10; 'State of the Irish poor in Manchester', in the *First Report of the Commission on the Condition of the Poor in Ireland*, PP 1836, XXXIV, Appendix GIII, pp. 54–7. This point is also considered in Chapter 5 for London

14 For further information on working-class housing conditions in Manchester see C. W. Chalklin, *The Provincial Towns of Georgian England* (London, 1974), pp. 89–98; T. R. Marr, *Housing Conditions in Manchester and Salford* (Manchester, 1904); but contemporary parliamentary reports provide the most graphic descriptions of living conditions

15 For information on the cotton textile industry and employment, see D. A. Farnie, *The English Cotton Industry and the World Market, 1815–1896* (Oxford, 1979); useful wage statistics are found in D. Chadwick, 'On the rate of wages in Manchester, Salford and Lancashire, 1839–59', *Journal of the Statistical Society* 23 (1860), pp. 1–36; and in R. Montgomery, 'A comparison of some of the social and economic conditions of Manchester in 1834 and 1884', *Transactions of the Manchester Statistical Society* (1884–5), pp. 1–30

16 In Manchester 47.2 per cent of adult females were in employment in 1851 compared to only 36 per cent in Liverpool

17 G. Rosen, 'Disease, debility, and death', in H. J. Dyos and M. Wolff (eds), *The Victorian City* (London, 1973), pp. 625–67

18 W. Brockbank, *The Honorary Medical Staff of Manchester Royal Infirmary*

(Manchester, 1965); R. Kargon, *Science in Victorian Manchester: Enterprise and Expertise* (Manchester, 1977)

19 G. Rosen, 'Historical trends and future prospects in public health', in G. McLachlan and T. McKeown (eds), *Medical History and Medical Care: A Symposium of Perspectives* (Oxford, 1971), p. 65

20 E. Chadwick, *Report on the Sanitary Condition of the Labouring Population of Great Britain* (1842, Edinburgh University Press, Edinburgh, 1965 edn); Engels (1845 and 1969) op. cit.; J. P. Kay-Shuttleworth, *The Moral and Physical Condition of the Working Classes Employed in the Cotton Manufacture in Manchester* (1832, Cass, London, 1970 edn)

21 *Fifth Report of the Medical Officer of the Privy Council*, PP. 1863 XXV pp. 299–399; C. Booth, *Life and Labour of the People in London* (London, 1902–4); B. S. Rowntree, *Poverty: A Study of Town Life* (London, 1902)

22 For information on the use of parish registers and Bills of Mortality, see J. T. Krause, 'The changing adequacy of English registration, 1600–1837', in D. V. Glass and D. E. C. Eversley (eds), *Population in History* (London, 1965), pp. 379–93; R. A. P. Finlay, *Parish Registers: An Introduction* (Geo Abstracts, Norwich, 1981); E. A. Wrigley and R. S. Schofield, *The Population History of England, 1541–1871: A Reconstruction* (London, 1981)

23 Detailed descriptions of Registrar General's data may be found in D. V. Glass, *Numbering the People: The Eighteenth-Century Population Controversy and the Development of Census and Vital Statistics in Britain* (Farnborough, 1973), pp. 118–205. See also Chapter 2

24 F. B. Smith, *The People's Health, 1830–1910* (London, 1979), p. 67

25 T. McKeown, *The Modern Rise of Population* (London, 1976), p. 53

26 For a discussion of the methods of classification of causes of death used by the Registrar General, see J. M. Eyler, *Victorian Social Medicine* (Baltimore, 1979), pp. 37–65. See Chapter 5

27 The work of Local Boards of Health in the Manchester area is summarized in E. C. Midwinter, *Social Administration in Lancashire, 1830–60* (Manchester, 1969), pp. 63–119

28 Salford Borough paid a fee to a Poor Law medical officer to do nuisance work for the Borough in the 1850s, but no medical officer of health was appointed until nearly twenty years later. Similarly, few of the Local Boards of Health in the Manchester area appointed medical officers until such appointments became compulsory under the 1872 Public Health Act in the newly-created Sanitary Districts. C. F. Brockington, *Public Health in the Nineteenth Century* (Edinburgh and London, 1965), p. 145; Midwinter (1969) op. cit., p. 91

29 During the period 1861–70, the Association analysed data relating to more than 700,000 cases of disease at public institutions in Manchester and Salford. For an account of their role in public health reform, see P. A. Ryan, *Public Health and Voluntary Effort in Nineteenth-Century Manchester, with particular reference to the Manchester and Salford Sanitary Association,* unpub. M.A. thesis, University of Manchester, 1974

30 E. A. Wrigley (ed), *Nineteenth-Century Society* (Cambridge, 1972); R. Lawton (ed), *The Census and Social Structure* (London, 1978)

31 The average annual age-specific mortality rates of each decade were used to calculate the numbers of deaths there would be if the population age structure and size in each decade were the same as that in the model decade, in this case 1891–1900. The standardized mortality rate per thousand population derived from this hypothetical number of deaths allows the influence of an ageing population structure on changing death rates to be discounted

32 Noble (1859–60) loc. cit.; *Tenth Annual Report of the Registrar General for 1847* (London, 1852), pp. xx–xxii; Registrars' notes for quarter ending September 30th, 1849, *Twelfth Annual Report of the Registrar General for 1849* (London, 1853), pp. 82–3

33 The calculation involves the use of a hypothetical population of one million, distributed by age as the Manchester area population of the decade 1891–1900. Using actual age-specific mortality rates for the decades 1851–1900, the number of deaths which would occur in each age group in each decade are calculated, and for each age-group the difference between the two decadal figures is expressed as a percentage of the total mortality change between 1851–60 and 1891–1900. After T. McKeown and R. G. Record, 'Reasons for the decline of mortality in England and Wales during the nineteenth-century', *Population Studies* 16 (1962), p. 101

34 For a summary of the epidemiology of tuberculosis and other diseases prominent in the nineteenth century, see Rosen (1973), op. cit.; a fuller treatment of the subject is given in T. McKeown (1976) op. cit., pp. 73–90 and 110–42. See also Chapter 4

35 *Papers relating to the Sanitary State of the People of England* PP 1857–8, XXIII, p. 78

36 For further discussion, see McKeown and Record (1962) op. cit., pp. 107–16; and T. McKeown, 'Fertility, mortality and causes of death: an examination of issues related to the modern rise of population', *Population Studies* 32 (1978), p. 540

37 For a discussion of the increasing differentiation during the nineteenth century of typhoid from typhus and relapsing fever, see Rosen (1973) op. cit., pp. 629–41 and Chapter 5

38 Beaver has concluded that a safe milk supply, available at a price from about 1900, was a major factor in the national reduction of infant mortality in the early twentieth century, as many disease pathogens thrive in milk. In Salford in 1904, the infant mortality rate per 1,000 live births varied from 128.6 among breast-fed children to 263.9 among those fed on cows' milk and 439.0 among those fed on other foods including condensed milk: this suggests that the quality of the milk supply and its subsequent handling were still causing major problems for child health. M. W. Beaver, 'Population, infant mortality and milk', *Population Studies* 27 (1973), pp. 243–54; M. Hewitt, *Wives and Mothers in Victorian Industry* (London, 1975), Appendix III; D. J. Oddy and D. S. Miller (eds), *The Making of the Modern British Diet* (London, 1976), pp. 125–7. The case of Bradford is considered in Chapter 6

39 Smith (1979) op. cit., p. 150

40 Kay-Shuttleworth (1832 and 1970) op. cit., E. Chadwick (1842 and 1965) op. cit., Engels (1845 and 1969) op. cit.; but local doctors like Thomas Percival were aware of the town's unhealthiness more than fifty years earlier. T. Percival, 'Observations on the state of population in Manchester' (1974, reprinted with an introduction by B. Benjamin, in *Population and Disease in Early Industrial England*, Gregg International, London, 1973)

41 For example, J. Roberton, 'Report on the amount and causes of death in Manchester', in *Second Report of the Commission on the State of Large Towns and Populous Districts*, P.P. 1845, XVIII, pp. 106–16; *Reports of the Officer of Health for Manchester* (Manchester Central Library); D. Chadwick, 'On the best means of recording the vital statistics of towns', *Transactions of the Manchester Statistical Society* (1860–1), pp. 70–81; and *Annual Reports* and *Decennial Summaries* of the Registrar General

42 Rosen (1973) op. cit., pp. 651–2; Smith (1979) op. cit., pp. 137–41

43 For example, a correlation of +0.87 was obtained between four major infectious diseases ('fever', scarlet fever, measles and smallpox) and the crude mortality rate of townships in the Manchester area, 1854–8; similarly, for the decade 1871–80, a correlation of +0.80 was obtained between mortality from five infectious diseases (as above, plus whooping cough) and crude mortality from all causes in the sub-districts and townships of Manchester Borough

44 Data are calculated from the summary pages of the census enumerators' books for Manchester, Salford and Chorlton registration districts

45 For contemporary descriptions of inner-city housing conditions, see Engels (1845 and 1869) op. cit. and Chadwick (1842 and 1965), op. cit.; on suburban development, see H. B. Rodgers, 'The suburban growth of Victorian Manchester', *Transactions of the Manchester Geographical Society* 58 (1962), pp. 1–12

46 On household definition, see M. Anderson, 'Standard tabulation procedures for the census enumerators' books 1851–91', in E. A. Wrigley (1972), op. cit., pp. 134–45

47 See for example, PP. 1845 XVIII, Appendix, Part 2, p. 106; A. B. Reach, *Manchester and the Textile Districts in 1849* (1849, reprinted by Helmshore Local History Society with an introduction by C. A. Aspin, 1972), pp. 1–9

48 Indices of net population and housing districts, multiple occupancy, people per house, household size, sex ratio, height above sea level and percentage of residential land were used in the analysis. See also table 8.8

49 A. E. Martin, 'Environment, housing and health', *Urban Studies* 4 (1967), pp. 1–21; G. Rosen, 'Social variables and health in an urban environment: the case of the Victorian city', *Clio Medica* 8 (1973), pp. 1–17

50 For a discussion of contemporary views of disease causation, see Pelling (1978) op. cit., and Eyler (1979) op. cit.

51 For example, one parochial committee actually minuted self-satisfaction with its policy of caution which had prevented the initiation of any costly public health undertaking. *Minutes* of the Withington Parochial Committee of *Chorlton Urban Sanitary Authority* 15 May 1976 (Manchester Central Library). See also Midwinter (1969) op. cit., pp. 63–119. On the controversy over a main drainage scheme, see A. Redford, *The History of Local Government in Manchester* (London, 1939–40) vol. II, pp. 377–401

52 For a summary of local housing legislation, see S. D. Simon, *A Century of City Government: Manchester, 1838–1938* (London, 1939), pp. 284–304; E. D. Simon and J. Inman, *The Rebuilding of Manchester* (London, 1935); and Redford (1939–40) op. cit.

53 S. M. Gaskell, 'A landscape of small houses: the failure of the worker's flat in Lancashire and Yorkshire in the nineteenth century', in A. Sutcliffe (ed), *Multi-Storey Living: The British Working-Class Experience* (London, 1974), pp. 95–109; Simon (1938) loc. cit.; Redford (1939–40), op. cit., pp. 410–23

54 For regulation of lodging houses, see *Report of the Officer of Health for Manchester, 1872*, pp. 20–2. (Manchester Central Library). Robinson cited the necessity for casual workers of a central lodging as a major cause of over-crowding in Manchester: G. T. Robinson, 'On town dwellings for the working classes', *Transactions of the Manchester Statistical Society* (1871–2), p. 69

55 Simon (1938) op. cit., p. 176

56 Manchester Corporation attempted to prevent the widespread adoption of water-closets in mid-century by extra charges on water rates. G. Greaves, 'Our sewer rivers', *Transactions of the Manchester Statistical Society* (1865–6), pp. 28–51

57 'Dolly Varden' was a popular scent of the time; the term was used ironically in this context. Simon (1938) op. cit., p. 178

58 For a summary of the development of sanitation in Manchester, see A. Sharratt and K. R. Farrar, 'Sanitation and public health in mid-nineteenth century Manchester', *Memoirs and Proceedings of the Manchester Literary and Philosophical Society* 114 (1971–72), pp. 50–69

59 Simon (1938) op. cit., p. 182

60 For a description of these schemes, see Redford (1939–40) op. cit., pp. 171–204 and 333–52

61 J. Hassan, *The Economic and Social Implications of Water-Resource Development in Manchester, 1568–1882*, Discussion Paper 10, Department of Economics and Economic History, Manchester Polytechnic (Manchester, 1980), pp. 11–12 and 17–19

62 On rising standards of living, see A. L. Bowley, *Wages and Income in the United Kingdom since 1860* (Cambridge, 1937) and Oddy and Miller (1976), op. cit., pp. 125–7

63 For development of this line of argument at a national level, see McKeown (1976) op. cit.; McKeown (1978) op. cit. and Chapter 1

64 Rosen (1973) op. cit.

65 See Figure 1.1 for a diagrammatic summary of some of these relationships

Chapter 8

1 T. McKeown and R. G. Record, 'Reasons for the decline of mortality in England and Wales during the nineteenth century', *Population Studies* 16 (1962), p. 120. See also Chapter 1. For related American studies see also E. Meeker, 'The improving health of the United States, 1850–1915', *Explorations in Economic History* 9 (1972), pp. 353–73; G. A. Condran and E. Crimmins-Gardner, 'Public health measures and mortality in U.S. cities in the late-nineteenth century', *Human Ecology* 6 (2) (1978), pp. 27–54; G. A. Condran and R. A. Cheney, 'Mortality trends in Philadelphia: age- and cause-specific death rates, 1870–1930', *Demography* 19 (1982), pp. 97–123

2 McKeown and Record (1962) op. cit., pp. 117–18

3 Ibid., p. 116

4 T. McKeown, *The Modern Rise of Population* (London, 1976), p. 56 and tables 3.1–3.5

5 J. A. Banks, *Prosperity and Parenthood* (London, 1954) and, *Victorian Values* (London, 1981)

6 J. Ralph, 'The best governed city in the world', *Harper's Monthly Magazine* (June, 1890) cited by Asa Briggs, *History of Birmingham*, vol. 2, *Borough and City, 1865–1938* (London, 1952), p. 67

7 John Nelson Tarn, *Five Per Cent Philanthropy* (London, 1973), p. 92

8 E. P. Hennock, *Fit and Proper Persons* (London, 1973), p. 112

9 Frederick Engels, *The Condition of the Working Class in England* (London, 1969), pp. 136–40. See also Chapter 7

10 R. A. Church, *Economic and Social Change in a Midland Town: Victorian Nottingham* (London, 1966)

11 J. M. Baynham et al., *Report on the State of the Public Health in the Borough of Birmingham by a Committee of Physicians and Surgeons* (London, 1841)

12 R. K. Dent, *Old and New Birmingham* (Birmingham, 1880); Hennock (1973) op. cit., p. 113

13 J. E. Vance, 'Housing the worker: the employment linkage as a force in urban structure', *Economic Geography* 42 (1966), pp. 294–325, and, 'Housing the worker: determinative and contingent ties in 19th century Birmingham', *Economic Geography* 43 (1967), pp. 95–127

14 S. D. Chapman and J. N. Barrett, 'The contribution of building clubs and freehold land society to working-class housing in Birmingham', in S. D. Chapman (ed), *The History of Working-Class Housing* (Newton Abbot, 1971), pp. 221–46

15 G. Stedman Jones, *Outcast London* (London, 1971)

16 Edwin Chadwick, *The Sanitary Condition of the Labouring Population of Great Britain* (London, 1842) (ed. M. W. Flinn, Edinburgh, 1965); E. P. Hennock, 'Urban sanitary reform a generation before Chadwick?', *Economic History Review*, 2nd Series 10 (1957), pp. 113–19

17 D. G. Watts, 'Public Health', in W. B. Stephens (ed), *Victoria County*

History of Warwickshire, vol. 7, *Birmingham*, pp. 339–50 (London, 1964). See Figure 8.7

18 Ibid., p. 344

19 T. McKeown and R. G. Brown, 'Medical evidence relating to English population changes in the eighteenth century', *Population Studies* 9 (1955), pp. 119–41; McKeown and Record (1962) op. cit.

20 J. H. Woodward, *To Do the Sick No Harm* (London, 1974); G. Rosen, 'Disease, debility, and death', in H. J. Dyos and M. Wolff (eds), *The Victorian City*, vol. 2, pp. 625–67 (London, 1973)

21 Watts (1964) op. cit., p. 345

22 McKeown (1976) op. cit., table 3.2; see also Figure 1.4

23 Briggs (1952) op. cit., p. 77

24 Geoffrey Best, *Mid-Victorian Britain, 1851–75* (London, 1973), p. 73

25 McKeown and Record (1962) op. cit., pp. 117–18

26 D. V. Glass, 'A note on the under-registration of births in Britain in the nineteenth century', *Population Studies* 5 (1951), pp. 70–88

27 N. Keyfitz and W. Flieger, *World Population: An Analysis of Vital Data* (Chicago, 1968), pp. 523–24

28 R. A. M. Case et al., *Chester Beatty Research Institute Serial Abridged Life Tables, England and Wales, 1841–1960* (London, 1962). See also Chapter 2 especially Figure 2.1

29 A. J. Coale and P. Demeny, *Regional Model Life Tables and Stable Populations* (Princeton, 1966)

30 McKeown (1976) op. cit., p. 96

31 M. W. Beaver, 'Population, infant mortality and milk', *Population Studies* 27 (1973), pp. 243–54

32 A. D. Cliff, P. Haggett, J. K. Ord and G. R. Versey, *Spatial Diffusion* (Cambridge, 1981), pp. 36–45; R. Higgs, 'Cycles and trends in mortality in 18 large American cities, 1871–1900', *Explorations in Economic History* 16 (1979), pp. 381–408

33 P. Laslett, 'Size and structure of the household in England over three centuries', *Population Studies* 23 (1969), pp. 199–223

34 M. S. Bartlett, 'Measles periodicity and community size', *Journal of the Royal Statistical Society* 120A (1957), pp. 48–70; Cliff et al. (1981) op. cit.

35 McKeown and Record (1962) op. cit., p. 117

36 Baynham et al. (1841) op. cit., p. 5

37 B. Benjamin, 'The urban background to public health changes in England and Wales, 1900–50', *Population Studies* 17 (1964), pp. 225–48

38 McKeown and Record (1962) op. cit., p. 120; see also A. S. Wohl, *Endangered Lives* (London, 1983)

Bibliography

(The bibliography contains the main references that appear in the chapter notes together with a number of other items on the social history of the nineteenth century, mortality, health care and the medical profession.)

ANDERSON, M. (1971) *Family Structure in Nineteenth-Century Lancashire* (Cambridge)

ANDERSON, M. (1972) 'Standard tabulation procedures for the census enumerators' books, 1851–1891' in E. A. WRIGLEY (ed.) *Nineteenth-Century Society*, pp. 134–45 (Cambridge)

ANDERSON, M. (1972) 'The study of family structure' in E. A. WRIGLEY (ed.) *Nineteenth-Century Society*, pp. 47–81 (Cambridge)

ANDERSON, O. W. (1953) 'Age-specific mortality differentials historically and currently: observations and implications' *Bulletin of the History of Medicine*, 27, pp. 521–9

ANDERSON, O. W. (1955) 'Age-specific mortality in selected Western European countries in the nineteenth century: observations and implications' *Bulletin of the History of Medicine*, 29, pp. 239–54

APPLEBY, A. B. (1975) 'Nutrition and disease: the case of London, 1550–1750' *Journal of Interdisciplinary History*, 6, pp. 1–22

ARMSTRONG, W. A. (1974) *Stability and change in an English County Town: A Social Study of York, 1801–51* (Cambridge)

ARMSTRONG, W. A. (1981) 'The trend of mortality in Carlisle between the 1780s and the 1840s: a demographic contribution to the standard of living debate' *Economic History Review*, 2nd Series, 34, pp. 94–114

ATKINS, P. J. (1980) 'The retail milk trade in London, c. 1740–1914' *Economic History Review*, 2nd Series, 33, pp. 522–37

AYERS, G. M. (1971) *England's First State Hospitals and the Metropolitan Asylums Board, 1867–1930* (London)

BALDWIN-WISEMAN, W. R. (1909) 'The increase in the national consumption of water' *Journal of the Royal Statistical Society*, 122, pp. 282–90

BANKS, J. A. (1954) *Prosperity and Parenthood: A Study of Family Planning Amongst the Victorian Middle Classes* (London)

BANKS, J. A. (1981) *Victorian Values: Secularism and the Size of Families* (London)

BARKER, T. and DRAKE, M. (eds) (1982) *Population and Society in Britain, 1850–1980* (London)

BARNET, M. C. (1972) 'The 1832 cholera epidemic in York' *Medical History*, 16, pp. 27–39

BEAVER, M. W. (1973) 'Population, infant mortality and milk' *Population Studies*, 27, pp. 243–54

BECK, A. (1959) 'Some aspects of the history of anti-pollution legislation in England, 1819–1954' *Journal of the History of Medicine*, 14, pp. 475–89

BEHLMER, G. K. (1979) 'Deadly motherhood. Infanticide and medical opinion in mid-Victorian England' *Journal of the History of Medicine*, 34, pp. 403–27

BENJAMIN, B. (1964) 'The urban background to public health changes in England and Wales, 1900–50' *Population Studies*, 17, pp. 225–48

BENJAMIN, B. (ed.) (1973) *Population and Disease in Early Industrial England* (London)

BEST, G. (1973) *Mid-Victorian Britain, 1851–75* (London)

BOOTH, C. (1902–4) *Life and Labour of the People in London* (17 vols) (London)

BOWLEY, A. L. (1914) 'Rural populations in England and Wales. A study of the changes of density, occupations and ages' *Journal of the Royal Statistical Society*, 77, pp. 597–652

BOWLEY, A. L. (1937) *Wages and Income in the United Kingdom since 1860* (Cambridge)

BRADFORD HILL, A. (1936) 'The recent trend in England and Wales of mortality from phthisis at young adult ages' *Journal of the Royal Statistical Society*, 49, pp. 264–7

BRAND, J. L. (1961) 'The parish doctor: England's Poor Law Medical Officers and medical reform, 1870–1900' *Bulletin of the History of Medicine*, 35, pp. 97–122

BRAND, J. L. (1963) 'John Simon and the Local Government Board bureaucrats, 1871–1876' *Bulletin of the History of Medicine*, 37, pp. 184–93

BREND, W. A. (1917) *Health and the State* (London)

BRIGGS, A. (1952) *History of Birmingham*, vol. 2, *Borough and City, 1865–1938* (London)

BRIGGS, A. (1961) 'Cholera and society in the nineteenth century' *Past and Present*, 19, pp. 76–96

BRIGGS, A. (1963) *Victorian Cities* (London)

BROCKINGTON, C. F. (1961) 'Public health at the Privy Council, 1831–34' *Journal of the History of Medicine*, 16, pp. 161–85

BROCKINGTON, C. F. (1963) 'Public health at the Privy Council, 1805–6' *Medical History*, 7, pp. 13–31

BROCKINGTON, C. F. (1965) *Public Health in the Nineteenth Century* (Edinburgh and London)

BROCKINGTON, C. F. (1965) *The Health of the Community* (London, 3rd edn)

BROWN, P. E. (1961) 'John Snow—the autumn loiterer' *Bulletin of the History of Medicine*, 25, pp. 519–28

BOURDELAIS, P. and RAULOT, J.-Y. (1978) 'La marche du choléra en France: 1832 à 1854', *Annales: E.S.C.*, 33, pp. 125–42

BRISTOWE, J. S. (1876) *A Treatise on the Theory and Practice of Medicine* (London)

BUER, M. C. (1926) *Health, Wealth and Population in the Early Days of the Industrial Revolution* (London)

BURKE, G. and RICHARDSON, P. (1978) 'The profits of death: a comparative study of miners' phthisis in Cornwall and Transvaal, 1876–1918' *Journal of South African Studies*, 4, pp. 147–71

BURNETT, J. (1968) *Plenty and Want: A Social History of Diet in England from 1815 to the Present Day* (London)

CARTWRIGHT, F. F. (1977) *A Social History of Medicine* (London)

CASE, R. A. M. et al. (1962) *Chester Beatty Research Institute Serial Abridged Life Tables, England and Wales, 1841–1960* (London)

CHADWICK, E. (1842 and 1965) *Report on the Sanitary Condition of the Labouring Population of Great Britain* (London, 1842; Edinburgh, 1965) (see FLINN, 1965)

CHALKLIN, C. W. (1974) *The Provincial Towns of Georgian England* (London)

CHAMBERS, J. D. (1972) *Population Economy and Society in Pre-Industrial England* (London)

CHAPMAN, S. D. (ed.) (1971) *The History of Working-Class Housing* (Newton Abbot)

CHECKLAND, O. and LAMB, M. (eds) (1982) *Health Care as Social History: The Glasgow Case* (Aberdeen)

CHERRY, S. (1972) 'The role of a provincial hospital: the Norfolk and Norwich Hospital, 1771–1888' *Population Studies*, 26, pp. 291–306

CHERRY, S. (1980) 'The hospitals and population growth: the voluntary general hospitals, mortality and local populations in the English provinces in the eighteenth and nineteenth centuries' *Population Studies*, 34, pp. 59–75 and 251–66

CHEVALIER, L. (ed.) (1958) *Le Choléra. La Première Épidemé du XIXe Siècle*, Bibliotheque de la Revolution de 1848, Tome XX (La Roche-sur-Yon)

CHEVALIER, L. (1973) *Labouring Classes and Dangerous Classes in Paris during the First Half of the Nineteenth Century* (London)

CHITNIS, A. C. (1973) 'Medical education in Edinburgh, 1790–1826, and late Victorian social consequences' *Medical History*, 17, pp. 173–84

CHURCH, R. A. (1966) *Economic and Social Change in a Midland Town: Victorian Nottingham* (London)

CHURCH, R. A. (1975) *The Great Victorian Boom, 1850–1873* (London)

CLARKE, E. (ed.) (1971) *Modern Methods in the History of Medicine* (London)

CLIFF, A. D. and ROBSON, B. T. (1978) 'Changes in the size distribution of settlements in England and Wales, 1801–1968' *Environment and Planning A*, 10, pp. 163–71

COALE, A. J. and DEMENY, P. (1966) *Regional Model Life Tables and Stable Populations* (Princeton)

COLLINS, E. J. T. (1975) 'Dietary change and cereal consumption in the nineteenth century' *Agricultural History Review*, 23, pp. 97–115

COLLINS, J. J. (1982) 'The contribution of medical measures to the decline of mortality from respiratory tuberculosis: an age-period-cohort model' *Demography*, 19, pp. 409–27

CONDRAN, G. A. and CHENEY, R. A. (1982) 'Mortality trends in Philadelphia age- and cause-specific death rates, 1870–1930' *Demography*, 19, pp. 97–123

CONDRAN, G. A. and CRIMMINS, E. (1980) 'Mortality differentials between rural and urban areas of states in the northeastern United States, 1890–1900' *Journal of Historical Geography*, 6, pp. 179–202

CONDRAN, G. A. and CRIMMINS-GARDNER, E. (1978) 'Public health measures and mortality in U.S. cities in the late-nineteenth century' *Human Ecology*, 6(2), pp. 22–54

CREIGHTON, C. (1894 and 1965) *A History of Epidemics in Britain* (2 vols) (Cambridge, 1894; London, 1965, 2nd edn)

CROSSICK, G. (ed.) (1977) *The Lower Middle Classes in Britain, 1870–1914* (London)

CROUZET, F. (1982) *The Victorian Economy* (London)

CROWTHER, M. A. (1981) *The Workhouse System, 1834–1929: The History of an English Social Institution* (London)

CRUICKSHANK, M. (1981) *Children and Industry: Child Health and Welfare in North-West Textile Towns During the Nineteenth Century* (Manchester)

CULLEN, J. (1975) *The Statistical Movement in Early Victorian Britain: The Foundation of Empirical Social Science* (New York)

DAVIES, S (1908) 'Twenty years' advance in preventive medicine' *Public Health*, 21, p. 116

DAVIN, A. (1978) 'Imperialism and motherhood' *History Workshop*, 5, pp. 9–65

DONNISON, J. (1977) *Midwives and Medical Men* (London and New York)

DUANNE, C. (1978) 'Infanticide: the worth of an infant' *Medical History*, 22, pp. 1–24

DUBOS, J. R. and DUBOS, J. (1953) *The White Plague: Tuberculosis, Man and Society* (London)

DUREY, M. (1979) *The Return of the Plague: British Society and the Cholera, 1831–2* (Dublin)

DYHOUSE, C. (1978) 'Working-class mothers and infant mortality in England, 1895–1914' *Journal of Social History*, 12(2), pp. 248–67

DYKSTRA, D. L. (1955) 'The medical profession and patient and preventive medicine during the nineteenth century' *Bulletin of the History of Medicine*, 29, pp. 401–19

DYOS, H. J. (1955) 'Railways and housing in Victorian London' *Journal of Transport History*, 2, pp. 11–21

DYOS, H. J. (1957–8) 'Some social costs of railway building in London' *Journal of Transport History*, 3, pp. 23–30

DYOS, H. J. and WOLFF, M. (eds) (1973) *The Victorian City: Images and Reality* (2 vols) (London)

ENGELS, F. (1845 and 1969) *The Condition of the Working Class in England* (Leipzig, 1845; London, 1969)

EVANS, W. A. (1896) 'Back-to-back houses' *Transactions, Epidemiological Society of London*, New Series, 16, pp. 87–99

EYLER, J. M. (1973) 'William Farr on the cholera: the sanitarian's disease theory and the statistician's method' *Journal of the History of Medicine*, 28, pp. 79–100

EYLER, J. M. (1979), *Victorian Social Medicine: The Ideas and Methods of William Farr* (Baltimore)

FARR, W. (1885) *Vital Statistics* (London)

FERGUSON, T. (1963) 'Public health in Britain in the climate of the nineteenth century' *Population Studies*, 17, pp. 213–24

FERGUSON, T., BENJAMIN, B. et al. (1964) *Public Health and Urban Growth*, Centre for Urban Studies, University College London, Report No. 4 (London)

FINER, S. E. (1952) *The Life and Times of Sir Edwin Chadwick* (London)

FINLAY, R. A. P. (1981) *Parish Registers: An Introduction* (Norwich)

FLINN, M. W. (ed.) (1965) *Report on the Sanitary Condition of the Labouring Population of Great Britain in 1842 by Edwin Chadwick* (Edinburgh)

FLINN, M. W. (1970) *British Population Growth, 1700–1850* (London)

FLINN, M. W. (1974) 'Trends in real wages, 1750–1850' *Economic History Review*, 2nd Series, 27, pp. 395–413

FLINN, M. W. (1974) 'The stabilization of mortality in pre-industrial Europe' *Journal of European Economic History*, 3, pp. 285–318

FLINN, M. W. et al. (1977) *Scottish Population History: From the Seventeenth Century to the 1930s* (Cambridge)

FLINN, M. W. (1978) 'Plague in Europe and the Mediterranean countries' *Journal of European Economic History*, 8, pp. 131–48

FLOREY, H. (ed.) (1970) *General Pathology* (London, 4th edn)

FORBES, E. L. (ed.) (1978) *Human Implications of Scientific Advance* (Edinburgh)

FORBES, T. R. (1972) 'Mortality books for 1820 to 1849 from the parish of St Bride, Fleet Street, London', *Journal of the History of Medicine*, 27, pp. 15–29

FOUCAULT, M. (1973) *The Birth of the Clinic: An Archaeology of Medical Perception* (London)

FRASER, D. (1979) *Power and Authority in the Victorian City* (Oxford)

FRAZER, W. M. (1950) *A History of English Public Health* (London)

GALE, A. A. (1959) *Epidemic Disease* (London)

GASKELL, G. A. (1890) *Social Control of the Birth Rate and the Endowment of Mothers* (London)

GAULDIE, E. (1974) *Cruel Habitations: A History of Working-Class Housing, 1780–1918* (London)

GIBSON, E. H. (1954) 'Baths and wash-houses in the English public health agitation, 1839–48' *Journal of the History of Medicine*, 9, pp. 391–406

GILBERT, B. B. (1965) 'Health and politics: the British Physical Deterioration Report of 1904' *Bulletin of the History of Medicine*, 39, pp. 143–53

GILBERT, B. B. (1966) *The Evolution of National Insurance in Britain: The Origins of the Welfare State* (London)

GITTINS, D. (1982) *Fair Sex: Family Size and Structure, 1900–39* (London)

GLASS, D. V. (1938) 'Changes in fertility in England and Wales, 1851–1931' in L. HOGBEN (ed) *Political Arithmetic*, pp. 161–212 (London)

GLASS, D. V. (1940) *Population Movements in England and Wales* (London)

GLASS, D. V. (1951) 'A note on the under-registration of births in Britain in the nineteenth century' *Population Studies*, 5, pp. 70–88

GLASS, D. V. (1964) 'Some indicators of differences between urban and rural mortality' *Population Studies*, 17, pp. 263–8

GLASS, D. V. (1973) *Numbering the People: The Eighteenth-Century Population Controversy and the Development of Census and Vital Statistics in Britain* (Farnborough)

GLASS, D. V. and EVERSLEY, D. E. C. (eds) (1965) *Population in History: Essays in Historical Demography* (London)

GLASS, D. V. and REVELLE, R. (eds) (1972) *Population and Social Change* (London)

GOLDBERG, B. (ed.) (1935) *Clinical Tuberculosis*, vol. 1 (Philadelphia)

GOODALL, E. W. (1934) *A Short History of the Infectious Epidemic Diseases* (London)

GREENWOOD, M. (1935) *Epidemics and Crowd Diseases* (London)

HABAKKUK, H. J. (1953) 'English population in the eighteenth century' *Economic History Review*, 2nd Series, 6, pp. 117–33

HABAKKUK, H. J. (1971) *Population Growth and Economic Development since 1750* (Leicester)

HAINES, M. R. (1977) 'Mortality in nineteenth-century America: estimates from New York and Pennsylvania census data, 1865 and 1900' *Demography*, 14, pp. 311–32

HAINES, M. R. (1979) 'The use of model life tables to estimate mortality for the United States in the late nineteenth century' *Demography*, 16, pp. 289–312

HAINES, M. R. (1979) *Fertility and Occupation: Population Patterns in Industrialization* (New York)

HAMILTON, D. (1982) 'The nineteenth-century surgical revolution: antisepsis or better nutrition?' *Bulletin of the History of Medicine*, 56, pp. 30–40

HARDYMENT, C. (1983) *Dream Babies: Child Care from Locke to Spock* (London)

HART, P. M. D'A. and WRIGHT, G. P. (1939) *Tuberculosis and Social Conditions in England with Special Reference to Young Adults: A Statistical Study*, National Association for the Prevention of Tuberculosis (London)

HAY, J. R. (1975) *The Origins of the Liberal Welfare Reforms, 1906–1914* (London)

HELLEINER, K. F. (1967) 'The population of Europe from the Black Death to the eve of the vital revolution' in E. E. RICH and C. H. WILSON (eds) *Cambridge Economic History of Europe*, vol. IV, pp. 1–95 (Cambridge)

HENNOCK, E. P. (1957) 'Urban sanitary reform a generation before Chadwick?' *Economic History Review*, 2nd Series, 10, pp. 113–19

HENNOCK, E. P. (1973) *Fit and Proper Persons: Ideal and Reality in Nineteenth-Century Government* (London)

HEWITT, M. (1975) *Wives and Mothers in Victorian Industry* (London)

HIGGS, R. (1979) 'Cycles and trends in mortality in 18 large American cities, 1871–1900' *Explorations in Economic History*, 16, pp. 381–408

HIGGS, R. and BOOTH, D. (1979) 'Mortality differentials within large American cities in 1890' *Human Ecology*, 7, pp. 353–70

HILL, A. (1879–80) 'Diphtheria and typhoid and their concomitant conditions in Birmingham' *Transactions, Society of Medical Officers of Health*, pp. 65–70

HILTS, V. L. (1970) 'William Farr (1807–1883) and the "Human Unit"' *Victorian Studies*, 14, pp. 143–50

HODGKINSON, R. G. (1956) 'Poor Law Medical Officers of England, 1834–1871' *Journal of the History of Medicine*, 11, pp. 299–338

HOEPRICH, P. D. (ed.) (1972) *Infectious Diseases* (London)

HOGBEN, L. (ed.) (1938) *Political Arithmetic* (London)

HOLLINGSWORTH, T. H. (1964) *The Demography of the British Peerage*, Supplement to *Population Studies*

HOLLINGSWORTH, T. H. (1977) 'Mortality in the British peerage families since 1600' *Population*, 23 (Special Number) pp. 323–52

HOLLOWAY, S. W. F. (1966) 'The Apothecaries Act, 1815: a reinterpretation' *Medical History*, 10, pp. 107–29 and 221–36

HOWE, G. M. (1972) *Man, Environment and Disease in Britain* (Newton Abbot)

HUNT, E. H. (1973) *Regional Wage Variations in Britain, 1850–1914* (London)

HUNT, E. H. (1981) *British Labour History, 1815–1914* (London)

IGNATIEFF, M. (1978) *A Just Measure of Pain: The Penitentiary in the Industrial Revolution, 1750–1850* (New York)

INNES, J. W. (1938) *Class Fertility Trends in England and Wales, 1876–1934* (Princeton)

JENSEN, J. V. (1970–1) 'The X-Club: fraternity of Victorian Scientists' *British Journal for the History of Science*, 5, pp. 63–72

JEWSON, N. D. (1974) 'Medical knowledge and the patronage system in eighteenth-century England' *Sociology*, 8, pp. 369–85

JOHNSON, J. H. and POOLEY, C. G. (eds) (1982) *The Structure of Nineteenth-Century Cities* (London)

KAY-SHUTTLEWORTH, J. P. (1832 and 1970) *The Moral and Physical Condition of the Working Classes Employed in the Cotton Manufacture in Manchester* (Manchester, 1832; London, 1970)

KEYFITZ, N. and FLIEGER, W. (1968) *World Population: Analysis of Vital Data* (Chicago)

KNIGHT, P. (1977) 'Women and abortion in Victorian and Edwardian England' *History Workshop*, 4, pp. 57–69

KNODEL, J. E. (1982) 'Child mortality and reproductive behaviour in German village populations in the past: a micro-level analysis of the replacement effect' *Population Studies*, 36, pp. 177–200

KRAUSE, J. T. (1965) 'The changing adequacy of English registration, 1600–1837' in D. V. GLASS and D. E. C. EVERSLEY (eds) *Population in History*, pp. 379–93 (London)

LAMBERT, R. (1962) 'A Victorian national health service: state vaccination' *Historical Journal*, 5, pp. 1–18

LAMBERT, R. (1963) *Sir John Simon, 1816–1904, and English Social Administration* (London)

LANGER, W. L. (1963) 'Europe's initial population explosion' *American Historical Review*, 69, pp. 1–17

LANGER, W. L. (1975) 'American foods and Europe's population growth, 1750–1850' *Journal of Social History*, 8(4), pp. 51–66

LAW, C. M. (1967) 'The growth of urban population in England and Wales, 1801–1911' *Transactions, Institute of British Geographers*, 41, pp. 125–43

LAWRENCE, C. J. (1975) 'William Buchan's medicine laid open' *Medical History*, 19, pp. 20–35

LAWTON, R. (1967) 'Rural depopulation in nineteenth-century England' in R. W. STEEL and R. LAWTON (eds) *Liverpool Essays in Geography*, pp. 227–55 (London)

LAWTON, R. (1968) 'Population changes in England and Wales in the later nineteenth century: an analysis of trends by registration districts' *Transactions, Institute of British Geographers*, 44, pp. 55–74

LAWTON, R. (1978) 'Population and society, 1730–1900' in R. A. DODGSHON and R. A. BUTLIN (eds) *An Historical Geography of England and Wales*, pp. 313–66 (London)

LAWTON, R. (ed.) (1978) *The Census and Social Structure: An Interpretative Guide to 19th Century Censuses for England and Wales* (London)

LAWTON, R. (1980) 'Regional population trends in England and Wales, 1750–1971' in J. HOBCRAFT and P. H. REES (eds) *Regional Demographic Development*, pp. 29–70 (London)

LEE, W. R. (1973) 'Emergence of occupational medicine in Victorian times' *British Journal of Industrial Medicine*, 30, pp. 111–17

LEES, L. H. (1979) *Exiles of Erin: Irish Emigrants in Victorian London* (Ithaca and Manchester)

LEWIS, J. (1980) 'The social history of social policy: infant welfare in Edwardian England' *Journal of Social Policy*, 9, pp. 463–86

LEWIS, J. (1980) *The Politics of Motherhood: Child and Maternal Welfare in England, 1900–1939* (London and Montreal)

LEWIS, R. A. (1952) *Edwin Chadwick and the Public Health Movement* (London)

LINDERT, P. H. and WILLIAMSON, J. G. (1983) 'English workers' living standards during the industrial revolution: a new look' *Economic History Review*, 2nd Series, 36, pp. 1–25

LOGAN, W. P. D. (1950) 'Mortality in England and Wales from 1848–1947' *Population Studies*, 4, pp. 132–78

LOMAX, E. (1977) 'Hereditary or acquired disease? Early nineteenth century debates on the cause of infantile scrofula and tuberculosis' *Journal of the History of Medicine*, 32, pp. 356–74

LONGSTAFF, G. B. (1884–5) 'The seasonal prevalence of continued fever in London' *Transactions, Epidemiological Society of London*, pp. 72–86

LOSCHKY, D. J. (1972) 'Urbanisation and England's eighteenth-century crude birth and death rates' *Journal of European Economic History*, 1, pp. 697–712

LOUDON, I. S. L. (1981) 'The origins and growth of the dispensary movement in England' *Bulletin of the History of Medicine*, 55, pp. 322–42

LUCKIN, W. (1977) 'The final catastrophe: cholera in London, 1866' *Medical History*, 21, pp. 32–42

LUCKIN, W. (1980) 'Death and survival in the city: approaches to the history of disease' *Urban History Yearbook*, pp. 53–62

MCCLEARY, G. F. (1935) *The Maternity and Child Welfare Movement* (London)

MCDONALD, J. C. (1951) 'The history of quarantine in Britain during the 19th century' *Bulletin of the History of Medicine*, 25, pp. 22–44

MCDOUGALL, J. B. (1949) *Tuberculosis: A Global Study in Social Pathology* (Edinburgh)

MCGREW, R. E. (1965) *Russia and the Cholera, 1823–1832* (Madison)

MACLEOD, R. M. (1967) 'The frustration of state medicine, 1880–1899' *Medical History*, 11, pp. 15–40

MACLEOD, R. M. (1970) 'The X-Club: a social network of science in Victorian England' *Notes and Records of the Royal Society*, 24, pp. 305–22

MCKEOWN, T. (1971) 'Medical issues in historical demography' in E. CLARKE (ed.) *Modern Methods in the History of Medicine*, pp. 57–74 (London)

MCKEOWN, T. (1976) *The Modern Rise of Population* (London)

MCKEOWN, T. (1978) 'Fertility, mortality and causes of death: an examination of issues related to the modern rise of population' *Population Studies*, 32, pp. 535–42

MCKEOWN, T. (1979) *Role of Medicine: Dream, Mirage or Nemesis?* (Oxford)

MCKEOWN, T., BROWN, R. G. and RECORD, R. G. (1972) 'An interpretation of the modern rise of population in Europe' *Population Studies*, 26, pp. 94–122

MCKEOWN, T. and RECORD, R. G. (1962) 'Reasons for the decline in mortality in England and Wales during the nineteenth century' *Population Studies*, 16, pp. 94–122

MCKEOWN, T., RECORD, R. G. and TURNER, R. D. (1975) 'An interpretation of the decline in mortality in England and Wales during the twentieth century' *Population Studies*, 29, pp. 391–422

MCLAREN, A. (1977) 'Women's work and the regulation of family size' *History Workshop*, 4, pp. 70–81

MCLAREN, A. (1978) *Birth Control in Nineteenth-Century England* (London)

MCNEILL, W. H. (1977) *Plagues and Peoples* (Oxford)

MARCUS, S. (1974) *Engels, Manchester and the Working Class* (London)

MARTIN, A. E. (1967) 'Environment, housing and health' *Urban Studies*, 4, pp. 1–21

MARX, K. (1976) *Capital*, vol. 1 (London, Penguin edition)

MEACHAM, S. (1977) *A Life Apart: The Working Class, 1890–1914* (Cambridge, Mass.)

MEEKER, E. (1972) 'The improving health of the United States, 1850–1915' *Explorations in Economic History*, 9, pp. 353–73

MIDWINTER, E. C. (1969) *Social Administration in Lancashire, 1830–60* (Manchester)

MINGAY, G. E. (ed.) (1981) *The Victorian Countryside* (2 vols) (London)

MITCHELL, B. R. and DEANE, P. (1976) *Abstract of British Historical Statistics* (Cambridge)

MITCHISON, R. (1977) *British Population Change Since 1860* (London)

MORRIS, R. J. (1976) *Cholera, 1832* (London)

MORTIMORE, M. J. (1969) 'Landownership and urban growth in Bradford and its environs in the West Riding conurbations, 1850–1950' *Transactions, Institute of British Geographers*, 46, pp. 105–19

MULLETT, C. F. (1951) 'The lay outlook on medicine in England c. 1800–1850' *Bulletin of the History of Medicine*, 25, pp. 169–77

MURCHISON, C. (1884) *A Treatise on the Continued Fevers of Great Britain* (London, 3rd edn)

MYERS, J. A. and GEISSLER, P. A. (1930) *Tuberculosis Among Children* (London)

NEWMAN, G. (1937) *The Building of a Nation's Health* (London)

NEWSHOLME, A. (1931) *International Studies on the Relation Between the Private and Official Practice of Medicine*, vol. 3, Milbank Memorial Fund (New York)

NEWSHOLME, A. (1935) *Fifty Years in Public Health* (London)

NOVAK, S. J. (1977) 'Professionalism and bureaucracy: English doctors and the Victorian public health administration' *Journal of Social History*, 6, pp. 440–62

ODDY, D. J. (1982) 'The health of the people' in T. BARKER and M. DRAKE (eds) *Population and Society in Britain, 1850–1980*, pp. 121–39 (London)

ODDY, D. J. (1983) 'Urban famine in nineteenth-century Britain: the effect of the Lancashire cotton famine on working-class diet and health' *Economic History Review*, 2nd Series, 36, pp. 68–86

ODDY, D. J. and MILLER, D. S. (eds) (1976) *The Making of the Modern British Diet* (London)

PATERSON, R. G. (1948) 'The Health of Towns Association in Great Britain, 1844–1849' *Bulletin of the History of Medicine*, 22, pp. 373–402

PATRICK, A. (1955) *The Enteric Fevers* (London)

PELLING, M. (1978) *Cholera, Fever and English Medicine, 1825–65* (Oxford)

PENNINGTON, C. I. (1979) 'Mortality and medical care in nineteenth century Glasgow' *Medical History*, 23, pp. 442–50

PETERSON, M. J. (1978) *The Medical Profession in Mid-Victorian London* (Berkeley)

PHELPS BROWN, H. and HOPKINS, S. V. (1981) *A Perspective on Wages and Prices* (London)

PINKER, R. (1966) *English Hospital Statistics, 1861–1938* (London)

POLLARD, S. (1981) 'Sheffield and Sweet Auburn-amenities and living standards in the British Industrial Revolution: a comment' *Journal of Economic History*, 41, pp. 902–4 (on WILLIAMSON (1981))

POYNTER, F. N. L. (ed.) (1968) *Medicine and Science in the 1860s* (London)

PRESTON, S. H. (1975) 'The changing relation between mortality and level of economic development' *Population Studies*, 29, pp. 231–48

PRESTON, S. H. (1976) *Mortality Patterns in National Populations* (New York)

PRESTON, S. H. (ed.) (1978) *The Effects of Infant and Child Mortality on Fertility* (New York)

PRESTON, S. H., KEYFITZ, N. and SCHOEN, R. (1972) *Causes of Death: Life Tables for National Populations* (New York)

PRESTON, S. H. and NELSON, V. E. (1974) 'Structure and change in causes of death: an international summary' *Population Studies*, 28, pp. 19–51

PRESTON, S. H. and VAN DE WALLE, E. (1978) 'Urban French mortality in the nineteenth century' *Population Studies*, 32, pp. 275–97

PYLE, G. (1969) 'Diffusion of cholera in the United States' *Geographical Analysis*, 1, pp. 59–75

RAZZELL, P. E. (1969) 'Population change in eighteenth-century England: a re-appraisal' in M. Drake (ed.) *Population in Industrialization*, pp. 128–56 (London)

RAZZELL, P. E. (1974) 'An interpretation of the modern rise of population in Europe: a critique' *Population Studies*, 28, pp. 5–18

RAZZELL, P. E. (1977) *The Conquest of Smallpox* (Firle, Sussex)

REDFORD, A. (1926) *Labour Migration in England, 1800–1850* (Manchester)

REEVES, M. P. (1913 and 1979) *Round About a Pound a Week* (London, 1913, reprinted 1979)

RICH, A. R. (1951) *The Pathogenesis of Tuberculosis* (Oxford, 2nd edn)

RICHARDS, D. and WOODWARD, J. H. (eds) (1984) *Health Professions and the State in Modern Britain* (London)

RIVERS, T. M. (ed.) (1952) *Viral and Rickettsial Infections of Man* (London, 2nd edn)

ROBSON, B. T. (1973) *Urban Growth: An Approach* (London)

ROWEN, G. (1958) *A History of Public Health* (New York)

ROSEN, G. (1971) 'Historical trends and future prospects in public health' in G. MCLACHLAN and T. MCKEOWN (eds) *Medical History and Medical Care: A Symposium of Perspectives* (Oxford)

ROSEN, G. (1973) 'Disease, debility, and death' in H. J. DYOS and M. WOLFF (eds) *The Victorian City*, pp. 625–67 (London)

ROSEN, G. (1973) 'Social variables and health in an urban environment: the case of the Victorian city' *Clio Medica*, 8, pp. 1–17

ROSENBERG, C. E. (1962) *The Cholera Years: The United States in 1832, 1849 and 1866* (Chicago)

ROSENBERG, C. E. (1966) 'Cholera in nineteenth-century Europe: a tool for social and economic analysis' *Contemporary Studies in Society and History*, 8, pp. 452–63

ROSNER, D. (1982) *A Once Charitable Enterprise: Hospitals and Health Care in Brooklyn and New York, 1885–1915* (Cambridge)

ROWNTREE, B. S. (1902) *Poverty: A Study of Town Life* (London)

SAUER, R. (1978) 'Infanticide and abortion in nineteenth-century Britain' *Population Studies*, 32, pp. 81–94

SAUL, S. B. (1969) *The Myth of the Great Depression* (London)

SAVILLE, J. (1957) *Rural Depopulation in England and Wales, 1851–1951* (London)

SCHOFIELD, R. S. and WRIGLEY, E. A. (1979) 'Infant and child mortality in England in the late Tudor and early Stuart period' in C. WEBSTER (ed.) *Health, Medicine and Mortality in the Sixteenth Century*, pp. 61–95 (Cambridge)

SCOTT, H. H. (1930) *Tuberculosis in Man and Lower Animals*, Medical Research Council, Special Report Series, No. 149 (London)

SCOTT-MONCRIEFF, W. D. (1909) 'River pollution: its ethics, aethetics and hygiene' *Journal of the Royal Sanitary Institute*, 30, pp. 165–72

SCULL, A. (1979) *Museums of Madness: The Social Origins of Insanity in Nineteenth-Century England* (London)

SHORTER, E. (1983) *A History of Women's Bodies* (London)

SIGERIST, H. E. (1943) *Civilisation and Disease* (Ithaca and London)

SIMON, J. (1858) *Papers Relating to the Sanitary State of the People of England* (London)

SIMON, J. (1887) *Public Health Reports* (2 vols) (London, ed. E. Seaton)

SIMON, J. (1890) *English Sanitary Institutions* (London)

SINGER, C. and UNDERWOOD, E. A. (1962) *A Short History of Medicine* (London, 2nd edn)

SMITH, D. (1982) *Conflict and Compromise: Class Formation in English Society, 1830–1914, A Comparative Study of Birmingham and Sheffield* (London)

SMITH, F. B. (1979) *The People's Health, 1830–1910* (London)

SOLOWAY, R. A. (1982) *Birth Control and the Population Question in England, 1877–1930* (Chapel Hill)

STEDMAN JONES, G. (1971) *Outcast London: A Study in the Relationship Between Classes in Victorian Society* (London)

STEVENSON, L. G. (1982) 'Exemplary disease: the typhoid pattern' *Journal of the History of Medicine*, 37, pp. 159–81

SUTCLIFFE, A. (ed.) (1974) *Multi-Storey Living: The British Working-Class Experience* (London)

SUTCLIFFE, A. (1982) 'The growth of public intervention in the British urban environment during the nineteenth century: a structural approach' in

J. H. JOHNSON and C. G. POOLEY (eds) *The Structure of Nineteenth-Century Cities*, pp. 107–24 (London)

TARN, J. N. (1973) *Five Per Cent Philanthropy: An Account of Housing in Urban Areas Between 1840 and 1914* (Cambridge)

TAYLOR, A. J. (ed.) (1975) *The Standard of Living in Britain in the Industrial Revolution* (London)

TELEKY, L. (1944) 'Certifying surgeons, examining surgeons, a century of activity' *Bulletin of the History of Medicine*, 16, pp. 382–88

THOMAS, B. (1954) *Migration and Economic Growth: Great Britain and the Atlantic Economy* (Cambridge)

TILLY, L. A. and SCOTT, J. W. (1978) *Women, Work, and Family* (New York)

TREBLE, J. H. (1979) *Urban Poverty in Britain, 1830–1914* (London)

TEITELBAUM, M. S. (1974) 'Birth under-registration in the constituent counties of England and Wales, 1841–1910' *Population Studies*, 28, pp. 329–43

THORNE, R. (1888) *The Progress of Medicine During the Victorian Era, 1837–1887* (London)

VAN DE WALLE, E. (1973) 'La mortalité de départements français ruraux du XIXᵉ siècle' in J. DUPÂQUIER (ed.) *Hommage à Marcel Reinhard*, pp. 581–9 (Paris)

VON TUNZELMANN, G. N. (1979) 'Trends in real wages, 1750–1850, revisited' *Economic History Review*, 2nd Series, 32, pp. 33–49

VAUGHAN, R. (1843 and 1972) *The Age of Great Cities* (London, 1843; Shannon, 1972 edition)

VINCENT, D. (1980) 'Love and death and the nineteenth-century working class' *Social History*, 5, pp. 223–47

VINOVSKIS, M. A. (1972) 'Mortality rates and trends in Massachusetts before 1860' *Journal of Economic History*, 32, pp. 184–213

WALL, R. (ed.) (1974) *Mortality in Mid-19th Century Britain* (Farnborough)

WALVIN, J. (1982) *A Child's World: A Social History of English Childhood, 1800–1914* (London)

WATKIN, B. (1975) *Documents on Health and Social Sciences, 1834 to the Present Day* (London)

WEBB, S. (1907) *The Decline in the Birth-Rate*, Fabian Tract No. 131 (London)

WEBER, A. F. (1899) *The Growth of Cities in the Nineteenth Century* (New York)

WEBSTER, C. (ed.) (1981) *Biology, Medicine and Society, 1840–1940* (Cambridge)

WEBSTER, C. (1982) 'Healthy or hungry thirties?' *History Workshop*, 13, pp. 110–29

WELTON, T. A. (1897) 'Local death-rates in England and Wales in the ten years 1881–90' *Journal of the Royal Statistical Society*, 60, pp. 33–75

WELTON, T. A. (1900) 'The growth of population in England and Wales and its progress in the period of ninety years from 1801–91' *Journal of the Royal Statistical Society*, 63, pp. 527–89

WELTON, T. A. (1911) *England's Recent Progress: An Investigation of the Statistics of Migrations, Mortality etc. in the Twenty Years from 1881–1901* (London)

WILLIAMSON, J. G. (1980) 'Earnings inequality in nineteenth-century Britain' *Journal of Economic History*, 40, pp. 457–75

WILLIAMSON, J. G. (1981) 'Urban disamenities, dark satanic mills, and the British standard of living debate, *Journal of Economic History*, 41, pp. 75–83 (see Pollard (1981))

WILLIAMSON, J. G. (1981) 'Some myths die hard—urban disamenities one more time: a reply' *Journal of Economic History*, 41, pp. 905–7

WILLIAMSON, J. G. (1982) 'The structure of pay in Britain, 1710–1911' in P. USELDING (ed) *Research in Economic History*, 7, pp. 1–54 (Greenwich, Conn.)

WILLIAMSON, J. G. (1982) 'Was the Industrial Revolution worth it? Disamenities and death in 19th century British towns' *Explorations in Economic History*, 19, pp. 221–45

WILLIAMSON, J. G. and LINDERT, P. H. (1980) *American Inequality: A Macroeconomic History* (New York)

WINTER, J. M. (1982) 'The decline of mortality in Britain, 1870–1950' in T. BARKER and M. DRAKE (eds) *Population and Society in Britain, 1850–1980*, pp. 100–20 (London)

WOHL, A. S. (1973) 'Unfit for human habitation' in H. J. DYOS and M. WOLFF (eds) *The Victorian City*, pp. 603–24 (London)

WOHL, A. S. (1977) *The Eternal Slum: Housing and Social Policy in Victorian London* (London)

WOHL, A. S. (ed.) (1978) *The Victorian Family: Structure and Stresses* (London)

WOHL, A. S. (1983) *Endangered Lives: Public Health in Victorian Britain* (London)

WOODS, R. I. (1978) 'Mortality and sanitary conditions in the "Best governed city in the World"—Birmingham, 1870–1910', *Journal of Historical Geography*, 4, pp. 35–56

WOODS, R. I. (1979) *Population Analysis in Geography* (London)

WOODS, R. I. (1982) *Theoretical Population Geography* (London)

WOODS, R. I. (1982) 'The structure of mortality in mid-nineteenth-century England and Wales' *Journal of Historical Geography*, 8, pp. 373–94

WOODS, R. I. and SMITH, C. W. (1983) 'The decline of marital fertility in the late nineteenth century: the case of England and Wales' *Population Studies*, 37, pp. 207–25

WOODWARD, J. H. (1974) *To Do the Sick No Harm: A Study of the British Voluntary Hospital System to 1875* (London)

WOODWARD, J. H. and RICHARDS, D. (eds) (1977) *Health Care and Popular Medicine in Nineteenth-Century England: Essays in the Social History of Medicine* (London)

WRIGLEY, E. A. (1972) 'Mortality in pre-industrial England: the example of

Colyton, Devon, over three centuries' in D. V. GLASS and R. REVELLE (eds) *Population and Social Change*, pp. 243–73 (London)

WRIGLEY, E. A. (ed.) (1972) *Nineteenth-Century Society: Essays in the Use of Quantitative Methods for the Study of Social Data* (Cambridge)

WRIGLEY, E. A. and SCHOFIELD, R. S. (1981) *The Population History of England, 1541–1871: A Reconstruction* (London)

ZINSSER, H. (1934) 'Varieties of typhus virus and the epidemiology of the American form of European typhus fever (Brill's disease)' *American Journal of Hygiene*, 20, pp. 513–32

ZINSSER, H. (1935) *Rats, Lice and History* (London)

Index

(The notes on pages 203 to 236 are referred to in *italics*.)